Studies in Major Literary Authors

Edited by
William E. Cain
Professor of English
Wellesley College

A Routledge Series

Studies in Major Literary Authors
William E. Cain, *General Editor*

"No Image There and the Gaze Remains"
The Visual in the Work of Jorie Graham
Catherine Sona Karagueuzian

"Somewhat on the Community-System"
Fourierism in the Works of Nathaniel Hawthorne
Andrew Loman

Colonialism and the Modernist Moment in the Early Novels of Jean Rhys
Carol Dell'Amico

Melville's Monumental Imagination
Ian S. Maloney

Writing "Out of All the Camps"
J.M. Coetzee's Narratives of Displacement
Laura Wright

Here and Now
The Politics of Social Space in D. H. Lawrence and Virginia Woolf
Youngjoo Son

"Unnoticed in the Casual Light of Day"
Philip Larkin and the Plain Style
Tijana Stojković

Queer Times
Christopher Isherwood's Modernity
Jamie M. Carr

Edith Wharton's "Evolutionary Conception"
Darwinian Allegory in Her Major Novels
Paul J. Ohler

The End of Learning
Milton and Education
Thomas Festa

Reading and Mapping Hardy's Roads
Scott Rode

Creating Yoknapatawpha
Readers and Writers in Faulkner's Fiction
Owen Robinson

No Place for Home
Spatial Constraint and Character Flight in the Novels of Cormac McCarthy
Jay Ellis

The Machine that Sings
Modernism, Hart Crane, and the Culture of the Body
Gordon A. Tapper

Influential Ghosts
A Study of Auden's Sources
Rachel Wetzsteon

D.H. Lawrence's Border Crossing
Colonialism in His Travel Writings and "Leadership" Novels
Eunyoung Oh

Dorothy Wordsworth's Ecology
Kenneth R. Cervelli

Sports, Narrative, and Nation in the Fiction of F. Scott Fitzgerald
Jarom Lyle McDonald

Shelley's Intellectual System and its Epicurean Background
Michael A. Vicario

Modernist Aesthetics and Consumer Culture in the Writings of Oscar Wilde
Paul L. Fortunato

Milton's Uncertain Eden
Understanding Place in Paradise Lost
Andrew Mattison

MILTON'S UNCERTAIN EDEN
Understanding Place in *Paradise Lost*

Andrew Mattison

Routledge
New York & London

Routledge
Taylor & Francis Group
270 Madison Avenue
New York, NY 10016

Routledge
Taylor & Francis Group
2 Park Square
Milton Park, Abingdon
Oxon OX14 4RN

© 2007 by Taylor & Francis Group, LLC

Routledge is an imprint of Taylor & Francis Group, an Informa business

Transferred to Digital Printing 2009

International Standard Book Number-10: 0-415-98134-4 (Hardcover)
International Standard Book Number-13: 978-0-415-98134-7 (Hardcover)

No part of this book may be reprinted, reproduced, transmitted, or utilized in any form by any electronic, mechanical, or other means, now known or hereafter invented, including photocopying, microfilming, and recording, or in any information storage or retrieval system, without written permission from the publishers.

Trademark Notice: Product or corporate names may be trademarks or registered trademarks, and are used only for identification and explanation without intent to infringe.

Library of Congress Cataloging-in-Publication Data

Mattison, Andrew, 1976-
    Milton's uncertain Eden : understanding place in Paradise lost / by Andrew Mattison.
        p. cm. -- (Studies in major literary authors)
        Includes bibliographical references (p.   ) and index.
        ISBN 0-415-98134-4
    1. Milton, John, 1608-1674. Paradise lost. 2. Eden in literature. 3. Place (Philosophy) in literature. I. Title.

PR3562.M38 2007
821'.4--dc22
        2006102721

ISBN10: 0-415-98134-4 (hbk)
ISBN10: 0-415-80301-2 (pbk)

ISBN13: 978-0-415-98134-7 (hbk)
ISBN13: 978-0-415-80301-4 (pbk)

Visit the Taylor & Francis Web site at
http://www.taylorandfrancis.com

and the Routledge Web site at
http://www.routledge.com

*For Susan Brisman
and
Ken Weedin*

Contents

Acknowledgments ... ix

Introduction ... 1

Chapter One
The Withdrawn Landscape: Vergil, Poetic Rereading,
and the Genre Problem ... 21

Chapter Two
The Environs of Imagination: *Paradise Lost* 7 and *8* ... 53

Chapter Three
Urgency and Delay in Eden: Description and the
Inverted Rhetoric of *Paradise Lost 9* ... 81

Chapter Four
Collapse and Consolation: The Postlapsarian Environment ... 115

Conclusion ... 155

Notes ... 159

Bibliography ... 183

Index ... 187

Acknowledgments

This book grew out of a long series of conversations with William Flesch, and owes much of its form and scope to those conversations and to Billy's ways of thinking about literature. Ramie Targoff and Jeff Dolven made essential suggestions regarding structure and approach; John Burt, Mary Campbell, and Christopher Ricks provided helpful comments on particular sections; and Alice Mattison read the entire manuscript with thoughtfulness and precision. Like so many Miltonists, of several generations, I am indebted to Roy Flannagan for his support. I am grateful also to Shannon Hunt, Tom King, Sue Lanser, Lisa Pannella, and Sarah Pikcilingis for advice and assistance, and to Mary Ellen Burd, Michael Gilmore, Evan Hirsch, Alan Levitan, Sara Lundquist, Ben Mattison, Edward Mattison, Meir Rinde, and Matthew Wikander for aid and encouragement. Throughout its development, this book, like its author, has benefitted from Lara Bovilsky's critical insight and erudition. For their patience and kindness, and for teaching me how to read, I dedicate this book to Susan Brisman and Ken Weedin, my teachers at Vassar College, with gratitude.

Chapter Two is a slightly longer version of an essay, "'Thine Own Inventions': The Environs of Imagination in *Paradise Lost* 7 and 8," previously published in *Milton Quarterly.*

Introduction

The last act that Adam and Eve commit in Eden, after they have drawn sustenance from it, nurtured it, defiled it, and caused its destruction, is an act of a different category: they look at it. They look at it indirectly, however, "looking *back*" (12.641; my emphasis),[1] with Eden behind them and "the World . . . before them" (646). The final lines of *Paradise Lost* describe a contrast between two places at two very different points in their histories: Eden in the moment of its destruction and the outer world at the point of its first discovery. Surprisingly, however, Milton introduces into the description of Eden a third place: a metaphorical landscape—the mist at evening—used to describe not Eden itself but the angels who are destroying it. The place within the metaphor is clearly modern (that is, postlapsarian)—it has a laborer, so labor must be long-familiar within it—and clearly static and quotidian. Milton uses figuration to evoke one context even while narratively portraying another.

The narrative context of this final passage is determined entirely by its finality. All of his lessons complete, Michael, backed by a numberless band of angels, leads Adam and Eve out of their paradise:

> . . . all in bright array
> The Cherubim descended; on the ground
> Gliding meteorous, as Ev'ning Mist
> Ris'n from a River o'er the marish glides,
> And gathers ground fast at the Laborer's heel
> Homeward returning. High in Front advanc't,
> The brandisht Sword of God before them blaz'd
> Fierce as a Comet; which with torrid heat,
> And vapor as the *Libyan* Air adust,
> Began to parch that temperate Clime; whereat

> In either hand the hast'ning Angel caught
> Our ling'ring Parents, and to th'Eastern Gate
> Led them direct, and down the Cliff as fast
> To the subjected Plain; then disappear'd.
> They looking back, all th'Eastern side beheld
> Of Paradise, so late thir happy seat,
> Wav'd over by that flaming Brand, the Gate
> With dreadful Faces throng'd and fiery Arms:
> Some natural tears they dropp'd, but wip'd them soon;
> The World was all before them, where to choose
> Thir place of rest, and Providence thir guide:
> They hand in hand with wand'ring steps and slow,
> Through *Eden* took thir solitary way. (12.627–49)

This moment is *about* place, and about the relationship between place's function in the world Milton describes and its function in the world in which he writes. The moment Adam and Eve leave Eden is the moment the definition of place changes permanently—the first event in the history of place as fallen humanity knows it. But Milton figures this complete transformation of place not ethically, theologically, or historically, but, in fact, *through* place. Figural descriptions of the laborer's evening and the Libyan air create a new place in order to help describe the old one, to the point that the richness of those descriptions threatens to interfere with the narrative function of the passage.

Place has a moral function in this passage—because Eden always has a moral function—but its figural function overwhelms its moral function. This book's principal thesis is that in *Paradise Lost* as a whole as in this passage the figural force of descriptions of place, and particularly of Eden, disrupt the moral logic the poem superficially invokes. The metaphor comparing the crowd of angels to mist is a clear example. There is a twofold analogy between the laborer chased home by the rising fog and Adam and Eve: a visual metaphor (the crowd of angels looks like mist) and a metaphor of circumstance (the laborer is hurried by mist in the same way that Adam and Eve are by the angels). Morally, however, the analogy does not hold up, and in fact represents a notable contrast, since Adam and Eve caused the hurrying mass behind them and the laborer is only reacting to a predictable effect of climate, season, and hour. Though labor itself is a postlapsarian function (sort of), the sheer *lateness* of the description—its clear placement in the modern world—separates it from the Fall.

So there is a dispersal of what place can signify—figural meaning and moral or theological meaning are moving in opposite directions. In fact,

Introduction 3

place represents at once at least four things in the passage: what has been lost (Eden as place rather than state: "thir happy seat" [642]), the catastrophe of its destruction ("to parch that temperate Clime" [636]), a metaphorical and imagistic description of the angels that herald the loss ("Ev'ning mist" [629]), and even the consolation for the loss ("The World was all before them" [646]). That last point is particularly significant, because in their very language the final lines point to the problem Milton's figuration creates. The world is before Adam and Eve, but what is behind is being insistently compared to an obviously postlapsarian country evening as well as Libya, so that the world in a figural sense is behind them as well. All four uses of environment point in different directions, so that place contributes to all that is challenging and ambiguous about this final moment. Those four distinct environmental aspects, however, also contain within themselves some measure of uncertainty.

Two separate environmental similes, in the opening lines of the passage, figure the effect of the horde of angels as a collaborative escort and deterrent. The mist that (in a distinctly georgic moment[2]) hastens the peasant home suggests the power of environment to meld together into a unified effect, even as it is antagonistic to the subject within it, a dual pattern we will see again and again. Meanwhile the flaming sword those angels carry introduces into the mythically active air of Eden the atmosphere of Libya. The unity of the cherubim, which is so complete that it can only be compared to mist, enables the fundamental discontinuity that they create in the Edenic landscape. Because they are themselves like the humid air of England or of Eden they can turn Eden into a desert. There is a logical leap between the cherubim's moral position and their position in relation to the environment, and Milton makes that leap by means of a metaphor that explains their power, but also reverses it. They dry Eden out (through the sword) by being like dampness, but also they create an epic cataclysm by being like a georgic, repetitive, image: an image that suggests the unchanging cycle of days and of seasons. Adam and Eve, looking back, do not know what they are looking at, because Eden is being destroyed even as they leave it, and Milton illustrates their confusion about place with metaphors of place that themselves confuse.

Libya is the metaphor, but the parching of Eden is real; in a typically Miltonic gesture—we will see it again in chapter 4 of this book, for example, with the "black Air" in and around Adam's conscience after the Fall [10.847])—the metaphor bleeds into the narrative. In looking back over the garden they have left, Adam and Eve see not Eden but the sword: Eden's destruction. In this same way, even their consolation is undermined; though

Adam and Eve are moving out of Eden and into the world, Milton arranges the description in reverse. The outside world is what they are looking at, and it contains not only labor but "a place of rest" (647); the world is described invitingly. Eden, however, is the last place mentioned in the poem. There is a double inversion. Once Adam and Eve were terrified to leave Eden for the outside world, but here the world functions as consolation for the loss and destruction of Eden: the first inversion. Still, strikingly, the newly foreboding, desiccated, burning Eden—once itself consoling but now tainted permanently by the Fall—ends the poem by obscuring the image of the freshness of the outside world. The new consolation looks back at the old consolation whose destruction made the new one necessary.

Doubt enters this passage, as (I will claim) it enters the poem as a whole, by means of place, but asserts through description and figuration a greater interpretive significance. This assertion through figuration is the key to the function of place in *Paradise Lost*—uncertainty about place governs the epic's interpretation not by any overt thetic status but by the sheer continuity of its presence. I will offer in this book a great deal of evidence for descriptions of place in *Paradise Lost* that are sufficiently at odds with the poem's most explicit theological points as to suggest doubts for that theology. I do not claim that there is an overarching structure to the presence of these descriptions—on the contrary, their presence undermines the poem's most superficial structure, working to disrupt easy conclusions about differences between Heaven, Eden, and the World. I will focus on the part of the poem surrounding the Fall because the disruption place creates is clearest in that part, since the basically postlapsarian mode of Milton's figuration deflects the Fall itself from its superficially central position. The final passage is an excellent example of this deflection—the passage is about Adam and Eve looking at Eden, but the description of Eden looks at it through the perspective of the modern world, instantiated in the mist and in Libya. The figure with which Milton describes the event recasts the narrative and Eden itself, creating a form of description that looks back at Eden through history.

Even when the narrative is set before the Fall, the figuration of Eden has that same backward-looking effect. This postlapsarian nature of Milton's sense of place is, I believe, its most misunderstood characteristic, in part because it is drawn from *Paradise Lost*'s poetic rather than theological provenance. It is in the descriptions of places, and of Eden in particular, that the epic's reliance on the literary tradition beginning with Homer and Vergil is strongest. Most critics understand that reliance to be simply a poetic tool toward some goal distinct (because of its religious nature) from the classical tradition, but to make that assumption is to ignore Milton's poetic technique as a topic unto itself, and also to read Miltonic place in too much isolation. My reading will suggest that Milton's intertextual descriptiveness allows him an understanding of place that extends beyond the theory of place as it existed in the period. Edward S. Casey argues convincingly that in the Renaissance, the philosophical discussion of place had given way to considerations—more in keeping both with Christian thought and with modern physics—of space as opposed to place.[3] In other words, by the Renaissance the problem of understanding one's immediate surroundings had been supplanted by a more abstract question about the nature of space as an extensive entity. Though post-Nietzschean philosophy, Casey demonstrates, has returned to the question of the relationship between the subject and his environment, in the seventeenth-century such a question was marginalized, though existing in memory through ancient philosophy. In the context of *Paradise Lost,* though Eden as a theological construct is an extremely abstract question and one that was covered extensively by thinkers of Milton's time (as Victoria Silver has ably demonstrated[4]), Eden as a potential setting for a poem would not have been considered a theological problem so much as a poetic problem. Thus, place raises a difficult interpretive question—to what extent do Milton's poetic strategies and choices affect the interpretation of the whole poem? After all, as I will argue in these chapters, Milton's descriptions of place work to unite the poem's prelapsarian and postlapsarian sections, while simultaneously taking part in trans-historical textual interchanges that blur the poem's relationship to the historical conditions of its production. As such, these descriptions pull interpretation in directions counter to current trends in Milton criticism, for which the poem's meaning is chiefly determined by its theodical content and political and social contexts. The danger of the universality of such readings is that much of Milton's specifically poetic agenda—his interpretive reuse of earlier materials—is ignored. By taking seriously Milton's poetic technique, even if that means investigating trans-historical and aesthetic logics along with theological and historicist ones, we can reanimate a nearly lost aspect of *Paradise Lost.*

In arguing that the poetic problem of the description of place disrupts Milton's theodicy, I am necessarily coming into conflict with the great majority of recent criticism on *Paradise Lost.* Most critics trust Milton's claim that the principal function of his epic is to "justify the ways of God to men" (1.26), to the point of thinking of *Paradise Lost* as a theodicy in the form of a poem, rather than the other way around. There is great confidence in Milton's claim, and criticism has generally assumed that such confidence is not only sincere in its explicit point, but applies to the whole poem. Milton's style and his scale also suggest, even in those moments when he is furthest from scripture or from seventeenth-century religious doctrine, an essential certainty in his subject matter. There is the possibility for disagreement, however, about how far that certainty extends. There is a long tradition—following C.S. Lewis, C.A. Patrides, and others with religious or historical justifications for endorsing Milton's orthodoxy—of reading Milton's certainty as absolute, universal within the poem, and coming directly from his confidence in addressing and representing God. There is an equally long tradition questioning that certainty, whether in the form of Samuel Johnson's criticisms of the poem's style and structure, Blake's brilliant but deeply personal inversions of his chief literary predecessor, or William Empson's influential and often-misunderstood discussion of the wickedness of Milton's God. However, because of the explicit confidence of the poem, certainty is always the default assumption among critics: particular evidence to the contrary is assumed to be necessary before any other possibility can be considered. As a result of this heuristic of universal underlying surety, the nature of environment or location or place in *Paradise Lost* has been thought to reflect the confidence of Milton's design. Whether critics read Milton's use of place within a general materialist philosophy (as, e.g., Christopher Kendrick does) or as referring specifically to the environment in the modern sense (as Ken Hiltner does), the various locations of the poem are treated as stable and knowable. In the midst of all this confidence, however, the poem's central figure, Adam, shares in none of it. As I will argue throughout these pages, Adam is profoundly uncertain about the nature of his surroundings, even well before the Fall, and that uncertainty, unappeased by God or by Raphael, grows and infects all of his thinking.

Thus, there is an analogy to be made between Adam's position—uncertain in the midst of confidence—and the position of the description or figuration of place within the poem. Adam's doubt within Eden is an emblem of the problem of environment in the epic—an environment that has one meaning when considered as a whole can have an entirely different meaning for a person within it. But what is within the environment and looking at it need not, as we will see, be an individual; as often as not, descriptive perspectives of environment exist abstractly in *Paradise Lost*, without referring to a particular person's point of view (see, for example, my reading of the description of Eden in Book 4 at the end of chapter 2, which describes Eden *while* Satan is looking at it but through the narrator's perspective rather than Satan's). So in the larger sense, description of place exists as an island of doubt within the poem's confident theodicy, as Adam's anxieties thrive within Edenic lushness and bliss.

I hope my reading of the final passage of *Paradise Lost* above may make clear the way I am using the terms at issue here, particularly *place* (the general

Introduction

term) and *environment* (my specific term for the surroundings—however they are described or figured—of a poetic character). I do not mean nature or ecology,[5] nor do I mean space in a strictly phenomenological sense. I also do not refer to the theological or cosmological definitions of the places in which Milton sets his poem—Heaven, Hell, Eden, the World, Chaos, and the liminal spaces in between—though I will often refer to the way those places function as environment. In fact, many of the particulars of my argument will involve my claim that all of those places have more in common than has generally been thought.[6] Environment here will refer to a subject's immediate surroundings—where the poem places its characters and figures—as they appear prosodically. Thus, the figurative environment of the misty river in the passage above belongs to the same category as the literal environment of Eden. The laborer, for example, becomes transiently reified, even though he is only present to complete the analogy, because Milton surrounds him with a vividly described environment. He *would* be merely a briefly mentioned type—he is only his occupation and lacks any substantive attributes—but by placing him, by giving him the context of a landscape, Milton makes him a person, and his eagerness to get home (caused by environment) is significantly analogous to Adam and Eve's need to get out. Images from Milton's similes and metaphors often emerge into the real landscape, but this trend is merely a subset of a larger and more significant issue. I will claim (particularly in chapter 3) that the rhetorical and poetic and tropic functions of place can subsume the narrative functions. Narrative can function through trope, and trope can interfere with narrative.

Much of this book will be concerned with evidence that the clear representation of the Fall, which theodical readings of *Paradise Lost* would seem to expect, is lacking. In particular, too many of Milton's anxieties about environment appear in similar manifestations before and after the Fall, and in reference to various states of being in relation to the Fall (so that in chapter 4, for example, I find that unredeemable Satan has much in common with both Adam and Samson). Through a reading of environment, we come to see a *Paradise Lost* in which the Fall is in competition with a host of other ways to interpret the human condition. My interest in that competition is behind much of my disagreement with the critical establishment. There is much contradiction in Milton, and a common critical response is to characterize any such contradiction as anticipating resolution. This characterization isolates two separate (but overlapping) strains within the criticism—on the one hand, readings that rely on assumptions about Milton's theology as the governing interpretive context, and on the other, readings that explore historical, theoretical, or intertextual contexts even at the expense of a unified theological interpretation. Though both strains exist, little attention has been paid to the basic contradiction between them, and one purpose of mine is to demonstrate that strict insistence on a resolution of everything within *Paradise Lost* into a seventeenth-century Protestant argument is futile. The sheer interpretive demands of the poem prevent that resolution.

In fact, a number of critics hint at the difficulty of reconciling *Paradise Lost's* complexity as a text with a simple ideological argument, even when that reconciliation is exactly what they are trying to achieve. Sharon Achinstein, for example, in a well-received attempt to connect Miltonic rhetoric with the political prose and particularly political allegory of his time, concedes the difficulty of her task even while insisting on its importance:

> *Paradise Lost* is no squib nor a polemical barb in some pamphlet war; it is, rather, an extraordinary epic poem, encompassing far more than simply a topical political intention . . . However, in its mission to justify the ways of God to men, and also to find a "fit audience . . . though few," Milton's poem is consistent with the ethical concerns voiced in his prose.[7]

Though Achinstein's political reading is useful, I must quarrel with this statement of the ultimate significance of that reading. Achinstein's claim, that it is only within "its mission" that the poem is "consistent with . . . his prose," implies that such a mission can be separated from its poetic instantiation. It cannot; what we have is a poem that states one mission but that in its poetic and—particularly for my purposes—descriptive details seems to stray from that mission. I believe that the evidence of intellectual discontent that will make up the chapters that follow undermines the force of Milton's initial statement of his goal.

Many Miltonists claim not only that the kinds of contradictions I identify do not exist in *Paradise Lost,* but also that it would not be possible to claim that they do. Kathleen M. Swaim's book *Before and After the Fall* focuses on the definition of fallenness, and covers some of the same material I do (Books 7 and 8 particularly). She begins the preface of her book thus:

> My starting point is a proposition about which there can be no disagreement: that *Paradise Lost* is about the fall and its antecedents and consequences and that the fall in Milton's epic makes a radical difference to humanity, to the physical universe, to human perception and communication, and to the relationship of humanity and God.[8]

Introduction 9

My complaint is not so much about the part of this sentence after the colon (I do disagree with it, but it contains the heuristic on which Swaim's argument depends), as it is about the first part. To assume that "there can be no disagreement" about the central subject of *Paradise Lost* is by necessity to cast aside those aspects of the poem that least effectively portray the Fall. More importantly, the "radical difference" the Fall makes is one aspect of the poem, but another is the difference the Fall does not make: the motivic structure that unites the whole poem and transcends its moral concerns. If Swaim is right that theology expects the Fall to create such a sharp disjunction, than an exploration of such universal motivic material must necessarily challenge the overriding importance of theology in the poem. Because the material I explore here creates such interpretive uncertainty anyway, the problems created by the presence of similar elements before and after the Fall are multiplied.

Perhaps the most cited contemporary Miltonist, Stanley Fish, also makes assumptions about Milton's chief concerns that have the effect of denying the validity of interpretations that are not morally and religiously centered, but unlike Swaim, Fish pursues that agenda openly. Writing of *Areopagitica* but clearly thinking of *Paradise Lost,* Fish says:

> The center of his theology is the doctrine of inner light, and his entire career can be viewed as an exercise in vigilance in which he repeatedly detects in this or that political or social or ecclesiastical program one more attempt to substitute for the authority of the inner light the false authority of some external and imposed rule.[9]

Fish does indeed view Milton's career "as an exercise in vigilance"; he believes that anything that contradicts the central doctrine must be corrected, or undermined, or retracted later, and invariably it turns out that the contradiction was only dangled in front of us to give Milton the opportunity to make a pedagogical point. My reading of Milton is virtually the opposite of Fish's; it asserts that poetic practice almost always overwhelms doctrinal intent. Because the two arguments are so clearly opposed, Fish will often function in these pages as a foil. The points in the poem at which my readings of Milton's ambiguities and anxieties most profoundly question his theocentricity are the points at which Fish most clearly excludes or ignores contradictions that, I feel, cannot be resolved so neatly.

On the other hand, there is a tradition in Milton studies going back at least to William Empson that holds that looking for contradiction in *Paradise Lost* can be a fruitful interpretive endeavor. Responding to critics who disparaged Milton for those contradictions, Empson says early in *Milton's God* that he will "accept the details of interpretation which various recent critics have used to prove the poem bad, and then try to show that they make it good."[10] Empson's basic goal has been echoed in a number of recent attempts to look at contradiction in Milton as a valid way of arriving at an interpretation. Victoria Silver cites Empson as a major influence in a work on a very non-Empsonian topic: Miltonic theology.[11] In his recent study of creativity in Milton, Gordon Teskey acknowledges the motivations behind Empson's thesis when he parenthesizes that "Empson was right to say this, even if the statement is not perhaps literally true."[12] Even when Empson is not cited, however, his call to think of Miltonic contradiction as a positive rather than negative aspect of his work seems to lie behind work that, in looking at contexts other than theology, necessarily finds the poem somewhat at odds with itself. Thus William Kolbrener discusses "Milton's ambivalences about political engagement" in his prose and poetry, and John Rogers looks for a "theory of organization" that *Paradise Lost* "does not consistently articulate" but which "is not missing altogether."[13] These critics share Empson's interest in a kind of consistent contradiction, a concept that works poetically but not necessarily theologically. These studies indicate particularly clearly the complex relationship between method and interpretation in Milton studies; method here demands a particular interpretation, since looking for ambivalence or pluralism necessarily questions the singularity of the poem's goal, and though these critics do not always concede this point, the interpretation demanded by their methods is not the established one.

Nor is contradiction in the poem necessarily incidental. Balachandra Rajan, in an undervalued essay, "The Uncertain Epic," argues that the genre of *Paradise Lost* is fundamentally ambiguous. Rajan articulates the value of inconsistency:

> . . . it should not be assumed that the purpose, or even the designed purpose, of generic multeity is always to contribute to the overall harmony, to show how many styles of discourse lead us to the one word, or to the unifying capability that is the "one word" of the poem. Multiple genres can provide the ingredients for subversion as well as for synthesis. Their purpose may be to show not the overall concord, but the fragmentation of any single style of understanding that unavoidably comes about when the fictive is brought into engagement with the actual.[14]

Rajan suggests that *Paradise Lost's* discontinuity reflects the depth of Milton's understanding of the world and his subject matter, a depth that prevents an ultimate resolution.[15] His interest in the "fragmentation" of an attempt to fictively interpret truth, not as a flaw in that attempt but as a strength, is a productive idea. Milton's well-documented willingness to stray from scripture in making his points can be seen as a tribute to scriptural truth through acknowledgment of the impossibility of a precise, final, or authoritative scriptural interpretation. Rajan's idea is particularly valuable for the explorations of place in this book. Environmental uncertainty works as a kind of gadfly against overly easy theological interpretation, and I will devote some attention to that issue, but it also reflects what I think is a central poetic response to the problem of the depiction of place. Those two functions exist continuously and simultaneously; they cannot be separated. Descriptions of place that are infused with doubt are a staple of Miltonic style and only assert their presence more volubly in *Paradise Lost's* context of doctrinal certainty.

Rajan's career as a Miltonist, to over-simplify, has been devoted to steering interpretation away from the temptation to read too direct a relationship between the idea and its reception. In his *Paradise Lost and the Seventeenth Century Reader,* published in 1947, he insists on a relationship between "public meaning" and "private significance"—the search for the former, he maintains, must never be confused with speculation (which is all that is available) about the latter.[16] As the methodologies and historical understandings have inevitably shifted over the many decades of his career, he has continued to emphasize that readers avoid too easy a finality of meaning, and Rajan's interest in Milton as a particularly clear example of permanently unsettled meaning has continued through the 80's and 90's. His most important proof-text, of course, is always *Paradise Lost,* but one of Rajan's most powerful arguments against the conclusion that Milton is "the poet of justification"[17]—the poet of truths that reveal themselves in experience as truths—is centered around *Areopagitica,* and specifically *Areopagitica's* description of a fragmented truth whose once-unified origin can never be reconstructed. Indeed, *Areopagitica* serves well as the basis of an argument for Milton's interest in the inherent indirectness of meaning, because it is in large part about the relationship between simplistic and sophisticated reading.

"A DISCREET AND JUDICIOUS READER"

Much of my argument in this book is about the moral inclusiveness of Miltonic description—the remarkable extent to which Milton's poetics does not constitute a direct bridge between intent and interpretation but rather creates a world of diverse meanings through which interpretation is given no more than the vaguest of direction. In *Paradise Lost* such a world emerges only through consideration of poetic choices as such, but in *Areopagitica* Milton's concept of interpretation is presented much more simply. Bad books, Milton goes so far as to say, can function as good books: they can "to a discreet and judicious Reader serve in many respects to discover, to confute, to forewarn, and to illustrate" (*YCP* 2: 512–13). This conception gives interpretation remarkable transformative power, and it is a crucial elaboration of Milton's analysis of the moral position of books in general, in which he admits that books could act and be judged

> as malefactors: For Books are not absolutely dead things, but doe contain a potencie of life in them to be as active as that soule was whose progeny they are; nay they do preserve as in a violl the purest efficacie and extraction of the living intellect that bred them. (492)

Of course, it is because books are to some extent living things that they can "discover, confute" and so on (513); but whatever they preserve must be tempered by the fact that, as Milton insists, they can act contrary to the original intentions of their authors. One of the requirements of the "purest efficacie and extraction" of an author's mind is that the extraction can be turned to some alternate purpose. The metaphor imagines a relationship between a fixed origin and a versatile and vulnerable ultimate effect. Its very purity makes it morally inconstant.

In that sense, the juxtaposition of the idea that books must occasionally be judged "as malefactors" and Milton's famous and rather effusive metaphor of the power of books is not the contradiction it has sometimes been taken for. Fish bases an entire chapter (drawn from a highly influential essay) about *Areopagitica* on that contradiction. He argues that ultimately Milton's insistence that virtue is an attribute of a person and not of a book undermines this passage, which apparently is here as some sort of trap for foolhardy booklovers. Milton's definition of virtue, Fish says,

> renders books beside the point: books are no more going to save you than they are going to corrupt you; by denying their potency in one direction, Milton necessarily denies their potency in the other and undercuts the extravagant claims he himself makes.[18]

The misreading is acute. Milton's argument is that books are alive not in the sense that they can have virtue but in the sense that they have multiple capacities as yet undetermined. The strength and expansiveness of the metaphor is

Introduction

germane to the idea that books are as capable of being used for ill as they are for good, because it is that "potencie of life" that prevents them from being permanently assigned to some particular morality. So Fish is partially right when he says of the metaphor:

> it is decidedly *un*-Miltonic; first because it locates value and truth in a physical object, and second because the reverence it apparently recommends toward that object is dangerously close to, if not absolutely identical with, worship.[19]

It would not be like Milton to locate truth in an object, but that is not the meaning of this metaphor, and it is very like Milton to appreciate that something can be powerful without being morally predetermined.[20] A book in that sense is like Satan's rhetoric in *Paradise Lost;* it *is* powerful, but its power does not mean that the intentions with which it was conceived govern its effects. Fish's misreading of *Areopagitica* is instructive for his misreading of *Paradise Lost,* because as this reading shows, his understanding of the function of metaphor is quite narrow. Milton *never* locates value in the thing, but *always* in the depiction of the thing—it is in the play between the thing and its figuration that meaning (and therefore truth) lies. This figural logic must always be remembered—to return to my central topic—in reading place in *Paradise Lost;* the fact of the place itself, whether Eden, Heaven, or Hell, is always capable of being trumped by the circumstances of its description.

On the other hand, the purity with which books preserve the spirit of their authors represents a central identity that is not nearly so flexible. That inflexibility is still consistent with the importance of process; for Milton versatility of effect can not only coexist with but depend on an inflexible origin. In *Paradise Lost* God reminds his Son, as a testament to the moral responsibility that Adam and Eve bear, that their freedom to fall is itself fixed:

> I form'd them free, and free they must remain,
> Till they enthrall themselves: I else must change
> Thir nature, and revoke the high Decree
> Unchangeable, Eternal, which ordain'd
> Thir freedom . . . (3.124–28)

The versatility of human beings, their potential to end either fallen or not, their very changeability, is itself more central than what is changeable; their mutability is "Unchangeable, Eternal" (127). Adam and Eve's freedom depends on its limitation; the only thing that guarantees their freedom is that they are defined through creation with certain attributes intact. God's list of capitalized qualifiers only highlights the discrepancy of "Till they enthrall themselves" (125): this is a decree so powerful that the choice it grants can undermine the freedom it requires. "High Decree" logically reflects God's power: he can create an unchangeable capability for change.

That flexibility of meaning applies particularly to place, as we have seen in the final passage. Neither Heaven nor Earth, in their respective moral hues, can govern the meaning of events that happen within those environments. Milton's description of the nature of the freedom of England is presented somewhat analogously to God's insistence on Adam and Eve's freedom of choice; England too is unchangeably free to change:

> If it be desir'd to know the immediat cause of all this free writing and free speaking, there cannot be assign'd a truer then your own mild, and free, and human government; it is the liberty, Lords and Commons, which your own valorous and happy counsels have purchast us . . . Ye cannot make us now lesse capable, lesse knowing, lesse eagerly pursuing of the truth, unlesse ye first make your selves, that made us so, lesse the lovers, lesse the founders of our true liberty. (*YCP* II:559)

Here the reminder goes the other way. Parliament cannot take away the freedom of thought of the English people because they have given that freedom on too deep a level to rescind it. Origin is important, but bad books can do good things; if we combine these two ideas, what we get is, to borrow a metaphor from John Donne, the monism of a compass, permanently centered yet infinitely variable.

Ideas then are always subject to motion. What is set and unchanging is only the range of the kinds of motion that are available. The motion of ideas is embedded in description and figuration, because descriptions and figures are not just expressions of the thing described but, inevitably, manipulations. Even the fixed origin that determines where an idea might go that is so central to Milton's conception of freedom in both *Areopagitica* and *Paradise Lost* is not always so important (see chapter 4, where I argue that even blasphemous intent cannot entirely determine the meaning of an idea). One of Milton's favorite examples is comedy. Milton is impressed enough with Plato's recommendation that a protege read Aristophanes (Socrates' literary enemy) that he mentions it twice in *Areopagitica,* the first time as evidence for the Athenians' generally liberal attitude toward books (495), and again in arguing that Plato's interest in censorship corresponds only to an ideal state; his practical interest in bad books is indicated by his perpetuall reading of *Sophron Mimus,* and *Aristophanes,* books of grossest infamy, and also [his] commending the latter of them though he were the malicious libeller of his chief friends, to be read by the Tyrant Dionysius, who had little need of such trash to spend his time on[.] (523)

Milton's characterization of Aristophanes is strongly worded not as a rebuke of Plato but to emphasize how bad an idea Platonic pedagogy could find use for. The juxtaposition of "such trash" and Plato's commendation is similar to the praise of books' "potencie" even while they may be punished for wrongdoing. Milton finds it worthwhile to comment on the central identity of a book even while allowing that such identity does not permanently mark its status. In fact, Milton intends the contradiction as praise, since for Milton, Plato's apparent waffling represents moral seriousness. Bad literature is banned in the ideal state of the *Republic* because there is no need for the entire process of converting bad to good, if everything is already perfect. In our own imperfect state, that process is central to any idea of moral development.[21]

The ability to make good use out of indifferent ideas, and the discursive openness that results, is much of what Milton has in mind when he says that it is better "to imitate the old and elegant humanity of Greece, than the barbaric pride of a Hunnish and Norwegian stateliness" (496). To back up his interest in Greece as well as his interest in making Christian use of non-Christian texts, he cites Paul, who also endorses the use of a pagan idea for Christian purposes, because he "thought it no defilement to insert into holy Scripture the sentences of three Greek Poets, and one of them a Tragedian . . ." (508).[22] In making the connection between English freedom of the press and Athenian debate, Milton invites the problem that referring to the pagan Athenians necessitates; his parallel both invokes a long history of the kinds of freedoms he calls for and reinforces those freedoms by making Christian use out of unchristian material. Similarly, Milton's interest in Paul's relationship with Athens is a reminder of Pauline doctrine at the same time as it celebrates Greek dialectic. Like the image of a people who cannot revert to dogmatism once their Parliament has freed them or a humanity that cannot lose the choice their creator has offered them, the motion that connects pagan ideas with Christian truth goes properly in only one direction. On the other hand, there is every reason to think that the end result of that motion is truly a synthesis. In chapter 1, we see this understanding of classical literature applied directly to the problem of description.

The most convincing accounts of Milton's pluralism involve the peculiar motion of pedagogy: the gradual and always partial transformation of the human mind. Donald Guss addresses the issue succinctly in his essay "Enlightenment as Process: Milton and Habermas." The word "process" is an appropriate one, I think; etymologically it is another figure of motion (*cedo* is the root: to withdraw, to move along). For Guss the process can refer both to Milton's idea of truth, which is pedagogical rather than doctrinal, and fluid rather than fixed, and also to the motion that Milton's own thought effects:

> What he does is to shift authority: from magistracy to rhetor, hierarchy to congregant; in the divorce tracts, from sacrament to married couple; ultimately, from laws and dogma to personal conviction and public persuasion.[23]

I would add to Guss's idea of a movement in Milton from the fixed and authoritative to the personal and dialectical an interpretive movement: a recognition that there is space to be traveled between the initial meaning of an idea stated barely and the final meaning of an idea stated in the context of poetry. Trope (etymologically another metaphor of motion) itself acts to distort meaning over a distance.

My compass figure applies to the reader of *Areopagitica* or of *Paradise Lost* as well; origin, in this case Milton's argumentative intent, cannot guarantee final effect, but it is still available. But in the case of the reader there are two distinct motions to contend with. There is the rhetorical motion that Guss discusses from thesis to dialectic, but there is also a motion from intention to reading, and both are governed by the relationship between a fixed origin and a flexible end. That relationship will be the key to my reading of *Paradise Lost* in several ways; the argument at the poem's center functions as one point of one compass, and the innocence of Eden functions as one point of a different compass, but in both cases considerable motion takes place before the idea arrives at the reader.

Earlier I cited God's insistence that the unchangeability of Adam's and Eve's origin guarantees their ability to choose to fall, and this idea of a specific origin for an unspecifiable motion is crucial to the poem. The question is how much the specificity of the origin governs or limits the motion, but Milton chooses frequently and crucially to highlight the contrast between a unique and specifically described origin and an uncertain outcome. In other words, Milton's specificity is one of origin, but he does not insist on a relationship between the particularity of origin and that of meaning. The difficulty of the relationship between origin and meaning, however, has led to a number of influential misreadings of the ultimate interpretive flexibility of *Paradise Lost,* of which Fish's has been most read. In *Surprised by Sin* the motion goes the other way from the kind of motion I am describing (or as Fish puts it, "the poem does not move, but the reader moves"[24]). Choice is abandoned in favor of doctrine, and at the same time, as Fish's reader realizes that the structure of the poem requires him to end in a particular place with a particular attitude toward the poem itself ("raised to an imaginative, almost mystical apprehension of what the poem has continually asserted . . ."[25]), he must also realize that his own importance, which seemed unshakeable at the beginning of Fish's book, has now been entirely supplanted by Milton's intention. Fish's desire for Milton to be absolutely in control of the reader undermines his own reader-response criticism: ultimately he is not interested in the reader at all, but in how Milton works, and indeed Fish has made this phrase the title of his more recent book on Milton.[26]

*

The lesson of *Areopagitica,* which is that meaning must always be determined at a distance, with a respect for the origin of a text but not a slavish commitment to origin's governance over final significance, becomes particularly relevant to *Paradise Lost* in light of the argument against the centrality of the Fall I will be making here. That is, though Eden itself may be prelapsarian and therefore located before the post-Babel complexity of signification that informs *Areopagitica,* there is something distinctly *post*lapsarian about the way Eden is figured, as we saw above in the georgic metaphor that creeps into the final passage of *Paradise Lost.* Eden was once Eden only, but for a modern reader looking back at Eden through its description, its significance must be created in the context of the modern world—the world of labor and of suffering. That world infuses all of Milton's descriptions of prelapsarian place, and draws *Paradise Lost* closer to its readers.

I begin by placing Milton in the context of the trans-historical Vergilian tradition that informs much of his description of place. My opening chapter outlines how criticism has handled the presence of Vergil in the Renaissance, arguing that Renaissance Vergilianism has previously been understood as a response to and further development of particular thematic strains within Vergil's poems, all of which must be reconsidered in a Christian context. The chapter will make a case for a new definition of Vergilianism in Milton and in other major Renaissance poets, based on common poetic techniques rather than the problem of the Christianization of classical poetry. I believe that the imitation of Vergilian description by these Renaissance poets significantly recasts Vergilian materials to demonstrate both an awareness of the autonomy of landscape in Vergil and also the possible disconnection between character and landscape in their own poems.

This darker strain of Vergilianism evident in Spenser and Marvell anticipates a more central and more extensive form of the same basic dynamic in Milton. Milton's early poems demonstrate an interest in the contradiction and conflicts inherent within the Vergilian description of landscape by placing contradictory ideas of landscape at close quarters. Not only is a broad range of conceptions of responsive landscapes available in the works before *Paradise Lost*, but, I find, Milton emphasizes the implications of that range by dwelling on their dissonant possibilities.

Those possibilities are clearest in the poem's central event—the conversation between the Archangel Raphael and Adam that fills all of Books 5 through 8. Throughout the conversation, I argue, both Adam and Raphael return to the issue of the difficulty of describing place—Adam is worried about his understanding of Eden and the surrounding world, and Raphael urges Adam not to overstep his intellectual bounds while constantly challenging him through his insistence that Adam try (even though he must fail) to imagine heaven. Superficially, the conversation is devoted entirely to one subject: the possibility of temptation. However, it is in the means of description within the conversation that its full scope is revealed.

Description, too, serves as the chief topic of my reading of Book 9, which builds on a simple observation: that in her argument with Adam about whether to work separately in the garden, Eve describes Eden as being hurried, suggesting that the basic nature of the place is imbued with a faster time than what comes naturally to her and to Adam. Eve's characterization leads to a debate between two competing descriptions with little or no common ground—Eve's of an Eden whose sheer speed of being is constricting and confining, countered by Adam's description of ample room and leisurely work within a basically stable and predictable place. The debate is characteristic of the whole of Book 9 in two ways: through its emphasis on rhetoric whose goal is reflection rather than persuasion, and its use of descriptions with competing senses of the time of Eden. The debate exemplifies the same inward-directed rhetoric that governs all of the causes of the Fall. No one convinces anyone of anything in Book 9—Adam breaks off in the middle of an argument against separation, without waiting for a response, to tell Eve to leave him; Eve, rather than respond to the Serpent's arguments to eat the fruit of the Tree of Knowledge of Good and Evil, creates her own arguments based merely on the ability of the Serpent to speak; and finally, Adam responds to Eve's fall with a long, inner monologue, in which he makes the decision to join her—despite understanding that she is mistaken about the

Introduction   19

implications of what she has done—based on reasons distinct from her arguments. Book 9 is about the failure of rhetoric—it is about communication that is irrelevant to action. At the same time, the book is characterized chiefly by descriptions that incorporate time into space; Milton seems to be working out through prelapsarian mouths the problem—for a modern mind—of conceptualizing a place before the postlapsarian sense of time.

My last chapter is chiefly devoted to Book 10 of *Paradise Lost*, a neglected part of the poem. Concerned with the immediate aftermath of the Fall, Book 10's depictions of despair, regret, and anger have generally been seen by critics as a kind of moral vacuum—a cathartic preparation for the final directedness of Books 11 and 12, in which the subject of messianic redemption is raised. The logic of despair in the book has not received comment, other than arguments to the effect that such logic is necessarily casuistic and sinful, and therefore to be displaced by later revelations. But the complexity of Adam's attempt to rethink place after the Fall suggests that even though Adam must later abandon the despair that informs his thinking in Book 10, that thinking cannot be entirely invalidated. On the contrary, I argue, in regard to the poetic description of place, Book 10 represents some of Milton's most advanced work.

In my first chapter, I discuss a pattern throughout the Vergilian tradition in which a character desires a consolation from the surrounding landscape that never quite materializes. This last explores an extreme version of that same pattern, in which Adam looks to the landscape for consolation for the Fall, and for his own death, which is made inevitable by the Fall. To some extent, he finds that consolation there, though he finds it in the most postlapsarian aspects of the new Edenic landscape, particularly fire. But Adam discovers that the only real and permanent consolation for the Fall would be a relationship with the environment in which there is no distinction between environment and self—a collapse into the environment beyond even that of death.

Chapter One
The Withdrawn Landscape: Vergil, Poetic Rereading, and the Genre Problem

"*It is impossible to imitate a text*," Gérard Genette says emphatically; "*one can imitate only a style: that is to say, a genre.*"[1] To imitate the text in a foreign context, he explains, necessarily means not just to repeat "its specific stylistic and thematic features" but to "constitute them as a matrix of imitation," creating in the act of imitation a distinct, generalized concept of what those features have in common. Genette means this statement, which he admits is blunt, to apply to pastiche, but his warning should be kept in mind when discussing allusion (and in the Renaissance, when poetic style often meant taking on—not just referring to—Latinate or Italianate style, the distinction between pastiche and allusion may be hard to maintain). To take a phrase, image, or familiar juxtaposition from Vergil, translate it, and insert into a completely distinct context is simultaneously to imply that there is something Vergilian about the new context, and to suggest a particular reading—a distinctive and arguable generalization—of the original.

Rethinking Miltonic description of place necessarily means rethinking Milton's position within the Vergilian tradition he invokes both explicitly and implicitly in all of his major works. The descriptions of place in *Paradise Lost* that I examine throughout this book get some of their heightened tension from Milton's experimentation with genre, and his imitation, in his epic, of the style of the *Eclogues* and *Georgics* beyond and contradicting his explicit imitation of the *Aeneid*. But as Genette's warning implies, all of those imitations are not allusions to a fixed Vergilian canon; they create in themselves a distinct understanding of what Vergilian description is in the first place. That understanding is itself based in a fluid and rapidly changing approach to reading Vergil, visible in a number of Renaissance poets within the Vergilian tradition. I will argue in this chapter that, in the Renaissance, the tension about the rereading that takes place when translated bits of Vergil's first two works make their way into English poetry already exists. Milton redoubles and intensifies that tension through the even greater generic complexity of *Paradise Lost*.

In the height of their desperate lovesickness, both Vergil's shepherd Corydon and Marvell's mower Damon look to landscape for consolation or direction, and both fail to find anything there that does not participate in their alienation. What seems like Marvell's direct translation of or allusion to a Vergilian original, however, is in reality a thoughtful and complex rethinking of his source. Descriptively, Marvell's version of the lovesick pastoral figure is significantly different—the landscape that surrounds Damon is figured as isolating him in a way that Corydon's environment is not. This off-putting landscape represents part of a rare, but important, tradition (or counter-tradition) in Renaissance poetry, reworking trends originally found in the *Eclogues*. In certain texts outside of the pastoral genre but relying on allusion to the *Eclogues*, the usually seamless relationship between pastoral shepherds (or their equivalents) and their idealized surroundings is occasionally disrupted. This disruption takes many forms and possesses many intensities—the landscape may be indifferent to humanity, humanity may be represented as hubristically attempting to control landscape, or a more fundamental difference in ways of being may divide the two.[2] In the following pages I examine several instances of this counter-tradition, in which characters expect or anticipate a landscape committed to their own lives and thoughts and find instead that landscape's response is divided, its attention coupled with indifference, and its dependence on man giving way to surprising self-reliance. Poets exploring this darker corollary to the pastoral tradition couple descriptions of a responsive landscape with brief images of a different kind of landscape, one less descriptively oriented toward humanity.

The difference between these two images of landscape lies not in the emotions represented—pastoral characters are always rather woeful—but rather in the tools used to describe pastoral settings. Vergil employs a number of pastoral or quasi-pastoral descriptions of landscape in which the relationship between shepherd and environment is disrupted, creating landscapes that are removed from human life. In fact, even the use of personification in describing landscape, as we will see, can end up creating separation between landscape and people, since the landscape's agency makes it less intertwined with human life. Though pastoral poetry provides a broad spectrum of similarly unsatisfying or incompatible relationships between environment and inhabitant, I refer to the collective poetic effect of such relationships as autonomy of landscape, because these examples characterize landscape as withholding the same kind of responsiveness or dependence on humanity that normally defines the pastoral genre, and therefore present the landscape as self-possessed, possessed of agency, and thus autonomous. Personification is central to this phenomenon: the autonomy that makes landscape more like people in one respect makes it ultimately less involved with human experience.

Poetic tensions between responsiveness and autonomy in landscape have not, I believe, been given previous attention, largely because critics have focused on human agents as the defining characteristic of pastoral rather than on the emotional relationship between character and landscape. Recent criticism of the pastoral tradition has stressed that what matters in the tradition is the shepherd or his equivalent rather than the landscape surrounding him. It is the shepherd's social position that gives pastoral its political message, his nostalgia that gives the genre its historiography, and his song that makes pastoral such an important genre for literary self-assertion and -identification. How shepherds describe their surroundings has been examined only insofar as it relates to those issues, which have come to seem central to the genre. There is an assumption in the criticism of pastoral that landscape is not an equal concern, much less an equal player in shaping who the shepherd is and what he means.

It is true that pastoral generally contains rural laborers. However, critics tend to assume that it follows from that trend that these pastoral characters define both the genre and its typical landscape; as Paul Alpers puts it, the "history of pastoral landscape is . . . an interpretation, a selective emphasis determined by individual or cultural motives, of the central fiction that shepherds' lives represent human lives."[3] Interest in that central fiction, though, has led some critics even to question the importance of the tradition in interpreting individual instances. Chris Fitter, in a book arguing for an ideological understanding of Renaissance landscape poetry, maintains that invocations of the classical tradition in this poetry represent "superficial continuities of landscape presentation," masking, in the Renaissance, a fundamentally new aesthetic of landscape.[4] Since description is always the most classically allusive aspect of pastoral, Fitter's insistence on the superficiality of such connections leads him to ignore description altogether; Fitter discusses the pastoral landscape without commenting on what it looks like.[5] Even in criticism sensitive to the specific continuities and differences within the tradition, however, the stress on character has resulted in an interpretation of pastoral that treats the landscape as necessarily interpretively subservient to character. Annabel Patterson has summarized the issue through a quotation from Servius; for both Patterson and the writers she discusses, pastoral is about some variation on the lament of Meliboeus in the *Eclogues* for the farm he must give up. Servius calls this pattern the "necessity of the lost lands" (Patterson 134).[6] In other words, the characteristic pastoral landscape matters because of the displacement of the people within it; for these critics, that displacement matters primarily in itself, not as part of a relationship between character and landscape.

To demonstrate the roots of Milton's anxious landscape, I will challenge the anthropocentricity of this critical history by examining several stages of the dispersal of the pastoral mode into other genres. Even in the *Eclogues* themselves, the landscape is not as unified around its inhabitants as has usually been thought; in quasi-pastoral uses in Spenser and Marvell that tension increases; and in Milton more than any of these poets we will see that in order for the landscape to fulfill the function a poem needs of it, landscape's relationship with the characters within it is far less immediate, far less concerned with or reflective of their lives (positively or negatively), than the characters themselves expect it to be. Thus Alpers's premise that the landscape can be understood by extension from its inhabitants must be amended; the landscapes that will emerge in this chapter will feature incomplete and ambiguous relationships between character and surroundings, relationships in which the differences or incompatibilities between inhabitant and environment become crucial. This use of the pastoral mode can best be understood by considering character and landscape to be of equal importance. In such a context, a particular kind of pastoral landscape emerges in which a description initially of a responsive landscape gives way to one that treats landscape and character more distinctly. In Spenser's "Epithalamion," for example, we will see one of the clearest instances of this overflowing of context—what begins as a landscape devoted to the wedding at its center becomes, at the moment of consummation, a surrounding too large and too distinct from its inhabitants to give the poem's bridegroom what he asks from it and expects from it.

Generally, the Renaissance poets I discuss here describe landscapes that counter their pastoral responsiveness to humanity with a contrary energy, which expands upon a similar energy derived from Vergil but is more prominent in these Renaissance poems. The Renaissance imitation of Vergilian description that I will focus on here derives from one reading of Vergil available in the period that stresses the autonomy that is always at least a potential aspect of the landscape of the *Eclogues*. That reading is complicated by Renaissance poets' awareness of similar and even darker material in the *Georgics*, which they then retroactively apply to the *Eclogues*. A focus on description will allow a new kind of relationship between Vergil and the English poets to emerge, in which far from being a restrictive influence, Vergil allows English Renaissance uses of pastoral to be even more versatile. I believe that the imitation of Vergilian description by these Renaissance poets significantly recasts Vergilian materials to demonstrate both an awareness of the autonomy of landscape in Vergil and thus of the possible disconnection between character and landscape in their own poems. The ultimate implications of this awareness vary from poet to poet; for Spenser, the autonomous landscape is only one form of a complex expression of gradually increasing anxieties about, in this case, marriage, while we will see a Marvellian example in which I will argue that the possibility of any relationship between man and landscape is questioned.

Milton displays in different ways this anxiety about the discrepancy between landscape's expected function and its actual effects, and some of his instantiations of this tension have been noted.[7] His concern about the possibility of connection with environment is particularly comparable to Spenser's because the Renaissance attempt to combine Vergilian pastoral with Christianity is always difficult, and landscape plays a crucial role in that difficulty. Landscape serves simultaneously as the context that allows the suspension of disbelief necessary for the allegory or conceit to work, and as a crucial part of the hermeneutic thrust of the poem. In other words, the difficulty of pastoral in a religious context is basically locative. But Marvell's concerns, despite a secular context, more closely anticipate Milton's, in part because, I believe, his reading of Vergil is closer to Milton's. The tension between the particular goals of a poet and his place within the tradition will be central to this chapter and to other chapters as well; we will see that neither can be interpreted independently from the other. Vergil's use of place functions as a kind of touchstone for the level of uncertainty about environment that Renaissance poets incorporate. In *Paradise Lost,* however, that basic Renaissance response becomes something else entirely, and though the Vergilian allusions are still there, they are in the service of a far deeper doubt, as other chapters will show.

As I have implied, this ambiguous and variable environment emerges when the Renaissance poets are read in the context of their ambiguous imitation and rewriting of Vergilian description. In the last ten years, criticism of Renaissance poetry has been marked by a burgeoning interest in—and a newly complex and sophisticated understanding of—the imitation and emulation of Vergil in English poetry. Old preoccupations with source and allusion have been replaced by a more dynamic model of intertextuality, so that John Watkins, for example, can claim about the *Faerie Queene* that "Spenser continually revises his understanding of his Vergilian identity within the context of a single poem," and Margaret Tudeau-Clayton that Vergilian meaning is mediated in the period by the circulation of contemporary illustrations of Vergilian texts.[8] Critics have shown, too, that the availability and relevance of the *Georgics* to Renaissance poets complicates the already unstable relationship between pastoral character and pastoral landscape. The use of composite or ambiguous genre in the Renaissance is familiar, but pastoral and georgic, because of their mutual interests in landscape and labor, are still more closely linked and often overlapping. Several distinct Renaissance preoccupations are colored by the complex relationship between the pastoral and georgic modes, preoccupations previously discussed by Patterson, Anthony Low, Jane Tylus, and others.[9] As Tylus has argued, Renaissance poetry's strong interest in the georgic mode develops, in part, because pastoral cannot quite account for the relationship between humanity and the surrounding environment. Georgic offers in labor a way for humanity to interact with a less responsive landscape, and thus to transcend pastoral. Still, Tylus has shown convincingly that, far from being a straightforward imitation of Vergilian pastoral, Spenser's *Shepheardes Calender* relies heavily on the *Georgics* for Spenser's complex analogy between agrarian and poetic labor. This reading demonstrates the possibility for a kind of Renaissance poetry that imitates one Vergilian form while referring thematically to another. Thus, Renaissance ideas of the Vergilian career lead organically toward broader questions of composite genre and intertextuality, questions that have not been rigorously attended to because of a desire for historical specificity as against trans-historical generic definition.

In fact, pastoral genre in itself often seems to be less clearly defined than other genres.[10] Patterson in particular has suggested that pastoral relies heavily, particularly in its later Renaissance manifestations, on essentially georgic modes. She identifies this trend as a fundamentally political one, but I will suggest that the poetics of pastoral as perceived by Renaissance poets already suggests the possibility of georgic, both because of the perceived integrity of the Vergilian career and because georgic offers a more pragmatic function for landscape. Tylus's example of Spenser also, it seems to me, shows that the georgic rethinking of pastoral is available at least to some poets throughout the Renaissance, not just, as Patterson argues, in the seventeenth century.[11] Thus, rather than adopt Patterson's view that developments in politics cause seventeenth-century readers to want pastoral to be more like georgic, we should recognize that these poets see the *Eclogues* themselves as insufficiently accounting for the relationship between man and landscape they describe. However, the Renaissance poets' responses to Vergil are highly individual, and I provide these not in order to make a claim for a period-wide epistemic perspective but on the contrary to demonstrate the possibilities for Vergilian imitation in the context of certain extremes of interpretation. The very existence of those extremes reflects even on more moderate responses; the status of the *Eclogues* and *Georgics* as poets interpreted them is unstable in the

Renaissance, and that instability suggests a variability in genre affecting both reading and writing.

"THE BIRTH OF EVERYTHING"

Interest in expanding the possibilities for the description of landscape within the pastoral mode begins before 1600. As we have seen, Spenser's relationship with Vergil has been a fertile area for criticism. *The Shepheardes Calender* has been the principal site for investigating that relationship, in part because its reliance on pastoral is so explicit. However, I wish to examine here a later poem, "Epithalamion," which is useful for understanding changes in the mode not because it is pastoral but because it is not—"Epithalamion" draws on pastoral elements en route to a generic shift. The landscape at the poem's opening is arranged around the nuptial couple and perfectly responsive to them, but that responsiveness gives way to a description of a landscape whose responsiveness to mankind is unreliable, an awareness of a scale of landscape so large as to be incompatible with human needs or meanings: a kind of landscape that reminds us of the *Georgics*. The generic uncertainty is particularly interesting given that the poem is so extravagantly structured—its careful repetitions and variations give it both a sense of poetic control and thematic continuity. But the implications of its repetitive refrain are not necessarily clear—two lines that sound the same, after all, do not necessarily have the same meaning in different contexts, and the use of a refrain does not necessarily indicate an emotional or philosophical consistency throughout the poem. In fact, I will argue below that the structure is somewhat misleading (and perhaps has misled critics in the past).[12] Within the precision of its intensely regularized stanzas, "Epithalamion" moves toward a darker and more sophisticated reading of the *Eclogues,* though the demands the narrator places on the landscape, specifically that it console humanity, lead eventually to the suggestion of a landscape too powerful and self-directed to perform that consolation or, indeed, to still be considered pastoral. In particular, a problem of scale is created, in which the landscape is figured as simply too huge and distant to be something with which a human being could directly interact, thus limiting the responsiveness of environment that is a hallmark of pastoral. In the process of that shift from small-scale to large-scale, I believe, an echo of the *Georgics* appears.

All these issues come to fruition at the crucial turning point in the poem—nightfall. At nightfall the repetitive refrain changes for the first time, from "all the woods them answer and their echo ring" (or very close variations) to a new silence: "The woods no more shal answere, nor your echo ring" (314).[13] But the silence alone does not yet signal the abandonment of the pastoral responsiveness of landscape. In his description of "welcome night," Spenser shows a sheer forcefulness that allows landscape in silence to have the same function as the echoing landscape:

> Spread thy broad wing over my love and me.
> That no man may us see,
> And in thy sable mantle us enwrap,
> From feare of perrill and foule horror free. (319–22)

The metaphor represents the connection between the couple and the landscape—through its sympathy with them—while also insisting on a direct relationship. The landscape is cooperative, but also acting as separation. Still, the image of safety easily overcomes any doubts that this strange metaphor—the night as a giant and very close bird—may suggest, even those created in the previous stanza by the necessary change to the refrain. The extraordinary physicality of the "sable mantle" metaphor postpones the emotional shift in the poem, allowing silence to function here not as the opposite of sound but as an extension. Spenser's genre shift from pastoral to georgic is carefully uneven—introduced and delayed simultaneously (like the grammatical delay we will see in the second stanza of Marvell's "Glowworms"). The interest in a responsive landscape is maintained, even while the specifically pastoral refrain changes, and separations begin to become evident. Both the new refrain, after all, and the image of wing and the "sable mantle" emphasize silence. The silence indicates that echo (and thus *Eclogue* I) has been abandoned, but the description of night is not yet as demanding or alienating as georgic.

Spenser's initial answer to the question posed by the change in the refrain, then, is that landscape can still be responsive to human needs, but that responsiveness is tied directly to the power that landscape has within itself—the suggestion is of a superior granting a favor to an inferior. It is *agape*—the love of the greater for the lesser or of the god for the man. But as the night continues, Spenser's description of it begins to shift into something entirely different—less responsive, less pastoral:

> But let the night be calme and quietsome,
> Without tempestuous storms or sad afray:
> Lyke as when Jove with fayre Alcmena lay,
> when he begot the great Tirynthian groome:
> Or lyke as when he with thy selfe did lie,
> And begot Majesty. (326–31)

Can the night that mothered Jove's child really be the same night that is the friend of newlyweds? In fact, the simile is really two similes recalling different forms. The second "lyke" (the anthropomorphic one) is different from the first, which is a pastoral simile, a simile of weather—the same kind of night (meteorologically) that accompanied that particular one of Jove's trysts. The second is a simile of historical occasion, referring to one specific night, not a sort of night. This moment is the central point of a gradual shift within the poem from its earlier, more strictly pastoral phase to its later doubts. Spenser's use of the third person in this first simile (as opposed to every other mention of night in the stanza, in second person) reinforces the passivity of night, and so enhances the surprise when night shifts from the accompaniment to love to the lover. Two functions of landscape come together here: personification (the metaphorical humanizing of the night through the image of "sad afray") becomes anthropomorphism (the mythological humanizing of the recollection of night's tryst with Jove). The moment of the shift from one to the other, when Spenser turns to Jove's encounter with Night herself, is specifically a turn away from the pastoral. The pastoral genre here, in fact, is functioning in its absence—the georgic mode of description that appears in the latter part of the poem works to highlight the earlier interest in a cooperative landscape, and thus the lack of that cooperation.

In fact, the encounter of Jove and Night recalls the marriage of earth and sky in *Georgics* II, and in both instances, the scale of the anthropomorphism makes a pastoral personification particularly unlikely—these sound like creation myths, not the myths of descents by Pan or Diana that fill pastoral. Vergil begins and ends his praise of Spring, for example, with discussions of the importance of Spring to farming, but in the midst of that description farming seems almost irrelevant, almost impossible:

> ver adeo frondi nemorum, ver utile silvis,
> vere tument terrae et genitalia semina poscunt.
> tum pater omnipotens fecundis imbribus Aether
> coniugis in gremium laetae descendit, et omnis
> magnus alit magno commixtus corpore fetus. (*Georgics* II.323–27)[14]

> Spring benefits the branches of trees, and the woods;
> in spring the earth swells and demands the fruitful seed.
> Then Sky, the almighty father, with his fecund showers
> descends into his joyful wife's lap, and
> the great one, mixing with her mighty body, feeds the birth of everything.[15]

The scale—culminating in a polyptoton of hugeness, "magnus alit magno" (the same adjective, magnus, describes both sky and earth)—is a reminder to the farmer that whatever his efforts, however hard he rows his boat, he is too small to make a difference in the world at large. The personification, since it allows for easier comparison with humanity, actually reinforces the distance between man and these figures. The passage is an extended sexual metaphor, but the metaphor does not refer back to humanity—it writes a human image too large on to the natural world. Sex in this case serves not to compare human life with nature but to enforce the distinction; this is a kind of sex that we cannot understand in relation to whatever kind we have. Rather than a narrative of decline, Vergil creates an image of essentially unchanging hardship. This image, in an essentially nostalgic poem, forces the reader to admit simultaneously a lost golden age and an eternal present.

In "Epithalamion" the consummation of the marriage ends the pastoral part of the poem—perhaps inevitably, since love in pastoral is really never consummated. It registers that disruption by reinterpreting its own descriptions of landscape, bringing up earlier modes and tropes in order to point out problems. The close proximity of myths of a landscape friendly to human life and human love with starkly contrasting images and allusions is no accident; "Epithalamion" ultimately questions its earlier depiction of a friendly landscape. How far that rethinking of pastoral can extend will be my next subject here. I think "Epithalamion" is a particularly clear example of a pattern in which the responsiveness of landscape to humanity is first offered and then withdrawn. As I have said, though, it is not necessarily clear whether that pattern as it appears in the Renaissance is a reinterpretation of the history and future of the genre or, in fact, an interpretation of the *Eclogues* themselves—that is, are these landscapes a reading of Vergil or a replacement with something new?

Genre is the necessary place to begin to answer that question, because all the elements involved in this darker version of pastoral exist in the Vergilian canon; the problem is only that they are not generally associated with pastoral. The first thing to do, then, is to establish the Vergilian model for the Renaissance autonomous landscape. If there is a continuum of the closeness or distance of the relationship between landscape and humanity, the extreme end of that continuum, for our purposes, is found in several famously dark passages in the *Georgics*. In the *Eclogues,* the disconnection between man and landscape ends up indirectly aiding landscape's ability to console, because it allows for the power of nature's response to man. In the *Georgics,* the disconnection between humanity and landscape is increased—in the *Georgics* environmental distance from humanity presents a serious practical problem—but at the same time the genre of georgic provides the idea of labor as a kind of supplement that can reinstate the consolation.[16]

A greater emphasis on labor allows georgic a new way of thinking about the landscape, which eases some of landscape's disconnections (we cannot make the trees sing, but we can prune them), while creating new ones. Specifically, though the personification of landscape is still present in different forms in the *Georgics,* the easy but dualistic pastoral relationship between man and nature has been replaced by an even more uneasy one in which man is always longing for something closer than what labor gets him.[17] At times, as in Book I's resigned complaint to the frustrations of farming, that longing is intense:

> sic omnia fatis
> in peius ruere ac retro sublapsa referri,
> non aliter quam qui adverso vix flumine lembum
> remigiis subigit, si bracchia forte, remisit,
> atque illum in praeceps prono rapit alveus amni. (I.199–204)
>
> Thus everything by fate
> rushes towards the worse, driven back, falling back,
> nor is the man different who barely pulls his boat
> with struggling oars; if his arms let up, he is sent back,
> and the current drags him headlong down the river.

Nature here represents that aspect of the universe most removed from human control, but there is still an immediacy to the personification; "rapit" (here, "drags," but the word often means "steals" and is the ancestor of our word "rape") is anthropomorphic in tone because of the violence of its usual connotations.[18] The landscape is being used in reference to human emotion, but it is not sympathetic. Rather than creating a connection by describing landscape in human terms, the use of emotion gives the landscape a tropic context for what is in fact a description of disconnection. The personification itself creates a relationship between humanity and the landscape even as the description suggests a disconnection, so that the trope is at odds with the image that contains it. Still, the trope functions as a heightened instance of the problem of the continuity of the personified landscape as it exists in pastoral. The fundamental nature of the disconnection is the same—nature's continuity, stressed here by Vergil's "omnia fatis" (everything by—or in the realm of—fate) pulls it away from mankind.[19] Though georgic's way of coming to terms with the problem is entirely different from eclogue's, the disconnection itself, as Vergil's totalistic vocabulary suggests, is inherent.

The potential for the personification of landscape to create distance from humanity rather than closeness is most evident in these passages in the *Georgics,* but traces of it, we will see, exist already in the *Eclogues.* Even in Vergilian pastoral, a personification of landscape that specifically produces consolation for humanity can still suggest an autonomy. In other words, I am suggesting that we read the *Eclogues* as I think some Renaissance poets did: with the *Georgics* in mind. We will see in the next section that the distinctly georgic image of a landscape whose human-like power over itself can separate it from humanity exists in subtle ways within the *Eclogues.* As in "Epithalamion," echo is central to that image. Echo can be thought of as the metaphor for tensions between landscape's response to humanity and its own distinct existence. The echo is always a response to the human singer that is not in his voice but in the voice of the surrounding woods.

"TEACH THE WOODS"

The central anxiety of the *Eclogues* is displacement, referring presumably to the Augustan land-confiscations that affected all of Italy including, to some extent, Vergil himself.[20] The anxieties about the loss of land that Meliboeus discusses in the first *Eclogue* are clearly intended to govern the perception of the land throughout, even in those of the poems that do not directly mention the confiscations. Rhetorically, however, the disconnection between landscape and shepherd is frequently expressed through the continuity of landscape. The status of pastoral landscape as an extension of the shepherds' lives, particularly their emotional lives, functions as an ever-present inversion of their displacement. We can see this two-sided relationship even in the opening lines of the first poem. Vergil opens his *Eclogues* with an image of contradiction; Meliboeus wonders how it can be that Tityrus can create a profound continuity even in the face of the discontinuity of place Melibeous (because he must leave) feels so strongly:

> Tityre, tu patulae recubans sub tegmine fagi
> siluestrem tenui Musam meditaris auena;
> nos patriae finis et dulcia linquimus arua.
> nos patriam fugimus; tu, Tityre, lentus in umbra
> formosam resonare doces Amaryllida siluas. (I.1–5)[21]

> Tityrus, lying in the shade of the beech tree,
> You practice your woodland muse on the thin reed;
> but we are to leave the pleasant, cultivated lands of our home country.

> We will flee our homeland; you, Tityrus, at ease in the shade,
> You teach the woods to echo 'Amaryllis'—Amaryllis the beautiful.

Melibeous surrounds his own disconnection from his environment with praise for Tityrus's ability to create connection. But the disconnection creeps into the last line. As Meliboeus is aware, part of the problem with echo is that, though controlled by the echoed singer, it is in fact located in the surrounding woods. "Resonare doces" ("you teach to echo") perfectly represents that tension. There is always something ambitious, sometimes over-ambitious, about the pastoral subject's interest in echo, as John Hollander observes.[22] Here, however, that ambition works, because the conceit as Vergil figures it does not require the woods to join too much in the emotional lives of their inhabitants. After all, Tityrus teaches the woods to echo, not to *sing*; his power over them is limited by the power that they already possess. Furthermore, echo has the power to conflate the sound that resonates through the woods with the shepherds themselves, further implanting the characters in their surroundings. I repeat the name "Amaryllis" in my translation to indicate a Vergilian zeugma; what is echoed is, of course, Amaryllis's name, but the adjective "formosam"—'beautiful'—refers to Amaryllis herself. Echo both is created by and represents the immersion of the pastoral subject in the pastoral landscape. But the choice of verb—"doces"—limits that immersion. The power to make all this happen comes equally from Tityrus's commonality with the woods—Vergil's word for his instrument here is "avena," literally "oat-straw," suggesting that he is playing a part of the landscape—and from his disconnection from them. The woods' inability to be completely determined by the interpretation of their inhabitants is what allows them to be taught to echo. The image is partly a contradiction and partly a circle—the native sympathy between the shepherd and his surroundings makes those surroundings a consolation for his troubles, but what allows that consolation to work is that the "pleasant, cultivated lands" do not in fact reflect or contain the pain of the impending exile. By thinking of Tityrus as the woods' teacher rather than as their fellow musician, Meliboeus allows for sympathy from the surroundings and disconnection at the same time.

The qualified distancing of the landscape from its human inhabitants, I believe, is a crucial feature of Vergilian pastoral. The relationship between the shepherds and their surroundings is symbiosis, not unity. The interpretive functions of the disconnection between inhabitant and landscape are many, allowing for important aspects of Vergil's political project, his poetic self-assertion, and his complex and ambivalent analogy between shepherd's song and his own written poetry.[23] But the peculiar technique of the *Eclogues* causes a paradox, in which description's role is as much a part of the disconnection between human and landscape as it is a part of the connection. That is, by focusing on description, we can reevaluate the place of the shepherd himself within the pastoral world, finding him at the center of the landscape but, to an extent, overwhelmed by its continuity apart from him. When Meliboeus recognizes that Tityrus's centrality exists at the expense of his own, his situation also suggests that the continuity of the landscape unto itself always has the potential to subdue rather than to emphasize the importance of the shepherd within it.

In the more intense personification of the landscape found in others of the poems, this tension becomes clearer. *Eclogue* VIII, as a way of accounting for landscape's always-qualified response to humanity, suggests a division between two kinds of landscape:

> Pastorum Musam Damonos et Alphesiboei,
> immemor herbarum quos est mirata iuuenca
> certantis, quorum stupefactae carmine lynces,
> et mutata suos requierunt flumina cursus,
> Damonos Musam dicemus et Alphesiboei. (VIII.1–5)

> [I sing] the muse of shepherds Damon and Alphesiboeus,
> at whom, as they competed, the cow wondered, unknowing,
> while the lynx were stupefied at their songs,
> and the changed rivers stopped their currents—
> I sing the muse of Damon and Alphesiboeus.

Vergil's relative pronouns are significant; he ascribes the changes wrought in the cows and lynx directly to the singers and their songs: "quos est mirata iuuenca" ("at [them] the cow wondered") and "quorum stupefactae carmine lynces." ("at [their] songs the lynx were stupefied"). The animals wonder at, by, because of, the music. The rivers, however, have no relative pronoun; *they* stop their currents: "mutata suos requierunt flumina cursus;" on the contrary, *requiesco,* rest, is almost always a word referring to an inner impulse.[24] However, Vergil stresses the cause of this event: the rivers have been changed ("mutata") by the songs. The first-foot spondee (we would expect "et" to be followed by two short syllables, but the first two syllables in "mutata" are both long) emphasizes the word. The attention of the animals contrasts with this fundamental change of the rivers. In the same way that Meliboeus's "teach the woods to sing" describes a landscape that is at once passive and active, the landscape in Eclogue VIII gives a divided response to the singers;

the animals here make up the passive element of nature, the rivers the active element. The distinction is between an agrarian landscape that responds more intimately to the song than does a reserved natural landscape, but these two are merely a division, clearer than usual, of responsive and unresponsive aspects of nature. The one is never without the other in the *Eclogues*, as if the pastoral world can only maintain its very close relationship with its human inhabitants by keeping something in reserve.[25]

The elements of landscape that, though examined as they respond to man, separate themselves from man—the self-contained, uncontrolled aspects of landscape—exist throughout the *Eclogues*. Our study of description has shown, however, that in the context of the even more distant landscape of the *Georgics*—the landscape that truly has the potential to alienate the human figure within by dwarfing him—those disquieting elements of pastoral become particularly clear. I believe that it is this reinterpreting context that Spenser introduces when he brings up, in an otherwise pastoral landscape, the dual description of a night that is within the scale of the landscape already created and well outside of it at the same time. Renaissance imitation of Vergil has the capacity to rethink its originals.

However, there is by no means a single perspective in the period of the status of the pastoral figure in relation to the pastoral landscape. In Marvell's Mower poems the imitation of Vergilian pastoral becomes an opportunity for a kind of landscape description utterly unlike the *Eclogues*. The introduction of a distinctively Marvellian topic—the mind—not only changes our interpretation of the figure at the center of the landscape, but rethinks the landscape itself, because the implied relationship between the two is so different. The mind is referred to in terms of place in the context of the pastoral landscape, as if to expect the Mower's mind to be the obvious center of that landscape, but in those moments when the consolation of a responsive landscape is most needed, the mind is displaced. Thus in Marvell, what was in Vergil and in Spenser a landscape with an at times troublingly ambiguous relationship with the central figures within it becomes a landscape with no center at all.

"SHE MY MIND HATH SO DISPLACED"

The built-in qualification of the landscape's response is a subtly expressed theme in the *Eclogues,* but Marvell's pastoral poetry induces us to think of that qualification as crucial. Thus, Marvell's imitation of Vergil is critical, and forms a critique functioning in several ways. Marvell suggests through his imitation that Vergil's pastoral already anticipates—or even needs—georgic (as I argued above that "Epithalamion" does), but it also questions the continuity of the relationship between subject and surroundings in pastoral itself. The potentially insufficient orientation toward humanity of Vergilian landscape becomes, in Marvell's Mower poems, the operative metaphor for a profound crisis, a crisis that asks to be read back on to Vergil. That crisis is an extreme version of the withholding of the consolation that the pastoral landscape seems to offer. But the crisis lies not in the thematic movement of the poems, which are superficially static, but in the mode of figuration. Marvell figures the landscape in such a way as to complicate Damon's relationship with his environment.

I am suggesting that the central problem of the Mower poems—Damon's sense of displacement—is not contained within Damon's mind but rather in the tenuous space between mind and landscape. By considering this possibility, we raise the question of whether the desire for a particular relationship with nature—which is Damon's principal subject other than the impossibility of getting what he needs from Juliana—locates that relationship in the self or in the surroundings. Victoria Silver, in a brilliant recent essay on ambivalence in Marvell's pastoral and lyric poetry, states the problem in such a way as to equivocate between a reading that finds the landscape or Damon as principally responsible for the failed relationship between them. As such, her reading similarly equivocates between that of an autonomous landscape and one more directly connected to its inhabitants. The Mower poems, she suggests, represent the clearest example of a trend uniting Marvell's pastorals; as with other Marvellian landscapes:

> the Mower's sweet fields purport to offer a retreat from the suffering desire itself brings upon humanity . . . Even in putative retirement, these figures still share this belief that they can withdraw yet further into some timeless because primal simplicity of nature that will more readily, intimately, and painlessly gratify their desires. But since the complication of desire by heterosexuality . . . is the invariable fact around which pastoral life turns, no such retreat is viable.[26]

So if the fields purport to offer a retreat that is—as it turns out—illusory, than is the failure (or the cause of the illusion) located in the fields or in the one who desires the retreat? To say that the problem is sexual is to remove it from the fields even as it is clear that the fields themselves, as Silver says, "purport to offer a retreat"—Silver replicates the personification of landscape with which Marvell expresses the very issue that interests her. If the problem is sexual desire, then what is to prevent landscape's offer from being real?

Silver clearly perceives rightly that there is something wrong with landscape's offer of retreat to begin with, even though what the poems actually represent as the obstacle is love. I would suggest, however, that by considering love as the *cause* of the problem with the offer of consolation, she is making a symptom the disease. It seems to me that the sexual failure is in fact merely the objective correlative of the failed consolation of landscape. What Damon wants, as Silver says, is a more complete and more immediate relationship with nature, and because he associates his inability to get it with Juliana, he concludes that Juliana has displaced his mind. But as we will see, the ideal place he imagines for his mind is dubious regardless of his relationship with Juliana. In mourning what Juliana has done to him, Damon describes the landscape as already containing the disruption that, nominally, he ascribes to her. In this sense, I believe that the interpretation of the Mower poems should not be based on the erotic situation they describe but on the modes of description they rely on.First, Marvell's rereading (or, perhaps, rewriting) of Vergil: the Mower poems reinterpret the pastoral personification of landscape not as a representation of a problem but as part of the problem. In a striking echo of the second *Eclogue,* the mower takes over Corydon's metaphor of the pangs of love as a kind of heat from which shade is no escape:

> This heat the sun could never raise,
> Nor Dog Star so inflame the days.
> It from an higher beauty grow'th,
> Which burns the fields and mower both:
> Which mads the dog, and makes the sun
> Hotter then his own Phaëton.
> Not July causeth these extremes,
> But Juliana's scorching beams. ("Damon the Mower" 17-24)[27]

Damon goes out of his way to stress that this heat is not the same as that of the sun, that the effects of Juliana are figured as environmental but are not in actuality environmental. Thus, the relationship between the heat of the sun and the heat of love that Damon insists upon—both burn the fields, etc.—works only to enforce the emphatic distinction: "*Not* July causeth these extremes" (23). The pun (July/Juliana) reinforces the distinction as well—however close the two sources of heat may sound, the difference between them is fundamental.

That distinction is not at all the point of Corydon's use of the same metaphor. For him, the personification of landscape is a way to express the depth of a problem clearly caused by love:

>   nunc etiam pecudes umbras et frigora captant,
>   nunc virides etiam occultant spineta lacertos,
>   Thestylis et rapido fessis messoribus aestu
>   alia serpullumque herbas contundit olentis.
>   at mecum raucis, tua dum vestigia lustro,
>   sole sub ardenti resonant arbusta cicadis. (*Eclogues* II.8-13)

>   Even now the cows seek shade and coolness,
>   even now the green lizards hide among thorns,
>   and Thestylis, for the weary harvesters emerging
>   from the fierce sun, pounds garlic and thyme
>   into her odoriferous herbs.
>   But only the shrill cicadas in the woods sing with me,
>   as I trace your footprints, under the burning sun.[28]

Corydon's stress is simply on his own isolation (caused by love) from all of the other creatures, human and animal, within the pastoral landscape. In fact, he focuses on the continuity of that landscape: both the physical continuity—everything is moving in the same direction, from sun to shade—and the temporal continuity—the repetition of "nunc etiam" (even now) suggests the opposite, that all of this shade-seeking happens primarily because it always does (or to put it another way, Corydon knows about it because it is the usual order of things). The continuity of landscape matters because it suggests that Corydon should be included but in fact is not. This much is not unusual, of course—the lover's sense of alienation from the landscape is familiar from other instances of pastoral.

On the other hand, there is something a little mysterious about that exclusion, since Corydon, the poem mentions specifically, is in the shade: "inter densas, umbrosa cacumina, and fagos "—"within the dense beeches, their pointed shades" (2.3). Editors read this discrepancy as hyperbole: an emphasis on the self-conscious extremity with which Corydon describes his situation.[29] But Marvell does not read it that way, or at least he does not imitate that part of the meaning of the original. Damon makes a distinction between two kinds of heat, including one that can burn a man even in the shade, in order to rethink the Vergilian landscape as something that cannot provide relief, not as something that happens not to provide relief. For Corydon seeking shade is prevented through a not very precise project, one that readers can easily take to be a pitiably over-exaggerated love. For Damon, seeking shade is a category error, and it creates within Marvellian pastoral a very different kind of landscape, one in which the failed consolation is inextricably embedded. Thus,

The Withdrawn Landscape 39

even while Damon's reaction to his situation—unrequited love causes him to think of the landscape as turning against him—is comparable to Corydon's, Marvell's figuration of the landscape ties Damon to a kind of thinking that is entirely unlike Corydon's. The allusion is not a thematic imitation but a descriptive innovation.

The relationship between lovelorn shepherd and pastoral landscape, however, is not the same in all of Marvell's pastorals. In some, as perhaps in "Damon the Mower," the possibility of some solution to the problem of the place of the mind in the landscape is left open, either through love or through labor. But the poems vary; in "The Mower to the Glowworms" no such possibility exists. The problem is expressed in terms of the same kind of discrepancy in scale that we saw in the *Georgics* and alluded to in the "Epithalamion," though in "Glowworms" the starkness of the disrupted relationship between pastoral landscape and inhabitant is much more pronounced. In fact, the form of the failure of landscape's consolation is more specific in "Glowworms" than in the other instances I have examined, because the Mower attaches that failure directly to his situation—he is the opposite of Melibeous, who has trouble making sense of Tityrus's connection to landscape even though he knows that his own displacement does not extend to Tityrus. The failure in "Glowworms" is tied directly to the displacement of the mind, and the literalization of that metaphor—that the mind has a *place* in the pastoral landscape and can lose it—should govern the interpretation of the whole poem.

The specificity of "Glowworms" is related to its very unusual compactness. It is not an epigram, but it is a single sentence, addressed to glowworms. Over the course of that sentence, however, a distinctive pattern of landscape's failure emerges, in which the landscape's unity of purpose is replaced by a problem in scale leading eventually to a complete disintegration of environment. It is not a coincidence, I believe, that the shortest and most formally simple of the Mower poems contains the starkest image of the impossibility of a consoling landscape. Thus, I offer my reading of "Glowworms" with the understanding that the severity of its depiction of pastoral landscape is beyond that of Marvell's other lyrics, even while I believe that this extreme form of disconnection between pastoral figure and landscape represents a tension that can be found in less pronounced versions in other poems. In other words, the doubts of "Glowworms" should be seen as differences in degree, not kind, from those of the Marvellian corpus as a whole.

The poem begins with an image of cooperation throughout the landscape:

> Ye living lamps, by whose dear light,
> The nightingale doth sit so late,
> And, studying all the summer night,
> Her matchless songs does meditate; (1–4)

The description is only of landscape; there is no human inhabitant yet. However, the stanza establishes the functions of pastoral landscape through the connection of the elements of that landscape with each other. The glow-worms and nightingale are working together to produce the familiar personified pastoral environment.[30] As often in Vergil, the metaphors themselves suggest possible connections with humanity as well. Simply to call the glow-worms "lamps" is to think of them in relation to human use of them, even though it is the personified nightingale who is using them. In this case, the personification of landscape excludes humanity altogether, not just the Mower himself, but this exclusion will later register together with Juliana's disruption. The continuity of the landscape represents the human figure's inability to connect with it, an inability that will later be repeated in terms of human interaction.

In the second stanza a further disconnection arises. The problem is scale—connection requires that two things be on the same level, and here (as in Spenser's two differently-scaled images of Night), the possibility of fundamentally incompatible levels appears. Marvell introduces a discontinuity of scale into the fluidly cooperative landscape:

> Ye country comets, that portend
> No war, nor prince's funeral,
> Shining unto no higher end
> Than to presage the grass's fall; (5–8)

The first stanza was an image of success; this is an image of failure, though not *yet* a significant failure—Marvell's joke is the hyperbole of his comparison. Still, the failure is there, and as in the opening stanza it is general; even before the speaker has introduced himself, the landscape is described specifically as something that does not respond to human crisis—any human crisis.[31] The verb, portend, signifies an attempt: its etymological root is *tendere*—to stretch. The objects the "country comets" stretch forth toward are in the negative—"portend / *No* war . . ." The objects are anticipated, and then are missing, so that the failure is withheld or delayed. The country comets, like all comets, try to portend, but because they are country they fall short.[32] The glowworms, within their limited pastoral world, are left with just enough power but no more: they fulfill their place in a world that needs all of its parts.[33] It is only the disruption of that world created, in this case, by love that makes important the meagerness of the glowworms' power of portending. Thus, love is specifically something to which an ordinarily responsive landscape does not respond.

The second stanza hints, in its acknowledgment of what the glowworms cannot do, that a scale problem exists; the third stanza reveals the problem in full:

> Ye glowworms, whose officious flame
> To wandering mowers shows the way,
> That in the night have lost their aim,
> And after foolish fires do stray; (9–12)

The suggestion, once again, is of small scale—fire is not officious unless it is strictly contained, as it is here figuratively by the glowworms' tininess and dimness—and that smallness anticipates the possibility of the landscape's inability to solve Damon's big problem. "Officious" is a peculiar word anyway; of its several meanings, the *OED* lists two, both current in the seventeenth century, which, though related, are essentially opposite in implication: "Doing or ready to do kind offices," and "Unduly forward in proffering services." The nature of the officiousness depends on whether or not the services are wanted, but in either case the offices are small. Here, of course, Damon would need the glowworms' services only if they were big enough to work for him. "Officious" indicates that the glowworms are not a stand-in for fire but a parody of fire. They represent fire no more than does the ignis fatuus—which "foolish fires" translates—the ignis fatuus whose distracting effect the glowworms are supposedly designed to overcome. Thus "foolish fires" is both a metaphor for love—what really causes the mower to be lost—with an applicable judgmental epithet, but within the image is the ignis fatuus itself—the light of the woods that is just as small but even more unstable than the glowworms. If a mower has lost his "aim"—his goal, but also his orienting landmark—the landscape must replace it. But the two possible aims in this stanza, the foolish fire which is rejected and the officious flame, are too similar. In this stanza, not only is landscape unable to respond to the problem, it is accused of contributing to the problem, through a discrepancy in scale between what the mower needs and what is provided.

Love is the most immediate but not the ultimate cause of this problem of scale. Under ordinary circumstances, a mower's hopes and his work are one and the same; his aim, the direction in which he is traveling, is not a distant point but his actual location: the field. The implication is a kind of perfect stasis, in which one is moving towards an ideal even as one is stationary. In that case, one's way *is* one's environment. Because Damon's needs, now that he is in love, require more of the glowworms than their usual function (providing reading light for nightingales), he creates a discrepancy, and he must question either the glowworms themselves or the new aim that they no longer support. A mower whose aim is an ignis fatuus still has an aim. If he is "wandering," then the aim he has lost is the stationary aim of mowing itself. But the problem is not solved by reinstating the mower's original aim. If the foolish fire the mower is chasing is an ignis fatuus, then the poem offers no reason to make a distinction between that fire and the glowworm's fire, which can only provide an aim through metonymy. But if the foolish fire is love, then the officiousness of the glowworms seems to be entirely on the wrong scale. Either way, the mower is lost. His world does not have enough significance to give him the kind of direction he recognizes in the nightingale. Being in love has caused him to lose the sense of a connected landscape altogether, not just his own place in that landscape.

The first three stanzas already establish an impossible situation—a natural connectedness between subject and landscape that has been irrevocably thrown off by the introduction of the as-yet-unmentioned foreign element. In the last stanza, however, Marvell introduces within that problem a further problem. He declares finally that the locative problem is a problem of mind:

> Your courteous lights in vain you waste,
> Since Juliana here is come,
> For she my mind hath so displaced
> That I shall never find my home. (13–16)

"Courteous lights" is a striking variation on "living lamps," "country comets" and "officious flame," since, the personification aside, it is not a metaphor; in fact, it is rather unambitious as epithets go. It contrasts markedly with the second half of the line, which is strongly negative. "Waste," the main verb of the only sentence in the poem, drops the suggestion of the first three stanzas that the pastoral world continues to fulfill its basic functions even if a member of it is suffering. In the first stanza in particular, the glowworms clearly maintain their utter connectedness within the landscape, even, it turns out, without the mower's participation. As the poem goes on, however, the perspective shifts to Damon's own, and here he now perceives a world whose function is no longer apparent. The vain waste is created by a displaced mind, a mind whose location—both literally and figuratively—is not

The Withdrawn Landscape 43

where it should be. If the image of the nightingale, with its scarcity of light, is an image of perfect equilibrium in which all of the necessary connections are made, the poem's final image is one of imbalance and disconnection. The glowworms are wasted, despite the many functions the poem lists for them, because Damon's mind is displaced, and thus there is no place for the glowworms to have their function.

External and internal collapse in this last stanza, as the displacement that, with the images of wandering lost in the woods, has always been an issue, finally locates itself in interiority. It is because of Damon's mind that the glowworms do not show him the way home. The displaced mind has caused the stark discrepancy between the cooperative landscape surrounding the nightingale and the uncooperative one surrounding Damon. Thus Marvell places the capacity of the mind to create the pastoral landscape at the center of that landscape; the mind is part of the framework of necessity that makes up the pastoral world. The poem presents us with an ambiguity that suggests a significant interpretive problem. If the poem is simply about love, than this is once again a condescending hyperbole. But the stanza itself, by bringing up the Marvellian concept of the world-making mind, suggests that the poem is not just about love but about the function of descriptive poetry itself.

That this world-making is, elsewhere in Marvell, an issue unrelated to the pastoral lover enforces the point. The creating mind whose displacement prevents the glowworms from functioning is closely related to the often-discussed mind of "The Garden," which distances itself from the world in order to create a better one. The form of "The Garden," however—its progression from an intensely physical garden to a kind of mental garden—is itself a way to stress poetry at the expense of nature, as Harry Berger tells us. Berger stresses that it is not often enough said because it is obvious that, over the course of "The Garden," "Marvell withdraws in, and into, a poem, not a garden."[34] In the context of the failed pastoral continuity of "Glowworms," that withdrawal would seem to be a comment on the inevitably of the failure. "The Garden" praises a mind whose greenness is independent of actual verdure:

> Meanwhile the mind, from pleasures less,
> Withdraws into its happiness:
> The mind, that ocean where each kind
> Does straight its own resemblance find,
> Yet it creates, transcending these,
> Far other worlds, and other seas;
> Annihilating all that's made
> To a green thought in a green shade. (41-48)

Marvell's "Yet" in line 45 is interesting. The mind has an ability to match kinds, to create categories for things, but "yet" suggests that the mind is able to make worlds not because of but in spite of that ability. To be observant of the continuity of the world does not give one the ability to make worlds within the self. The ability to see a nightingale or evening as part of a continuous environment, assembled *a priori* to the individual things but by the mind, is not the same as the ability to recognize evening or the nightingale or even the daily cycle of which both are a part. The "yet" and the talk of transcendence suggest already two levels of the mind's activities, of which analogy—finding resemblance—is the lower and place-making the higher.

Empson comments usefully on this passage, suggesting that this hierarchy of thought depends on the scope of thought. He finds three levels of thought in "The Garden," and ultimately those levels must "rise through a hierarchy of three sharply contrasted styles and with them give a more and more inclusive account of the mind's relation to Nature."[35] He begins his exploration of these levels by pointing out an ambiguity in "annihilating": it can mean "either contemplating everything or shutting everything out," a combination of the conscious and unconscious nature. For Empson the contradiction leads to a greater understanding of the world, precisely because the kind of mind Marvell discusses is the kind that can handle the contradiction Empson points out. This inclusive mind, I think, is the kind of mind that is presented as the ideal in "Glowworms," but that in that poem cannot be reached, and is thus mourned. "The Garden" makes the larger-scale, darker reading of the ambiguous final stanza of "Glowworms" more likely.

I asked earlier whether, for Marvell, the failure of landscape to console its inhabitants is located in the landscape or in the individual. But the relationship suggested, in the end of "Glowworms," between landscape and mind implies that the distinction between subject and surroundings is itself ambiguous, since the mind is described in terms of place even while the surroundings are affected by the mind's displacement. The poem is not just a pastoral application of the idea of mind Marvell suggests in "The Garden," because the mind of "Glowworms" is concerned with surroundings in a way that (as Berger argues) the mind of "The Garden" is not. I believe that this different kind of mind in "Glowworms," to which place is so important, is there as part of a significant and pointed reading of Vergil. When Meliboeus remarks, in the first *Eclogue*, that Tityrus's connection to environment continues even when Meliboeus is displaced, he is commenting on the tragedy of a landscape whose continuity remains when that connective power is no longer aimed at a particular human subject. The opening of "Glowworms" reflects a similar idea; the nightingale and glowworms maintain *their* pastoral relationship even without human interaction. But finally the displacement of love (as opposed to the more pragmatic form of displacement in Vergil) threatens to overwhelm the continuity of landscape itself. In Marvell's version, even Meliboeus's (or Cordyon's) observation of a pastoral life continuing without him is impossible.

By inserting a distinctly Marvellian idea of mind into the pastoral landscape, Marvell not only personalizes that landscape but transforms it into something that (in "Glowworms" at least) is not quite pastoral—is more like a wistful remembrance of pastoral. What the last stanza of "Glowworms" denies—the place of the mind at the center of the pastoral landscape—is what defines pastoral, and thus Marvell elides the whole. But to say that therefore the poem does not belong to the genre to which it blatantly and unquestionably refers (as Empson says, "Marvell was not hiding his source with any care"[36]) is to maintain an unacceptably simplistic idea of what genre is. On the contrary, the examples I have discussed here show that texts that not only rephrase but rethink Vergilian pastoral are all the more inextricable from the long history of the genre, precisely because by rethinking they are also always rereading. The Renaissance did not universally read Vergilian pastoral as containing an autonomous landscape. What Renaissance pastoral did contain was the *potential* for a concept of landscape in some ways alien to the genre itself, a potential that appears to a greater or lesser extent in different poets, but which, over the course of the period, can explain at least some of the slipperiness and the mutability of the early modern uses of the *Eclogues*.

"THE GOD OF THE PLACE"

There is a pattern in these poems involving personification and the difficulty of connection to landscape: the personification of landscape is a reflection of human thought but in its actual use makes the landscape more of a distinct entity. For Milton, even in his early work, the pattern is of greater significance than for any other poet in the period, and anticipates the later, full-fledged anxiety about place that is the principal topic of this book. Before *Paradise Lost*, the issue of an autonomous landscape is presented not as the paradox it later will become but as a simple dichotomy—a set of alternatives between one reading of landscape and another. Unlike in Spenser, Milton's description of landscape emphasizes not the contrast of pastoral and non-pastoral but fluidity. Thus, in "L'Allegro" and "Il Penseroso" descriptions of a kind of landscape that includes man alternate easily with descriptions of one that isolates him. Even in these poems about and exemplifying stark contrasts no such contrast is allowed between these two kinds of landscape.

Milton's double invocation of the moon in "Il Penseroso" is perhaps his clearest example of this fluidity between ideas of landscape:

> And the mute Silence hist along,
> 'Less *Philomel* will deign a Song,
> In her sweetest, saddest plight,
> Smoothing the rugged brow of night,
> While *Cynthia* checks her Dragon yoke
> Gently o'er th' accustom'd Oak;
> Sweet Bird that shunn'st the noise of folly
> Most musical, most melancholy!
> Thee Chantress oft the Woods among
> I woo to hear thy Even-Song;
> And missing thee, I walk unseen
> On the dry smooth-shaven Green.
> To behold the wand'ring Moon,
> Riding near her highest noon.
> Like one that had been led astray
> Through the Heav'n's wide pathless way;
> And oft, as if her head she bow'd,
> Stooping through a fleecy cloud. (55–72)

As in Spenser's "Epithalamion," Milton makes a musical landscape and a silent one almost equivalent. There are two separate descriptions here—in the first landscape with its singing bird, the moon is stopped (like the rivers in Vergil's Eighth *Eclogue*), while in the second, silent landscape, the moon is still "wand'ring" (67). The two descriptions are perfectly parallel, both turning to the moon as the image of solitude. They take place in apparently the same time; in fact, the word "oft" appears at essentially the same point in the final couplet of each description. Yet the two figures are clearly not the same; Cynthia is still, and the moon is in motion. The first moon is on the same scale as the narrator and the bird he is listening to; they all participate as similar agents in the same world. The second is astronomical; it *has* a "highest noon," and heaven here is not the one whose host was led by Venus in Spenser but the enormous sky that Adam contemplates. The personification of the second moon, other than the pronoun "her," is only half suggested; "as if her head she bow'd" is a simile; the only metaphor is "stooping." This subtle personification makes the previous one, with its dragon and its tree, seem hyperbolic.

Neither of these landscapes is directly responsive to the narrator, but both involve him (and the reader) through their personification, though in entirely different ways. One is a responsive personification, the other a sympathetic but distinctly unresponsive personification, and even a distant one; the moon in the second description seems smaller and farther away. As in the doubling of "L'Allegro" and "Il Penseroso" themselves, the point of the doubling of this description is not that either one is the real one but that both alternatives, by being so different, cancel out the ultimate authoritativeness of the other. Neither the responsive nor the autonomous landscape is permitted to have the final place of prominence in "Il Penseroso," and that careful equivocation, I believe, applies as well to Milton's handling of genre and the place of the Vergilian tradition in his poetry. Pastoral, georgic, and epic are evident in all of Milton's major poems, not just to enforce the comparison with Vergil but to use Vergilian devices in the service of Milton's greater generic flexibility.[37]

However, Milton's manipulation of his Vergilian materials extends beyond this composite use of genre, particularly in relation to the description of landscape. The culmination of the theme of the relationship between man and nature is in the fourth *Georgic*'s retelling of the Orpheus myth, a passage particularly influential in the Renaissance. Within the period, as Charles Segal says of *Georgics* 4 itself, "the interplay between man's control over nature and nature's independence—often destructive independence—from man" is centered on the Orpheus story.[38] Significantly, Milton imitates the Orpheus passage while intensifying aspects that, though decidedly Vergilian, are less pronounced at this particular moment of the *Georgics*. Personification, once again, is the issue. When Vergil uses emotionally charged epithets for place in order to surround an elegiac singer with an appropriate environment he resists personification in favor of a simple continuity between human emotion and natural cycle, a continuity that still preserves the disconnection between Orpheus and his surroundings:

> te, dulcis coniunx, te solo in litore secum,
> te veniente die, te decedente canebat. (*Georgics* 4.465–466)
> "You," he sang, "sweet wife, you" alone on the shore
> "You" at the rising of the day, "you" at its falling.

There is an emphasis on landscape in these lines, with the repetition of natural place and natural time, carefully arranged as parallels, so that the reader necessarily imagines the beginning and end of the day occurring *at* the shore where Orpheus is singing. There is an ambiguity within those repetitions, however. This could be someone unusually embedded in landscape—the repetitions suggesting that the song is arising out of natural time and place—

or ignoring it. After all, the song does not change. The contrast between responsive and autonomous landscape is inverted here—it is Orpheus whose responsiveness to the landscape is unclear.

That ambiguity explains the slight instability with which the well-known passage enters English poetry. Though there is no suggestion in the *Georgics* that the day rises or falls for any reason other than that it does, Milton can allude to this passage and replace its sympathies with true personification:

> Thee Shepherd, thee the Woods, and desert Caves,
> With wild Thyme and the gadding Vine o'ergrown,
> And all their echoes mourn. ("Lycidas" 39–41)

Milton's personification is not the pathetic fallacy, or at least is not merely the pathetic fallacy, because it is built in to the sense of location that Vergil describes, even though Vergil avoids personification. In other words, the personification of place in "Lycidas" can be defended by its relationship with the pathos of place in Vergil, because that pathos even in the *Georgics* is never far from personification. By reading personification into Orpheus's surroundings, Milton violates Vergil's disconnection between man and landscape, but in a way that chooses one possible reading of the passage over another.[39] At the same time, it creates some distance from Vergil (and hence from Orpheus); it is, in essence a *re-pastoralization* of Vergil's georgic Orpheus, recalling the imagistic mechanics of Vergilian eclogue in order to rethink the georgic aspects of the poem.[40]

Milton's critical imitation in this passage is similar in kind to Marvell's discussed above—both reread Vergil necessarily as they reuse Vergilian resources—but Milton's is far more ambitious, as other passages in "Lycidas" show. Unlike Marvell, Milton is willing to recall a level of anthropomorphism associated with the *Aeneid*. In the *Eclogues* and *Georgics*, Vergil created a range of subtly different ways to figure the relationship between man and landscape. In the *Aeneid*, the full range is at work at once, and this epic use of a simultaneous large continuum of possible figurations of environment will be influential for Milton. Landscape retains aspects of both the pastoral cooperative personification and the divine scale of the *Georgics*. In Aeneas' conversation with the Tiber, for example, Vergil seems to be unsure which way he wants to go:

> nox erat et terras animalia fessa per omnis
> alituum pecudumque genus sopor altus habebat,

The Withdrawn Landscape 49

> cum pater in ripa gelidique sub aetheris axe
> Aeneas, tristi turbatus pectora bello,
> procubuit seramque dedit per membra quietem.
> Huic deus ipse loci fluuio Tiberinus amoeno
> populeas inter senior se attolere frondes
> visus (eum tenuis glauco velabat amictu
> carbasus, et crinis umbrosa tegebat harundo),
> tum sic adfari et curas his demere dictis . . . (VIII.26–35)

> It was night, and through all the earth deep sleep took hold
> of the tired animals, the herds and flocks of every kind,
> while lord Aeneas, on the cold riverbank under the sky's axis,
> his heart troubled by the emotions of war,
> stretched out and gave evening rest to his limbs.
> The god of the place, the pleasant river Tiber, came to him,
> raising his old face among the poplar leaves;
> a thin robe of gray flax covered him,
> and reeds shaded his head;
> then he spoke, and removed care with words.

The two interactions with nature in this crucial, somewhat difficult passage are as different as possible. The image at first is of continuity; weariness and sleep are everywhere, from man to animal to landscape, without division. Aeneas is placed in his environment as if it is an extension of himself, and he of it. The anthropomorphic god, however, forms a connection beyond that even of pastoral. It may be that this is no longer landscape, that this is not about the poem's setting but about its religious center, but even in that case the god's leafy image still refers back to a landscape that can not only echo, but speak. One gets the feeling that the cooperation of the sleeping landscape with the sleepy hero (and vice versa) is necessary for the prophetic vision to function; there is some basic similarity between Vergil's sympathetic landscape and his compassionate god. But the image of the raising of the god also interrupts the original, continuous image. In the instant of the appearance of the anthropomorphic god, the personification of landscape is no more, and the leaves and reeds are inert accompaniments to the god. In epic, the personification of landscape found in pastoral has become simultaneously less and more pronounced; what was bold image has become spare suggestion, while what was vague religious background has become divine vision. The connection problem of pastoral is acknowledged and dealt with here by replacing the simple personification of landscape with a distinctly religious anthropomorphism.

This competitive variety of connections is comparable to that in "Lycidas," in which the elegiac task requires the cooperation of incompatible anthropomorphisms. For a time it seems that Milton will be content to echo Vergil:

> Next *Camus,* reverend Sire, went footing slow,
> His Mantle hairy, and his Bonnet sedge,
> Inwrought with figures dim, and on the edge
> Like to that sanguine flower inscrib'd with woe. (103–06)

This is a northern Tiber; like the god Tiber, Camus is clothed in his own landscape. But in the *Aeneid* the river god interrupts and forces a rethinking of an existing pastoral-sounding landscape. Here, Camus represents the landscape which is interrupted by the even greater god, Peter, an interruption whose force is felt mostly at its end: "Return, *Alpheus,* the dread voice is past / That shrunk thy streams . . ." (132–33). Not only does "Lycidas" not take place in a pastoral world, but the elements that remove it from pastoral are themselves in conflict. In transforming the Vergilian motif for a Christian use, Milton allows the landscape to recede somewhat (a recession represented by Alpheus's shrinking streams). The elegiac and Christian needs of the poem cause the perfectly interconnected landscape it initially suggests ultimately to be dubious. In *Paradise Lost,* we will see a fundamentally similar but far greater crisis caused by the impossibility of that fully responsive landscape.

As has been noted elsewhere, all three of Vergil's major poems are available as source material for *Paradise Lost*.[41] Thus all of Vergil's conceptions of the relationship between man and environment are available as well: the continuity of the *Eclogues* in which metaphors of disconnection and images of connection can function together, the discontinuity of the *Georgics* in which similar tropic connection enforces the distance of an aloof and inaccessible nature, and the various combinations and compromises between these. Two themes persist throughout: the capacity for disconnection or doubt, which we will see many times, and the predominance of personification as both a means of connection and disconnection. Two of the Vergilian passages I have discussed here are particularly significant for this book (and for *Paradise Lost*): the opening of the first *Eclogue,* including Meliboeus's phrase "resonare doces . . . silvam" ("you teach the woods to echo"), and the great simile from *Georgics* 2 of the farmer as a rower working against a current too powerful for him.

Though there are similarities between Milton's and Marvell's handling of Vergil, at least two major factors in *Paradise Lost* separate that poem's use of Vergilian resources from Marvell's and from those of other poems I have discussed. The first, of course, is Milton's explicit religious project; the relationship between that project and his ambiguous use of Vergilian landscapes will be an important strain in all of the remaining chapters of this book. I believe that the relationship is an uncomfortable one—the description of environment and the relationship of landscape and the subject constitute two of the aspects of *Paradise Lost* that are least compatible with the attempt to "justify the ways of God to men" (1.26). The other element of the poem that makes *Paradise Lost* such a different kind of treatment of Vergil than any other poem I have examined is Milton's poetic ambition, his pursuit of "Things unattempted yet in Prose or Rhyme" (1.16). This ambition reveals itself in large part in the form of competition with Vergil, and as a result in Milton's case Vergilian materials are used not just to reinterpret the originals but to outdo them. But there is one more factor that separates *Paradise Lost* from "Epithalamion" or "The Mower to the Glowworms": Adam himself, whose understanding of his environment will be central to my argument for the remainder of this book. Unlike Spenser's ambiguously anxious groom or Marvell's pitiable Mower, Adam says very sophisticated things about the relationship between his surroundings and himself, and his own observations of the difficulties of coming to terms with his place in the landscape will be as significant as the narrator's descriptions of the landscape. In fact, I will ultimately argue that Adam has a genius for the uncertainty an autonomous landscape can create, a capacity with the power to undermine Milton's explicit religious goal and to infect the ethics of the Fall itself.

Chapter Two
The Environs of Imagination: *Paradise Lost* 7 and 8

Raphael's descent to Eden, which takes up most of the middle four books of *Paradise Lost,* is an extraordinary gesture of solidarity from a fundamentally alien being. Milton describes Raphael's long conversation with Adam as "Venial discourse unblam'd" (8.5); the suggestion of kindness and freedom points to the contrast between this conversation and the later trouble between Heaven and humanity, but it also emphasizes that the "discourse" is an exception to the usual order of things. However, there are several moments, particularly in Books 7 and 8, in which Raphael's anxieties about Adam's capacity to understand and interpret make him a little less kind and a little quicker to blame than Milton's summary suggests. Notable among these moments is Raphael's description of angelic song, which is introduced with the warning that heavenly song's structure is not comprehensible "to human ears" (7.177); rather than stressing the similarity between the praise-songs of angels and those that Adam and Eve sing, he is careful to point out the basic inaccessibility of angelic song. Similarly, Raphael reacts harshly to Adam's attempt at astronomy in Book 8, warning him to "be lowly wise" (8.173); as angelic song was inaccessible to his ear, astronomy is inaccessible to "earthly sight" (8.120). Both of these instances are warnings against intellectual hubris, but against a very particular kind of hubris: the human attempt to understand an inaccessible place, whether heaven or the outer reaches of the created Universe. Though Raphael's ostensible subject is disobedience, much of his anxiety seems to be directed at place.

The conversation begins as a warning about the possibility of the Fall, and most criticism (following the lead of Stanley Fish and Regina Schwartz) has assumed that that warning governs the interpretive status of the whole.[1] I will argue in this chapter, however, that much of the conversation becomes a dialectic about the ethics of locative imagination: the obligations and risks associated with Adam's understanding of his own surroundings and, more so, his imagination of Heaven. As the conversation goes on, both participants find issues of place to be of greater and greater consequence. In order to warn Adam about Satan, Raphael must describe events in Heaven; in order to narrate those events, he must confront the question of Adam's ability to understand a place unlike the created world. Though the warning's chief content is about action, in the telling the warning necessarily brings up a problem that seems to be more difficult for Raphael: the human understanding of place. That understanding poses risks, but what makes place particularly a problem is that Raphael, Adam, and God (as Adam describes him) all seem to have different notions of what those risks are. For this reason, I believe that Raphael's original purpose does not end up governing the entire conversation, as issues distinct from the Fall become central.

Raphael frequently demonstrates his concern that Adam is too eager to imagine things he cannot understand. Even the praise-songs, which are the Heavenly events closest to Adam's own experience since they resemble the prayers and songs Adam and Eve create themselves, are affected by Raphael's difficulty in translating them into a human sense of time and place. By asking Adam to imagine events in Heaven, Raphael is already creating a problem for his own message. When Adam's imagination of place is the subject, what is otherwise a confident tutorial becomes a cautious, contradictory, and subtle debate about the limitations of Adam's ability to understand Raphael's subject. Those limitations focus not on events but on the environment of those events; it is harder, it seems, to imagine an inaccessible location than it is to understand any particular event in history, even the history of angels. The problem of environment informs the entire conversation, and in different ways the entire poem; the imagination of place is much more vexing and ultimately much more significant in *Paradise Lost* than the imagination of events. In Book 8, Raphael questions Adam's attempts to understand his own Universe apart from Heaven, implying that any large-scale understanding of place, not only heavenly place but worldly place as well, is inaccessible to human thought.[2]

The problems I will investigate here—Raphael's attempt to tell a narrative whose setting he thinks is off-limits to Adam and Adam's simultaneous contrition for and defense of his curiosity—suggest a more dialectical and less catechistic understanding of the conversation, since much of what Raphael and Adam say is informed by a group of related concerns that they share and that Adam has apparently already been considering. Contrary to what God's intentions might lead us to expect, many of the central concerns of the conversation are not introduced by Raphael as part of his warning but are introduced by the two conversants as consequences of their attempts to share their knowledge. These shared concerns suggest that the impending Fall is not the only issue in the conversation; both Adam and Raphael are already concerned about potential disconnections between Heaven and Eden. Rather than Fish's idea of Raphael's demonstration of a proper and balanced worship, or a crucially misunderstood warning (about Satan, about appropriate and inappropriate forms of knowledge, or about sin—a chief exponent of this reading is R.A. Shoaf) to Adam by Raphael, I read the conversation as one in which both Raphael and Adam (and, by extension, Milton as well) are struggling with the problem of how to reconcile Adam's overreaching imagination with a Universe that simultaneously requires his ignorance and celebrates his imagination.[3]

The difficulty of understanding place in *Paradise Lost* further complicates several already tense issues in Milton criticism. Conflicts between historicist approaches and the study of poetics, which have characterized criticism of the entire period, has melded with existing debates in Milton studies between readings of *Paradise Lost* based principally on ideas of coherent theology with those exploring the poem's moral ambiguities. Ultimately, the problem of historicizing *Paradise Lost* is inseparable from the perennially vexing question of the poem's religious identity. As Bill Readings points out, Eden is the principal problem in any attempt to historicize the poem, because Eden is always inherently earlier than any history, and the basis of any history.[4] As I will discuss in detail in this chapter, however, Eden's conceptual status is not the extent of the problem; in fact, I will focus on similarities between problems of description relative to the larger created Universe and Heaven as well as Eden. These similarities suggest that place itself is a fundamental site of the resistance of description and of interpretation in *Paradise Lost*. In subsequent chapters, I will argue that throughout the later books of *Paradise Lost*—the parts of the poem most directly concerned with the Fall of Man—the human inability to make adequate sense of environment intrudes frequently at the most urgently moral points in the narrative. Despite *Paradise Lost*'s explicit interest in the moral questions of the Fall, in the moment those questions tend to be deflected toward a question of description.

Indeed, the difficulties of the imagination of place affect the Miltonic narrator, as well as Raphael and Adam, and create a point of doubt in the transmission of divine insight. In recognizing this fundamental instability, I intend to resuscitate one part of William Empson's argument about *Paradise Lost*: that the theodicy of the poem—or as Empson calls it, the effort "to make his God appear less wicked"—is more of a struggle or a search than it is a treatise.[5] In particular, Milton must leave the definition of prelapsarian imagination ambiguous, not because it suits a rhetorical goal, but because the nature of that imagination is itself made ambiguous by the problem of place. My reading of this conversation suggests a *Paradise Lost* which is not in any way intended to reassure, but which demonstrates, through the complexity of the problems it explores, the difficulty of the poem's project. The poem's defense of itself, I believe, is more earnest than its defense of its subject. Like Empson, I find that there is a fundamental discontinuity in Raphael's tutorial: that its length, complexity, and ambiguity interfere with its ability to realize straightforwardly the divine commandment that caused it. That discontinuity, I must stress, does not mean that the Fall is Raphael's fault or anyone else's, but it prevents any reading in which Raphael is seen as a purveyor of a divinely sanctioned truth of which Adam and Eve are unable to take advantage, a reading most famously defended by Stanley Fish. Fish has summarized succinctly this reading of Raphael as mouthpiece: "Everything Raphael says is an expansion and reformulation of God's crucial and controversial characterization of the unfallen state: 'Sufficient to have stood, though free to fall' (III, 99)."[6] That characterization cannot sufficiently account for all of the decisions Raphael makes; as we will see, Raphael's unease about Adam's ability to understand the context of his unfallen state becomes a part of the subject of the conversation itself. In other words, the inherent difficulty of explaining Adam's state to him means that the possibility of temptation and Fall cannot after all be the only issue in the conversation.

Milton critics have been aware for some time that much of what Raphael says is tinged with an awareness of the possibility of its failure.[7] That awareness, charged from the start, becomes even greater in the latter half of the conversation, in which Raphael answers Adam's questions about creation and the nature of the created world.[8] But the idea of Raphael's imminent failure demands an examination of what Raphael is trying to do in the first place, particularly in those latter books. Fish finds the most succinct statement of Raphael's goal in his request that Adam view "the Heav'n's wide Circuit" in a way that can "speak / The Maker's high magnificence" (8.100–101). For Fish the passage indicates a more Miltonic way of reading the heavens.[9] But the passage comes after Adam's attempt at astronomy, and I would read it as responsive: a part of Raphael's correction of Adam's hubris. Raphael's adjectives, "wide," "high," attempt to mold Adam's understanding of environment on a basic level; he wants Adam to read width as height—that is, to understand the great size and complexity of the Universe as indicating its remoteness from human understanding. It may be that Adam is willing to accept that reading, at least temporarily, of the heavens as they are in relation to Eden, but Raphael's own narrative prevents Adam from thinking of the Heaven of angels in the same way. The size of the sky might encourage praise of God, but the remoteness of Heaven makes praising God harder.

The contradiction between the necessity of praise and the impossibility of understanding is central to Adam's idea of place. In Adam's most conciliatory acceptance of Raphael's warning of the danger of imagination, he uses place as a metaphor for the risk of the hubristic attempt to comprehend too much:

> But apt the Mind or Fancy is to rove
> Uncheckt, and of her roving is no end;
> Till warn'd, or by experience taught, she learn
> That not to know at large of things remote
> From use, obscure and subtle, but to know
> That which before us lies in daily life,
> Is the prime Wisdom . . . (8.188–94)

To speak of imagination as "roving" is already to suggest what the problem is for Raphael and Adam both: at least on a figurative level, Adam is assuming here that when one imagines something, one's imagination is effectively there. Thus Adam's metaphor for safe thinking is "That which lies before us": suggesting not only "daily life" but also, to take the metaphor literally, one's immediate physical surroundings; Adam seems not to make the distinction between the literal and figurative meanings. Adam's rejection of "things remote / From use," beyond the etymological extension of "unusual," is a metaphor of place. Milton's line break is meaningful; Adam is concerned about "things remote": the imagination of place beyond the garden. In fact, the main thing he is apologizing for here is his own inquiry into astronomy (a passage I will discuss in detail below), and the word "remote" is in his mind in that context. Raphael earlier explained the distorting effects of astronomical observation using the same word; he says of the stars:

> By tincture or reflection they augment
> Thir small peculiar, though from human sight
> So far remote, with diminution seen. (7.367–69)

For Raphael, then, remoteness is specific to perception, not just location: the stars are "remote" "from human sight." Adam (with or without Raphael's encouragement) associates literal remoteness (remoteness from human perception) with figurative remoteness (remoteness from human understanding). Because of that association, the gratitude Adam implies in response to Raphael's warning not to worry about "things remote" would seem to conflict with the gratitude he continually expresses for Raphael's accounts of things to which he would not ordinarily have access. In fact, Dennis Danielson, who is principally concerned with theodicy, praises Adam's ability to imagine the remote.[10] Adam's eager acceptance of Raphael's warning is not final; on the contrary, it is qualified if not countered by the rest of the conversation.

Despite Raphael's stated desire to influence Adam's thought, he does not make much effort to control the content of the conversation, which is remarkably interactive; its latter half consists mostly of Raphael's responses to Adam's questions. For that reason, the imaginative curiosity for which Adam is so apologetic in the lines quoted above actually governs the entire exchange, which is about knowledge beyond "what concerns thee and thy being" (8.174); in fact, the ostensible reason for the conversation is that the danger of temptation makes it necessary for Adam and Eve to consider some larger issues than those of their daily life. Raphael's function in these books is to provide Adam with precisely the kind of knowledge he tells Adam not to want.

For Raphael, the discrepancy between the need to answer Adam's questions and his concerns about the appropriateness of Adam's intellectual ambition prevents him from answering those questions with much confidence; he is eager to avoid becoming an authority on the kinds of knowledge that are only partially available to Adam and Eve. When introducing to Adam the subject of the history of Heaven, and frequently thereafter, Raphael warns him of the difficulty of describing Heaven within "the reach / Of human sense" (5.571–72), as if to apologize in advance. (When Raphael calls telling the story of the war in heaven a "sad task and hard" [5.564], he is offering a similar apology both for the inaccessibility of the subject matter and for his own emotional difficulty in relating it.) Thus, throughout the conversation, Raphael reminds Adam of the inherent problems in a conversation designed to both enhance and check Adam's knowledge, by reiterating warnings for Adam not to overstep his intellectual bounds while requiring Adam's full creative participation in the conversation.

What Raphael offers to Adam is a locative dualism, in which places inaccessible to Adam can be understood only through fuzzy analogies with accessible places. Against the difficulty of describing heavenly events to a human ear Raphael rather tentatively offers the unity of creation:

> . . . what if Earth
> Be but the shadow of Heav'n, and things therein
> Each to other like more than on Earth is thought? (5.574–76)

Raphael's consolation suggests the way he is thinking about the problem of imagining Heaven from Adam's point of view: things and events are determined by their setting, so that what goes on in Heaven is, to Adam, merely "invisible exploits" (5.565); Raphael contrasts that invisibility with the more expressible life on Earth. Raphael's formulation shows that the representation of angels or other heavenly occupants is not in itself the problem for his narrative. Just as Adam can accept that Raphael is a spirit in corporeal form, Raphael expects Adam to imagine that the things he is describing are superficially similar even if fundamentally different from the way that Adam must imagine them. The problem is Heaven itself: he is trying to locate a narrative in a setting that, because time and space are not structured there as they are on Earth, resists narrative.[11] This anti-narrative context, however, is not Raphael's problem alone; Adam experiences something very similar in trying to describe Eden back to Raphael. Raphael wants Adam to make an ironclad distinction between Earth and Heaven, but to Raphael, Adam's attempt to make sense of the divine logic of creation suggests that he is either unwilling or unable to make that distinction.

"CELESTIAL CHOIRS"

Well before Adam's troubling thought experiments, Raphael is already struggling with the presentation of events whose surroundings are not accessible to Adam. Raphael's descriptions of angelic song, far from being the emblem of perfect worship (as Schwartz has read them), are in fact loci of the intensity of Raphael's anxiety about the human imagination of Heaven.[12] Raphael does seem to intend song to be the aspect of creation most comprehensible to Adam; he considers praise, its basic subject, to be one with which Adam ought to be concerned. But he also stresses, both directly and indirectly, that the audience of angelic song is itself necessarily angelic. Because angelic song is sung in heaven, it is already too remote for Adam to fully understand.

Part of the function of these songs is to describe the culture of heaven; they are glimpses into the way creation works. After all of Raphael's talk about the esotericism of creation, Adam might expect a description of an obscure, isolated creator. Instead, after God's announcement that the Son will take charge, Raphael reiterates the impossibility of human knowledge within an image of a rather public creation:

> So spake th'Almighty, and to what he spake
> His Word, the Filial Godhead, gave effect.
> Immediate are the acts of God, more swift

> Than time or motion, but to human ears
> Cannot without process of speech be told,
> So told as earthly notion can receive.
> Great triumph and rejoicing was in Heav'n
> When such was heard declar'd the Almighty's will;
> Glory they sung to the most High . . . (7.174–82)

The requirements of that publicity seem to be at odds with Raphael's understanding of the temporality of creation. The progression of ideas here sounds like non sequitur: if the acts of God are indeed "more swift / Than time" then there could not be enough time for the apparently centrally significant angelic song. Both the temporal and conceptual connotations of the word "immediate" (176) cause a certain amount of puzzlement here: if the actualization of God's creation is indeed instant, then it is not clear when the "triumph and rejoicing" takes place (180), but there is a broader question of immediacy as well, since one wonders what the function of the singing is if not to provide some form of mediation—an explanation, an interpretation, or at least a confirmation of God's acts.[13] On the contrary, the effect of the problem of time is to divorce the praise of the act from the act itself, since the praise is available to "human ears" (176) only in a way that does not fit with Raphael's narrative of creation. Raphael's description of creation emphasizes its instantaneousness, and it is clear that whatever knowledge Raphael is attempting to convey to Adam, the idea of the instantaneousness of God's acts matters to that knowledge. If song, translated into human language, is not instantaneous, then it would seem that Raphael is making a distinction, already, between Adam's understanding of creation itself and Adam's knowledge of the angelic response to creation. Raphael requires him to understand that creation is instantaneous, but does not seem to think that he could imagine song as anything other than extended. The sheer presence of song acts as a means of connection between Adam's worship and angelic worship, but the instantaneousness of the context of the song interferes with that connection and prevents Adam from understanding heavenly music in terms of his music.

Complicating the temporal issue, Raphael says that the Son began his mission during the song:

> Meanwhile the Son
> On his great Expedition now appear'd . . . (7.192–93)

Raphael's insistence on the difference between the immediate reality and the necessity of time in his narration suggests that the duration of the song is a

The Environs of Imagination

convenience for Adam's sake, and that the Son in fact appears in his chariot immediately upon God's pronouncement. The contradiction stresses the physical nature of Raphael's speech "to human ears" (177). The idea of an instantaneous action that takes more time to be told than to happen makes sense to anyone, but according to "earthly notion" (179), that model cannot be applied to music; music's interest in repetition (an interest reflected in the very organized structure of Raphael's songs) means that it exists by definition in time. Just as Raphael refers to speech literally even as he uses "His Word" as a metaphor, the song here is in part a metaphor as well, in this case a metaphor for some instantaneous expression by the singers.

The angelic songs Raphael discusses are more than simply praise of creation, because they are so carefully placed in close proximity to creation itself. They are, in fact, responses to creation, further demonstrating the distinction between heavenly song and Edenic song, which is simply praise. The specificity of the songs' function requires Raphael to comment on the formal aspects of the song: structure and audience. Those aspects give him trouble, as becomes clear in the most specific song, the one just before the beginning of creation. The past perfect tense of the verbs describing God's actions indicates that Raphael reports rather than quotes the content of the song:

> Glory they sung to the most High, good will
> To future men, and in thir dwellings peace;
> Glory to him whose just avenging ire
> Had driven out th' ungodly from his sight
> And th' habitations of the just; to him
> Glory and praise, whose wisdom had ordain'd
> Good out of evil to create, instead
> Of Spirits malign a better Race to bring
> Into the vacant room, and thence diffuse
> His good to Worlds and Ages infinite.
> So sang the Hierarchies . . . (7.182–91)

The song begins and ends with God's current project, the world and "future men"; in between it covers recent heavenly history (hence those past perfects). The theme of the song is the relationship between that history and God's project—"Good out of evil" (187). The song's climax is contained simply in the word "thence"—"thence diffuse / His good" (189)—which connects the "vacant room" of the past with the "Worlds and Ages" of the future, and succinctly suggests the continuity of all of God's actions. If this song happens instantaneously, and if music here is a metaphor for something else, the content of the song would suggest that the metaphor is for the angels' acknowledgment of the continuity of divine decision-making. The song indicates and celebrates the angelic understanding of the unity of the divine project, which depends on the angels' access to the whole; its instantaneousness, its ability to present itself at once to its heavenly audience, allows this vision of the glory of creation. In that sense, the songs of praise are Raphael's careful reminder to Adam that earthly praise is not the same as heavenly praise. On the other hand, the triple repetition of "Glory," always at the beginning of the line and with one more line between the second and third than between the first and second, is choral; it suggests not only repetition but structured repetition, so that even with Raphael's heavenly non-time the musical ordering of time still applies. But the structure is more than simple repetition. The last sentence, from the last "Glory," opens up into a larger phrase with a grand crescendo, rising over two enjambments: the rapid movement from the small space of the "vacant room" to the massive one of "Worlds and Ages infinite" (189–90). The structure suggests an expanding sound in the moment of an expanding Universe.

The structure of the "glory" song is mirrored in the final song in Raphael's narrative of creation:

> Open, ye everlasting Gates, they sung,
> Open, ye Heav'ns, your living doors; let in
> The great Creator from his work return'd
> Magnificent, his Six days' work, a World;
> Open, and henceforth oft; for God will deign
> To visit oft the dwellings of just Men
> Delighted, and with frequent intercourse
> Thither will send his winged Messengers
> On errands of supernal grace. (7.565–73)

Once again, the crucial word, "Open," is repeated three times; once again, there is more space between the second and third than between the first and second, and as with "Glory," the final repetition is followed by a longer coda. This repeated structure is significant. It cannot be coincidence that the two songs have the same form; the repetition implies genre. But the genre is not traditional song form, which would be ABA: two similar entities interrupted by a contrasting middle section. The form of Raphael's angelic songs is AAB; the traditional organization is reordered. In both songs, the third statement connects the first two to a larger time-scale and a larger function, and incorporates a much more complex metaphysics; to describe the world as "Magnificent" is praise; but to imagine "the dwellings of just Men" (570) is an extracurricular bit

The Environs of Imagination

of prophecy. The form of the angels' song, established by repetition, includes a final idea that moves beyond praise, and the AAB form enforces that movement, putting the emphasis on the final outside element rather than returning (as one would expect) to praise.[14] Even as he urges praise, Raphael makes clear that praise cannot be separated from the greater anxieties caused by the limits of human understanding.

Not only the angels' image of themselves but also the speed of the change in image and the hurriedness of the three enjambed lines suggests the familiar image from Sonnet 19 (which also runs over a noticeable enjambment):

> Thousands at his bidding speed
> And post o'er Land and Ocean without rest:
> They also serve who only stand and wait. (Sonnet 19, 12–14)

In the sonnet, though it represents a consolation, the contrast between the fleet angels and the flat-footed man is clear; in Raphael's song the same contrast applies, but in this case it is enforced by the grand choral execution of both songs. Both musically and locomotively these angels are doing something that Adam cannot; Adam and Eve can sing, but not on this scale. The specificity of the form of Raphael's angelic songs tells Adam two things: that structure matters in heaven, however time works there, and that praise is not separable from the larger issues that Raphael discusses, in particular, the inaccessibility of Heaven from Adam's point of view. The problem of describing place interferes with Raphael's pedagogy of praise by creating a discontinuity within the world of worship that is supposed to contain both Heaven and Earth.

Ultimately, the issue of the temporality of the song cannot be separated from the song's function. Music, of course, is interactive, since its structure only functions as structure if it is comprehended, and comprehension needs an audience to do the comprehending. Elsewhere in Milton, angelic song has a clearer audience, usually because it has a human audience, and a human motive, as in *Lycidas:*

> There entertain him all the Saints above,
> In solemn troops, and sweet Societies
> That sing, and singing in their glory move,
> And wipe the tears for ever from his eyes. ("Lycidas," 178–181)

Regardless of whether these singers are singing for anyone else in addition, it is clear enough that they are singing to Lycidas in particular; the content of their songs seems to be contained in its effect: perfect and final consolation.

The physical space may still be ambiguous, however; since "singing in their glory move" (180) is as vague as the "above" in "all the Saints above." Milton avoids a physical description of heaven, which might undermine the power of the relationship between the angels as singers and Lycidas as audience. Rather than the acoustics of the singing, he stresses the effect of the singing (including the clear allusion to Revelations 21.4 in line 181); the simplicity of that effect requires that the singing not be grounded in place.

In *Paradise Lost* the function of singing is more complex, since it seems to be both a response to and a participation in creation. Thus singing must be placed; its narrative function is not just about the relationship between God and Man, but also about the function of the world as an environment for that relationship. Praise is not an abstract activity devoid of context—it is located like any other activity, and its location affects it. The question of audience is also more complicated; Raphael intends his descriptions of song to benefit Adam, and humanity is indeed mentioned in some of them, but even though the songs are responses to creation the angels do not seem to be thinking of creation itself as the audience. The first song after the beginning of creation is a good example:

> Thus was the first Day Ev'n and Morn:
> Nor pass'd uncelebrated, nor unsung
> By the Celestial Choirs, when Orient Light
> Exhaling first from Darkness they beheld;
> Birth-day of Heav'n and Earth; with joy and shout
> The hollow Universal Orb they fill'd,
> And touch'd thir Golden Harps, and hymning prais'd
> God and his works, Creator him they sung,
> Both when first Ev'ning was, and when first Morn. (7.252–59)

Everything in this passage happens at once; Raphael's double negatives ("Nor . . . uncelebrated, nor unsung" [253]) serve to prevent the song from being assigned to a particular time, while "when . . . first" and "Both when" (259) have contrary effects with ambiguous results, since either the song that marks the appearance of light is repeated twice, or evening and morning happen at the same time (the heavy "Thus" of line 252 might suggest that anyway), in which case the "Both" becomes puzzling. The overall effect is the one suggested by "The hollow Universal Orb they fill'd": in both time and space song fills creation. That effect gives one the feeling that this song overflows the passage that describes it; like Creation itself, the angelic song is something Raphael describes despite the inadequacy of the description. Filling the orb is exactly what Adam cannot do; it involves a totally different kind of relationship between song and place. Adam can sing in a place, but he cannot sing to take over a place.

With that inadequacy in mind, the extraordinary syntactical compression of "Creator him they sung" suggests, rather than a moment of awkwardness, a moment of unusually indescribable music. "Creator" looks like an apposition to "him," but one would then expect some kind of preposition (or at least another object: they sang him something); another possibility is that "Creator" is akin to an object of proclamation (as in, they proclaimed him ruler).[15] In any case, the meaning depends on the audience for the reported song in question. If the "Celestial Choirs" are singing directly to God, then I do not know what the effect of singing him creator is supposed to have. Furthermore, the setting is different here from the earlier song: this song is sung not in Heaven but in the created Universe. That setting removes the song from a direct association with God; the angels must be singing to each other, and "Creator him they sung" is an apostrophe. In this case, since Raphael describes rather than quotes the song, it is a reported apostrophe, creating a double remove. Raphael asks Adam to imagine a specific space that does not include God (though God is immanently present through his creation of it) but in which God can still be apostrophically invoked. The angels affirm among themselves that God is the creator, but they do so by addressing God (effectively in absentia) as creator, and Raphael's phrase is meant to contain both of these functions. The difference between human and angelic song that Raphael insists upon by describing the space-altering potential of angelic song is exactly what "Creator him they sung" represents—a song that can fill all space is a song that can reinforce the very creatorship of God, exactly the kind of song that angels can sing and Adam cannot.

The apostrophe's compression represents the complexity of the function of this singing in the created world. The apostrophe is not entirely unlike the one in Adam and Eve's prayer at 5.157–208 ("These are thy glorious works, Parent of good . . ."), and as such suggests something Adam can take part in, but at the same time that apostrophe is attached to the overwhelming, world-filling scale of angelic song, which emphasizes its remoteness. The space Raphael's description imagines is cut off in two directions; it is not heaven (a place unimaginable to Adam), but it is not Eden either. In fact, the song's content, praise, includes Adam even as its form, in scale and in the nature of its address, excludes him. Raphael's song includes a lesson about place that anticipates his later reluctance to talk about the far reaches of the created world; while the most important distinction of place is that between the world and Heaven, there is a further distinction to be made between

Adam's immediate surroundings and a larger creation which, though worldly in some sense, is still inaccessible to him. Place matters here more than events, because there is a distinction to be made between problems of knowledge (such as those John Tanner discusses[16]) and those of description.

Raphael describes angelic song as having a subject, praise, that is accessible to Adam, a form that both includes him and moves beyond what Raphael thinks of as his capabilities, and a context that is inaccessible to human beings. Neither time nor space functions in Heaven as it does on Earth, and music needs to be heard in time (or it has no structure) and space (or it has no audience, not to mention acoustics). The contradictions in Raphael's account of angelic song represent the greater contradictions involved in the relationship he describes between Heaven and Eden. Raphael never gives Adam, in Book 7, a clear idea of what the boundary is between the two, even as he repeatedly insists on the importance of that boundary. For this reason, it is not surprising that when Adam begins discussing his own experience and observations he is primarily concerned with location, since that is the issue with which Raphael has left him the greatest doubt. Not only is Adam not sure where he is, he does not even know to what extent he can know where he is. Raphael does not help him.

"NUMBER FAILS"

Adam's questions, some of which Raphael answers and some of which he suggests Adam should not have asked in the first place, structure Book 8. Most of those questions concern place, and in fact most come back to the very question I have suggested Raphael has trouble with himself: whether it is possible, and whether it is necessary, for Adam to understand the nature of environment, both his own and the angels'. Adam's inquisitiveness relates directly, I believe, to Milton's formal difficulties—the question of the description of the prelapsarian world, which is Milton's question, is also essentially Adam's.

The first question of Adam's life, as he narrates it to Raphael, is the question of place, which continues to occupy him during the conversation:

> Thou Sun, said I, fair Light,
> And thou enlight'n'd Earth, so fresh and gay,
> Ye Hills and Dales, ye Rivers, Woods, and Plains
> And ye that live and move, fair Creatures, tell,
> Tell, if ye saw, how came I thus, how here? (8.273–77)

Adam seems to make a direct connection between the characteristics he observes of the natural world around him—its variety, its beauty, its brightness—and his decision to ask that world his question. In that sense, he is suggesting that the two questions he asks, how did I become and how did I become *here* (277), are versions of the same question; that is, if Adam understood how he came to be a part of the "enlight'n'd Earth," he would understand necessarily how he came to be at all. As we will see, this version of Adam's basic question is aptly placed after Raphael's description of creation and warnings not to think too much about the nature of the Universe. For Adam, the separation Raphael calls for between his understanding of himself and his function and his understanding of the world around him is essentially impossible.

Of course, Adam mostly accepts Raphael's insistence that the solution to the problem is simply not to try to imagine the unimaginable. However, I believe that there is a significant sub-strain within Adam's conciliation, particularly in his account of the creation of Eve. Adam's portrayal of a God who not only approves of but responds materially to Adam's imagination is a defense of his ability to understand his location. The defense never becomes explicit, however, because Adam has no answer to Raphael's warnings of the danger his intellect presents. It is not altogether clear whether the amount of thought about environment that is necessary simply to live in and understand Eden might itself carry a fair amount of risk. Adam proceeds carefully, presenting alternatively ambitious and self-effacing interpretations of his environment, as if testing for Raphael's approbation. Ultimately, however, his previous conversation with God indicates that Adam is determined not to give up on his attempts to make sense of his surroundings.

Place is crucial to Adam's autobiography in Book 8. From the moment of his creation, Adam thinks of himself as a part of a larger landscape:

> As new wak't from soundest sleep
> Soft on the flow'ry herb I found me laid
> In Balmy Sweat, which with his Beams the Sun
> Soon dri'd, and on the reeking moisture fed. (8.253–56)

At first glance there are two distinct connections with the landscape here. "The flow'ry herb" describes a passive environment, the sun an active one. But there are several features that combine the two into an environment in which Adam's place is difficult to determine. The use of "soft" as an adverb here is surely more than just slightly elevated diction: within ordinary Miltonic hyperbaton,[17] the line can also suggest "soft" as an adjective modifying "herb." "Laid" can have at least two meanings, one directly transitive, assuming that someone as yet unknown had laid Adam in that spot, as well as an intransitive one that only implies that Adam is lying there (the *OED*, as one meaning of "to be laid," gives "to lie down," including Renaissance citations). Thus, the care with which God has placed Adam, Adam's relaxation, and the malleability of the surface he is resting on all exist in the word "soft." Adam perceives the world as personified, and at the same time, the world is charged with the deliberate choices of its creators. The personification both connects Adam to his environment by suggesting that the environment cares for him, and disconnects him by making the process of that care so mysterious, a paradox to which Geoffrey Hartman has called our attention.[18] From Adam's birth, then, he has reason to be confused about his own place in the landscape.

Immediately after this moment Adam discovers the whole world at once:

>   . . . about me round I saw
> Hill, Dale, and shady Woods, and sunny Plains,
> And liquid Lapse of murmuring Streams; by these,
> Creatures that liv'd, and mov'd , and walk'd, or flew,
> Birds on the branches warbling; all things smil'd,
> With fragrance and with joy my heart o'erflow'd. (260–266)

Here, the personification ("all things smil'd") explicitly refers to the entire landscape, physical, vegetable, and animal, at once. Adam discovers the world as a place as friendly to him as whoever put him there. Adam's instant reckoning of landscape at the moment after his creation anticipates a natural world that will continue to include him. Adam expects a kind of pathetic fallacy turned true, a landscape that both smiles at him and smiles with him. But he discovers very early in his life that he is not going to get that perfect environmental connection; almost immediately after this passage, Adam's discovery that "answer none return'd" to his call (285) makes him "pensive" (287). The beginnings of Adam's loneliness, which he describes to God a few lines later, are so close to his discovery of landscape as to be inseparable; Adam's wonder leads directly to his anxiety. As his doubts about astronomy will demonstrate, that anxiety is still developing after the creation of Eve. After the Fall, Adam has many more significant doubts than these about man's connection to the environment, but his uncertainty about landscape exists even before the fall. That uncertainty could be considered evidence—as Fish has suggested—of a fall that is already clairvoyantly present, but the problems Adam raises in his conversation with Raphael actually suggest that the Fall as a philosophical problem is not *sui generis*. The Fall is the most significant but not the most obvious or immediate of a related group of concerns that exist within Adam's world because they are fundamental to the world God created.[19]

The persistence of the problem of location in Adam's description of his birth should be kept in mind throughout Book 8. Whereas Book 7 was an extended metaphysical tutorial with Raphael as master and the unity (however complex and obscure) of the world as subject, Book 8 is a dialogue in which Adam brings up increasingly pointed doubts about the unity of the world from his own perspective. Hoping that Raphael will assuage these doubts (". . . only thy solution can resolve" [8.14]), Adam begins with a question about the proportions of the respective motions of planetary bodies:

> When I behold this goodly Frame, this World
> Of Heav'n and Earth consisting, and compute
> Their magnitudes, this Earth a spot, a grain,
> An Atom, with the Firmament compar'd
> And all her number'd Stars, that seem to roll
> Spaces incomprehensible (for such
> Their distance argues, and their swift return
> Diurnal) merely to officiate light
> Round this opacous Earth, this punctual spot,
> One day and night; in all thir vast survey
> Useless besides; reasoning I oft admire,
> How Nature wise and frugal could commit
> Such disproportions, with superfluous hand
> So many nobler Bodies to create,
> Greater so manifold to this one use,
> For aught appears, and thir Orbs impose
> Such restless revolution day by day
> Repeated, while the sedentary Earth,
> That better might with far less compass move,
> Serv'd by more noble than herself, attains
> Her end without least motion, and receives,
> As Tribute such a sumless journey brought
> Of incorporeal speed, her warmth and light;
> Speed to describe whose swiftness Number fails. (8.15–37)

Adam responds to Raphael's complex and esoteric pedagogy by creating the most syntactically sophisticated sentence of his short life. After Raphael's at times elegant and complex depiction of creation, Adam wishes to show that he can describe his own surroundings with comparable skill, but at the same time the complexity of his argument reveals the extent of his uncertainty. The main verb of the sentence is "admire" in line 25, a verb of so much doubt that even its doubtfulness is uncertain, and Raphael uses it in the other, certain meaning in response, warning that God has prevented "His secrets to be scann'd by them who ought / rather admire" (8.74–75). The *OED* cites line 29 as its first use of the word "roll" in this peculiar, transitive meaning. Invention and complexity are everywhere here, but there is considerable caution in the rather vague "commit /such disproportions" (26) and considerable anxiety about the remoteness of creation revealed in the distance between the charged word "create" (27) and its subject, the neither divine nor not divine "Nature"(25). However, though his doubts bother Adam, it is also clear to him and to Raphael that he is very good at expressing them.

What bothers Adam in particular is proportion: the heavenly bodies move such distances and at such speeds "merely to officiate light / Round this opacous Earth."[20] Adam's "merely," like Yeats' "mere anarchy," refers more to the greatness of what is notably absent than to the paucity of what is present; he is not denigrating the earth, but having gotten a sense of the vastness of the universe, he now understands relativity. He could accept more easily that he is the center of the world if that circumstance did not seem to require such effort of the universe. Of course, Raphael's decidedly large-scale description of creation reinforces the discrepancy between the small but needy earth and the huge and generous cosmos.

That troublesome proportion is in part a form of inefficiency ("in all thir vast survey / Useless besides"), but he is also very aware that the universe's inefficiency is the product of his own, and the earth's, uniqueness. It is interesting that Adam questions speed and not motion. He does not argue that the unity of the world prevents any motion within it (the thesis of Parmenides); his logic is not even necessarily metaphysical, in that the essence of astronomical bodies does not concern him nearly as much as how they behave in relation to him. He questions not what the stars do but how much they do. His image is almost of a laboring universe, and he thinks of that labor in terms of its product. In that sense, Adam is relying on personification to understand the relationships among heavenly bodies. For a human being, to travel a greater distance is always more tiring.

On the other hand, when Adam remarks that his current understanding of the universe would require the planets to possess "Speed to describe whose swiftness Number fails" (37), he is talking not about impossibility but about indescribability. The choice is significant, since Adam is already experimenting with ways of describing relativity: "this Earth a spot, a grain, / An

Atom," searching for the best and smallest metonymy, suggests a very sophisticated understanding of perspective. The implication is that Adam could use a relative measurement to describe the speed of the planets, but even that measurement would be insufficient. By imagining the scale of the universe through analogy or metonymy, he can get a sense of its impressiveness, but his inability to conceive of a mathematics that would go up, so to speak, to the speed that would be necessary for the model he has in mind still seems to him to be a failure. He expects from Raphael either a different model, which would be comprehensible for what knowledge of physics Adam commands, or a different methodology for understanding the current model, which would require a still more powerful sense of relativity in description.

To a limited extent, Raphael gives him both. He describes various other possible structures for the relationship between Earth and the other bodies, but at the same time, Raphael wants to move Adam closer to an idea in which he could be the center of nature and dwarfed by it simultaneously, without contradiction:

> Yet not to Earth are those bright Luminaries
> Officious, but to thee Earth's habitant.
> And for the Heav'n's wide Circuit, let it speak
> The Maker's high magnificence, who built
> So spacious, and his Line stretcht out so far;
> That Man may know he dwells not in his own;
> An Edifice too large for him to fill . . . (8.98–104)

The final two lines of this passage contain the essence of Raphael's paradox: the purpose of the nature of the universe is human development and education, but the actual lesson is humility, and of course Raphael is preaching a kind of blind acceptance; he does not appease Adam's doubts so much as urge Adam not to have them. "Let it speak / The Maker's high magnificence" (100–01) is a command to think of significance as distinct from description. Raphael attempts to change Adam's understanding of meaning in relation to environment to one in which all meaning is essentially praise. In doing so, he poses what becomes a central question of Book 8: is praise sufficient, or is knowledge needed distinct from praise? According to Raphael's method, if a workable model of the cosmos is impossible, God is that much more impressive. Raphael clearly understands that the question of the layout of heavenly bodies is only part of the problem; Adam's expectation that he can formulate a science that will account for that layout is the reason for Raphael's talk about knowledge.

When Adam tells Raphael his own story somewhat later on, it becomes clear that Raphael's lesson was not sufficient, if only because Adam's ideas about his place in the world are already more sophisticated. Adam perceives instantly that he must be humble, but that perception does not prevent him from questioning his status (though this level of questioning is acceptable to both God and Raphael). But through that questioning Adam returns to the idea that a sophisticated understanding of place, in particular the difference between Heaven and Eden, is necessary in order to live as God wishes. This idea is a version of Adam's anxiety over the speed of astronomical bodies: what understanding he has impresses him, but it does not satisfy him.

Adam understands the significance of God's statement that "all the earth / to thee and to thy race I give" (8.338–39). He is not ungrateful; he genuinely appreciates

> all this good to man, for whose well being
> So amply, and with hands so liberal,
> Thou hast provided all things . . . (8.361–63)

Adam does have a knowledge of the complexity of the Universe that functions, like Raphael's description, as praise. But he cannot stop there; he cannot limit his understanding of his surroundings to a notion of their generosity. Adam sees himself surrounded, yet alone, because he sees his surroundings not as extensions and aids to himself, but as arrangements of discrete entities. He only recognizes that the animals are arranged in pairs, for example (in a passage quoted below), because he is interested in them in relation to each other and not just to himself. This interest is perhaps not so remarkable in itself, but the speed with which Adam arrives at it is; within moments of recognizing his place in the world, he perceives that his solitude is unique, and assumes that, being unique, it must also be undesirable:

> In solitude
> What happiness, who can enjoy alone,
> Or all enjoying, what contentment find? (8.364–366)

If Adam's question about astronomy demonstrates the way his mind works, the leap to loneliness here makes sense. The peculiar type of personification Adam employs, one in which the personified landscape is always divided into discrete entities comparable to himself, leads him to object, once again, to a perceived discrepancy between him and everyone else.[21] Without the personification of the animals, he would have no comparison that would allow him to conceptualize solitude.

God's response suggests that Adam should get companionship enough from the world God created for him:

> What call'st thou solitude? is not the Earth
> With various living creatures, and the Air
> Replenished, and all these at thy command
> To come and play before thee; know'st thou not
> Thir language and thir ways? (8.369–373)

Unlike Raphael, God does not ask Adam to see his environment without distinctions between discrete parts. The difference between Adam's and God's understandings of the Garden here has to do with the kinds of connections possible. God wants Adam to recognize connections of all types, and take different kinds of comfort in different ones. But the only connections that Adam sees are, essentially, sexual ones:

> . . . the brute
> Cannot be human consort; they rejoice
> Each with thir kind, Lion with Lioness;
> So fitly them in pairs thou hast combin'd . . . (8.391–94)

Just as the description of the universe meant to Adam accounting for the relationship between earth and the planets, the categorization of fauna means rethinking relationships between categories. If all animals were unique, Adam might be willing to accept a simple hierarchy, but since all animals other than Adam arrange themselves in pairs, Adam perceives something from which he is excluded that is built into his environment. God's suggestion that the world exists for Adam's enjoyment is belied, for Adam, by the very existence of "kind" (393). God's term, "Replenished" (371), indeed implies a much vaguer sense of creation than Adam's "combin'd," as if God preferred to think of reproduction as independent from species, and from sex. But Adam reminds God that this state of affairs is his doing; the extra clause—"So fitly them in pairs thou hast combin'd" (394)—is not actually relevant to Adam's argument that species determines social compatibility, nor is it intended as mere flattery; the word "fitly" is a reminder to God that arranging things in pairs is actually a more logical way of doing it. It also represents a certain amount of imaginative ambition on Adam's part, since to define one way of being as "fit" is necessarily to imagine and reject other ways of being: Adam can picture himself in a pair, or can picture the animals in his solitary state. Though this observation of God's power is in the form of praise, beyond praise it is interested in the way that power is put to use.

Remarkably, God's response to Adam's imaginative ambition is to suggest an even more ambitious act: imagining God himself. If Adam can take no pleasure in solitude, God wonders:

> What think'st thou then of mee, and this my State,
> Seem I to thee sufficiently possest
> Of happiness, or not? who am alone
> From all Eternity, for none I know
> Second to mee or like, equal much less. (402–06)

God's characterization of himself is the opposite of the rather mystical praise Raphael had in mind; he is asking Adam to think about the nature of God's relationship to his creation, not simply his status as its creator. The question is a *reductio ad absurdam,* a form that depends on imagining other perspectives. God asks Adam to experiment, to hypothesize, in thinking about divine nature. Responding to Adam's interest in making connections between things of disparate categories, God makes a connection so stretched as to create what a logician would call a category error: the application of a predicate to a subject that does not belong to the category of things that take that predicate. To question whether God is happy is surely an absurd degree of anthropomorphism. God's question goes in two directions at once; on the one hand, it mocks Adam's willingness to think of the bestial pleasure in sexual connection as one necessary for his own happiness by comparing it to a clear category error. On the other hand, by asking Adam to think about whether or not it is possible to imagine the emotional life of an infinite being, God is approving Adam's willingness to think beyond the immediate—his own state—and to consider himself authorized to contemplate the greatest questions.

Of course, Adam's answer is the only one possible:

> To attain
> The highth and depth of thy Eternal ways
> All human thoughts come short, Supreme of things . . . (412–14)

It is the necessary answer, but by phrasing his answer in this way Adam does point out a distinction between imagining the state of God and imagining alternatives to his own state. That is, his answer is not that the analogy God has made is of a sort that cannot or should not be made; he says only that he cannot answer it because it happens to be beyond his abilities. He never abandons (and God, unlike Raphael, never asks him to abandon) his theoretical framework for understanding the relationship between himself and his environment.

Eventually God admits that the sexual connection is indeed more close than the connections Adam has available to him already, and in fact asserts that he had always planned to provide Adam another human:

> Thus far to try thee, *Adam,* I was pleas'd,
> And find thee knowing not of Beasts alone,
> Which thou hast rightly nam'd, but of thyself,
> Expressing well the spirit within thee free,
> My Image, not imparted to the Brute,
> Whose fellowship therefore unmeet for thee
> Good reason was thou freely shouldst dislike . . . (437–44)

What separates Adam from the animals, the freedom of his soul, is the same thing that allows Adam to recognize that separation. In other words, God affirms that it is only by thinking about the world around him not just as it relates to his use and pleasure and to the praise of God but in itself—that it is only by contemplating the meaning of the world around him—that Adam achieves his humanness. Given that Adam reports this conversation immediately after Raphael tells him not to worry about astronomy, it does not seem like much of a stretch to read Adam's anecdote as a very subtle and very polite rebuke to Raphael's instruction, and as evidence that Adam's apologetic acquiescence to that instruction was, at best, temporary.[22] It is important to Adam that his imagination of place has not only been acceptable to God in the past, but has actually done him some good.

Adam uses his conversation with God to defend himself from Raphael's accusation that he is thinking too much, but God still leaves Adam in a somewhat precarious intellectual position. The creation of Eve answers Adam's immediate question, since it abates his loneliness, but it notably fails to respond to the underlying question: what is supposed to be the relationship between human and environment?[23] How close does God expect that connection to be? Adam and God seem to agree that the kinds of connections that God has with the world, the connection of creator to create, are not available to Adam. But Adam refuses to find the kind of connection he has with Eve in his landscape. His need to observe and describe nature prevents him from a completely cooperative model, in which nature's ability to provide for him would not need examination. Throughout his life, Adam makes a distinction between what merely sustains him and what cannot be taken for granted.

Of course, the whole problem seems to be something God wants Adam to go through. In their debate, God demonstrates why he delays introducing Eve: he wants Adam to conceive of the possibility of multiple forms of connections. In particular, he wants Adam to be able to recognize an incomplete connection and long for a better one, a basic skill of any religious person. But the process leaves Adam with a problem; since he does not know what to do with the incomplete connection, he has particular trouble understanding how to relate to landscape. This problem puts Raphael in a difficult position, since he must simultaneously give Adam a larger idea of his surroundings by describing the history of Heaven while trying to put some limits on Adam's investigations of the nature of the world. It is reasonable for Raphael to ask Adam to concentrate on the local, since the remote is the problem, but the local inevitably involves the remote. If the remote is at issue in any discussion of place, and if the remote is dangerous in itself, then there does not seem to be any safe way for Adam to think about his surroundings.

If it is unsafe for Adam to contemplate the nature of the environment, and unsatisfactory if not dangerous for Raphael to describe a physically inaccessible environment, then the poetic description of that environment, after the fact, would seem to come under question as well. Milton's ambition to create a comprehensible version of both Heaven and Eden puts him in a similar position to Raphael's. As much as the physical distance and strangeness of Heaven, remoteness of time is a problem for Milton, a problem he acknowledges by never quite making the distinction between the prelapsarian time he is describing and the history that has passed since. His description of Eden seems to have trouble sticking to a particular kind of temporal setting. It is clearly important to him (as it is to Adam) to stress the interconnectedness of the Edenic landscape:

> Another side, umbrageous Grots and Caves
> Of cool recess, o'er which the mantling Vine
> Lays forth her purple Grape, and gently creeps
> Luxuriant; meanwhile murmuring waters fall
> Down the slope hills, disperst, or in a Lake,
> That to the fringed Bank with Myrtle crown'd
> Her crystal mirror holds, unite thir streams.
> The Birds thir choir apply; airs, vernal airs,
> Breathing the smell of field and grove, attune

> The trembling leaves, while Universal *Pan*
> Knit with the *Graces* and the *Hours* in dance
> Led on th' Eternal Spring. (4.256–267)

Milton's vines are almost seductive and the presence of Pan fascinating, but the birds are even more striking. Milton interprets birdsong simultaneously as formal and formed music and as so much a part of the landscape itself that it induces a double synesthesia: smell becomes the breath of song; leaves shaking in the wind become harmonic vibration. Air (surely the pun is deliberate)[24] can exist in a distinct natural state to be smelled even as it takes on the already personified musical agenda of the birds in order to extend their music, in the style of an Aeolian harp, to the leaves.[25] As the waters "unite thir streams" (263), Milton's "Breathing" in line 265 unites the birds, the air, the fields, and the leaves into a single musical project. Infinite complexity—those grapevines, "mantling" themselves over everything (257), "Luxuriant" (259), are principally responsible for the feeling of excess in this passage—and infinite unity are in accord.

That wildly tamed personification occurs at the end of the description, encircling it with descriptive immediacy. It begins, however, with a different kind of immediacy: the nearness to Eden both of creation and of fall:

> . . . in this pleasant soil
> His far more pleasant Garden God ordain'd;
> Out of the fertile ground he caus'd to grow
> All Trees of noblest kind for sight, smell, taste;
> And all amid them stood the Tree of Life,
> High eminent, blooming Ambrosial Fruit
> Of vegetable Gold; and next to Life
> Our Death the Tree of Knowledge grew fast by,
> Knowledge of Good bought dear by knowing ill.
> Southward through *Eden* went a River large,
> Nor chang'd his course, but through the shaggy hill
> Pass'd underneath ingulft, for God had thrown
> That Mountain as his Garden mould high rais'd
> Upon the rapid current . . . (4.214–227)

The rhetorical device of "he caus'd to grow," and the metaphor involved in "God had thrown / That Mountain," are hard to describe (the latter suggests, in comparison to a potter's wheel, that the motion involved is circular, physical, and quick, whereas the former is gradual and organic). Milton begins with a grand anthropomorphism, making God a gardener and also, with the interest in "sight, smell, taste" (217), someone who appreciates what he tends, as Adam and Eve will later. He ends with a description of river and hill that suggests personification, so that God seems to be grappling with a landscape that plays along. The juxtaposition is striking, and the description of the two trees makes clear why it is there: Eden is so saturated with meaning that the immediate association of the Tree of Knowledge with our death takes nothing away from the power of the Tree of Life.

The description of Eden has a number of concerns; the prelapsarian meaningfulness of the Edenic landscape is one of those concerns, while the postlapsarian futility of landscape is another. To refer to the tree specifically as "Death" (221) is to introduce a suggestion of a different kind of landscape, the kind that will later emerge starkly in Book 10, at the very center of Eden. The different gardens present are intertwined; death, bacchic exuberance, the heavy presence of Creation, and pastoral unity all exist at once. I quote the description out of order to suggest that there is no linear direction governing these contradictory elements; they are parallel. Death, in the form of the Tree of Knowledge, comes before the Eternal Spring, but it could just as easily go the other way, and certainly the reader is expected to remember that temporally the order is as I have quoted it, not as Milton writes it.

In attempting to account for Milton's inclusion of a clearly postlapsarian description of the landscape of Eden, it is not sufficient to say that the description is not from Adam's point of view and his innocence does not apply to it. The ambivalence of the description so closely mirrors Adam's own ambivalence about landscape in Book 8, in which there seems to be no way to describe the world that does not include danger, that the landscape's lack of innocence seems to apply retroactively to Adam. Adam seems to be responding to a property of landscape that is built into it throughout *Paradise Lost*, even though both he and Raphael identify the problem as having to do with the limits of his knowledge. Like Adam, Milton cannot seem to find a way to describe Edenic landscape that does not include the possibility of the Fall, as if a truly innocent Eden were literally unimaginable. But it is not necessary to ascribe the presence of the Fall to the potential of the Fall; landscape itself, as Milton describes continually, reaches toward the Fall.

Milton cannot intend his readers to disregard Raphael's warnings about ambitious imagination, but he is careful to include with those warnings a sense of the necessity of the kind of imagination that is so dangerous, along with an acknowledgment that Milton's project itself depends on that imagination. This duality informs *Paradise Lost* as a whole; the poem has much in common with Raphael's praise songs, but its praise exists in a very unsettled context. For Milton's readers to take sides, as it were, in the conflict between praise and ambitious knowledge would be beside the point; Milton includes both because the two are inseparable. But the conflict inevitably comes back to environment. The problem with angelic song is not the subject of the song but the setting of the song in heavenly time and space; the problem with Adam's understanding of astronomy is not the scientific principle involved but the anxiety inherent in the human relationship with the Edenic landscape. Both of these examples are about the ethics of imagination: the moral difficulty involved in understanding something inaccessible. However, Milton's own difficulties in describing Eden demonstrate that environment is not by happenstance a representation of intellectual conflicts in the poem but that environment is itself the locus of those conflicts. The difficulty of imagining the inaccessible, I would suggest, is not ultimately a moral problem in *Paradise Lost;* it is a problem of description. The conflicts and contradictions I have outlined here arise from Milton's project itself: the poetic depiction of prelapsarian Eden. The remoteness of Eden renders its description essentially impossible; Milton hedges against that problem by including a sense of future in the description in the form of the reference to the Fall: a connection to, and therefore beyond, the transforming event that has caused the inaccessibility of Eden. But the hedge works only partially, because there is no way to separate Raphael's and Adam's dialectic from the inaccessible settings it continually invokes. Because remoteness is a quality of place, the setting as a distinct poetic entity is more affected by inaccessibility than anything located within that setting. In that sense, one possible response to Raphael's advice that the greatness of the Universe should signify the greatness of God is that the greatness of God is easier to make sense of; place cannot be a route toward religious understanding if place is itself incomprehensible. Raphael is doomed by his own project; he is trying to use place—the immediacy of Adam's function within Eden—to create certainty, but the project is undermined by the uncertainty that governs environment throughout. Raphael's predicament shows the power of place: the indescribability of Eden presents a serious obstacle to a discourse of the human condition and the Fall.

Chapter Three
Urgency and Delay in Eden: Description and the Inverted Rhetoric of *Paradise Lost 9*

In Books 7 and 8 of *Paradise Lost*, as we have seen, Milton presents place as a problem of the imagination; Adam complains repeatedly of the difficulty of conceiving of the world in which he finds himself, and despite his assurances to Raphael that he is satisfied by the archangel's explanations, I am convinced, as I have said, that he is not. However, the problem of imagining place is only one of the aspects of place that Milton confronts in the poem, and it relates to the particular context of the discourse within Books 7 and 8. Adam's conversation with Raphael is, by and large, a speculative one; once Raphael's warning has been given, the conversation turns to the nature of the world and Adam's budding philosophical investigations of it. In Book 9, Adam engages with Eve in a very different kind of conversation—a debate about what to do and how to do it—which leads to similar kinds of debates surrounding the Fall itself, whether between the two human beings or between Eve and the Serpent. Place is still central to that conversation, but as a result of that shifting context, the aspect of place that matters in Book 9 shifts as well, from a speculative approach to a rhetorical one. At the same time, imagination itself is no longer discussed, and instead the *description* of place becomes the dominant issue. Two particularly salient features of that issue will emerge in this chapter: that the various debates in Book 9 are characterized by distinct, incompatible, competing descriptions of Eden, and that in general, the description of place is rhetorically unstable, contributing to a generally ineffective and self-contradictory rhetoric throughout this part of the poem.

When Eve complains, at 9.205ff., that plants in Eden grow faster than they can be bound back, she gives us perhaps the best description of Eden we get. It is pragmatic and clear; she lives in a garden, and she needs to understand how it is constructed. The lushness and extravagance of Eden has often been discussed, and those aspects appear as early as Book 4, but Eve's description, as we will see later on, treats lushness as an effect of an underlying quality of the garden rather than as a cause. In Book 9 what emerges is an effect of time that creeps into descriptions of Eden. There is an urgency that is basic to the place; destined to exist only briefly, Eden hurries all of its functions. It is not incidental, I believe, that a discussion between Adam and Eve of this urgency—the infamous 'separation scene,' which is rife with disagreement about what Eden looks like—leads directly or indirectly (depending on the reader's view of it) to the Fall itself. This effect of time is the key to the rhetorical problem of description in the book. The difficulty Eve confronts when she insists to Adam that something must change is the great challenge of describing what surrounds her. That challenge informs her actions, and leads her into temptation and into death. What matters most, from our point of view, is that she is right.

Eden's urgency makes itself clearest in two parallel moments in Book 9. When Eve eats the fruit of the tree of knowledge of good and evil, Nature reacts immediately and clearly, as to an action whose impact is so great that its implications are not only felt throughout eternity but are felt at once. When Adam eats, the reaction is the same. The other results of the Fall—Adam's and Eve's growing guilt; God's punishment; the implications for Satan, for Eden, and for all the world; and most importantly, the human death that is made possible by the Fall—all take place gradually, so it is significant that Nature's response is instant. That instantaneity is particularly noticeable in that Eve cites the overwhelming presence of nature, the lushness of vegetation, as the original reason for the separation that allows Satan access to her; the speed of Eden's growth is a problem. The immediacy of nature's response is also causally significant: Eve expects that the punishment for the Fall will be instant and that expectation is a principal reason why she does not believe in the punishment for the Fall. Since the serpent has eaten and lived, she reasons, eating cannot cause death; since she eats and lives, she argues to Adam, the original warning must be incorrect. A delayed death never occurs to her.

But Eve is right about the urgency of Eden; the poem's own understanding of the world's relationship to Heaven (and the narrator's relationship to its divine subject) suggests an additional problem in the form of an even more significant discrepancy between the urgency of Eden and the mediatedness of Heaven. Heaven is not governed by instantaneity, but rather by the delay inherent in communication between two unequal states. As I said at the outset, that discrepancy is clearest in the immediate aftermath of Eve's eating the fruit:

> her rash hand in evil hour
> Forth reaching to the Fruit, she pluck't, she eat:
> Earth felt the wound, and Nature from her seat
> Sighing through all her Works gave signs of woe,
> That all was lost. (780–84)

This is a stark image of immediacy; the crime is so severe that its implications reach the edges of the created world instantly (editorial opinions on the punctuation vary, but most editors put Nature's response in the same sentence as Eve's eating, and Hughes's punctuation here is identical to that of the standard Columbia edition's[1]). The immediacy is all the more important because it is limited to Eden; God does *not* respond instantly to the Fall. The delay of God's punishment and its form as mortality as opposed to immediate death, suggest a discrepancy—one that Eve draws attention to when she uses her realization that God has not immediately killed her as an argument to Adam in support of eating the Fruit. All of this difference suggests that we should read the word "Nature" not as the inclusive, universal term it seems to be on first glance, but rather as a term of specification. Nature reacts instantly, but God does not. In this most central moment of the epic, Milton makes a fundamental distinction between earthly and heavenly environment. On the other hand, it surely matters that Nature's reaction is not available for humanity to sense (whether inherently or because as a result of their sin is not clear). The reaction, though crucial narratively, seems to have no effect on Adam's and Eve's experience of the Fall. The intimacy with which Eden responds to its inhabitants does not benefit them.

Nature's reaction is a perfect indication of the dynamic created by a kind of descriptiveness, bound to time, that exists outside of rhetoric. The reaction to Eve's fall is one of a pair, in fact: this and the reaction to Adam's fall form a non-rhetorical, even anti-rhetorical frame surrounding the bizarre non-debate in which Adam agrees to eat the fruit. In that conversation, rhetoric is replaced by an inward-directed form of persuasion that bears little resemblance to communication. As a context for this communicative disconnection, Nature's twin responses demonstrate the inability of rhetoric to respond to or encompass the Fall. The immediacy of description marks a specifically unpersuasive utterance—Nature's response is ignored.

The personification of Nature in the aftermath of Eve's eating of the tree lies in more than just the reaction itself: Nature's response is vocal—a sigh. The voice of the landscape, caught in urgent time, is a voice that signifies only in its existence, without content. That limitation is intensified among the multiplication of voices in Nature's response to Adam's fall:

> Earth trembled from her entrails, as again
> In pangs, and Nature gave a second groan,
> Sky low'r'd, and muttering Thunder, some sad drops
> Wept at completing of the mortal Sin
> Original; while *Adam* took no thought . . . (9.1000–4)

The wordless and unheard groaning and muttering of the world here, a further disintegration of the somewhat more hermeneutically active sighing in the first response, is a reflection of the disruption that the climax in the conflict between kinds of time has forced upon speech. It follows a conversation in which two people in agreement are speaking entirely at odds. In the last debate before Adam's fall, persuasiveness is dissolved, replaced by a simple and stark rhetoric of actions and inner conversations.

This assumption of instantaneity, together with the garden's sheer speed of growth, is the most blatant and ultimately important representation of Eden's basic urgency. Throughout Book 9, Adam and Eve must confront the difficulties that Eden's urgency creates for their own lives. The problem is that the opposite of urgency—delay, mediatedness—characterizes Milton's depiction of Heaven and of God; God's decisions are delayed, his truths only slowly and painstakingly understood. The disruption caused by the disparity between these two conflicting forms of time is everywhere in the final books of *Paradise Lost,* both before and after the Fall. But that disruption is associated with the impossibility of a coherent relationship between Eden and Heaven; Heaven's intrusion into Edenic life—through Raphael, through the moral significance of the Tree of Knowledge, and even through human reason itself—is an intrusion of a delayed time into an urgent time. In that sense, the problem of timeliness in Eden is in fact not a condition of time but a condition of place, and thus for the poem a problem of description. It becomes impossible to distinguish between the temporal effect of description and the time involved. This impossibility is particularly eminent in the suggestive hints of Heaven in Book 3, because the evocations of time (and there are many) serve to slow down and space out time in relation to a place that, as Raphael tells us, tends to experience things instantaneously. In other words, Milton chooses tropes that are directly contrary to the time within his description. There are two things that follow from this choice: one is that descriptiveness and time have an uneasy relationship, but the other is that the contrast between the urgency of Eden and the delay of Heaven is one created tropically, not theologically or cosmologically. This importance of trope in Book 9 creates an unusual rhetorical context, in addition to its unusual descriptive context.

Nature's rhetoric at the moment of the Fall is itself inverted; if the response had been to Satan's arguments it might have done Eve some good, but instead Nature is merely addressing itself, and in fact, neither Eve nor Adam seems to hear the response.[2] Most crucially, this inverted rhetoric appears in Adam's inexplicable reversal during his debate with Eve about working separately in the garden—Adam turns away from argument at the moment of his rhetorical climax, essentially retracting everything he has just said, as if the purpose of the rhetorical energies he had thus far displayed were to clarify something for himself, not to persuade Eve. The reversal is not a change of mind; Adam is not convinced by anything that Eve says. But it also indicates a profound lack of confidence in his own persuasive power; just as he is not convinced, he believes that Eve cannot be convinced either. Taken in by the immediacy of Eden, Adam believes that Eve should simply agree with him by default; lacking that connection, his rhetoric becomes one of distance.

Eve's objection to Eden is that things grow too quickly there; at 9.211 she complains of its "wanton growth." She thinks of that problem as a gardener's problem, but it is also a rhetor's problem—she is, after all, trying to persuade Adam at that moment—and thus it is also a poet's problem. Milton's Eve, I think, finds Eden difficult to describe because Milton does, and wantonness—its sheer speed of growth—is the principal obstacle. Description tends to be static, and the garden refuses to sit still. So the problem of Eden's urgency is specifically a problem of description, introduced by a generalized difficulty of reconciling description with narrative time; as Michel Beaujour points out, that relationship is never an easy one.[3] In order to make sense of the descriptive urgency of Eden with which Eve struggles, we must place it in the context of the temporal problem of description.

The problem is not unique to Milton nor to poetry; description is a discipline with a complex and uneasy relationship to time, heightened in the descriptions of Eden in Book 9 but fundamentally familiar from other (particularly later) texts. The theory of description, other than a brief fad in the early 1990s, has never enjoyed much standing as a distinct critical approach, but consensus does emerge about certain key features, and the problem of time is one of them. Gerard Genette's influential work on Proust, from his *Narrative Discourse,* can provide a useful model that, with caution, might be allowed to pose a general question. Genette expresses the effect of descriptiveness on narrative in terms of the speed or tempo of narrative; in a descriptive pause, what Genette calls "narrative time" increases infinitely in proportion to "story time."[4] This descriptive version of time is available even to an epic poet. When Milton describes the urgency of Eden at length, there is necessarily a similar discrepancy between the time of narration and the time within the narrated object. On the other hand, Genette comes to the conclusion that in Proust descriptive pause is notably absent, on the grounds that Proust treats description as part of the narrative:

> So we see that in Proust contemplation is neither an instantaneous flash (like recollection) nor a moment of passive and restful ecstasy; it is an activity—intense, intellectual, and often physical—and the telling of it is, after all is said and done, a narrative just like any other. What we are compelled to conclude, therefore, is that description, in Proust, becomes absorbed into narration, and . . . the descriptive pause does not exist in Proust, for the obvious reason that with him description is everything *except* a pause in the narrative.[5]

For Genette, then, there are two kinds of description: narrative (which is the less usual kind outside of Proust) and non-narrative. What distinguishes narrative description is that the time of the narration has a direct relationship to a kind of time inherent in the description itself. The effect of descriptiveness on narrative time depends on the amount and kind of notice that is taken of description within the narrative. In other words, regardless of the level on which the descriptiveness is occurring (the level of character or of narration), descriptiveness for Genette represents a disjunction in time between a speedy undescribed place and a slow described place. Genette's distinction between different types of the motion of time at different levels of narration, associated with descriptiveness, suggests a closer association between time and the subject of the description. His distinction between a descriptiveness in Proust that corresponds to story time and a descriptiveness elsewhere that does not implies two different conceptions of described landscape. All description is slow, but what is described in Proust has a slowness relative to character, and what is described elsewhere has a slowness relative to narration but not to character.

Description itself affects time, in other words; the extent of that effect is the chief lesson to be learned from Genette's study. Though the relationship between narrative time and story time might be affected by the incorporation of descriptiveness into narrative, the disjunction that description creates is not. For Eve, the kind of time already present in what is being described means that she is unusually troubled by the temporal problem of describing it. The timeliness of a particular landscape, revealed in description but still conceptually associated with the landscape itself, varies. In Book 9, the overflowing descriptiveness of Eden causes language itself to seem slow, but later we will see also that in his own narration in Book 3, Milton considers the relationship between descriptiveness and timeliness, particularly in relation to Heaven, of which all descriptiveness seems necessarily delayed.

Most of the work done on description over the last 30 years (by or responding to Genette, Philippe Hamon, Harold Mosher, and Alexander Gelley, among others) has focused on the novel, and in particular on the narrated description of the third-person novel. The extent to which those findings, or any unified theory of description, can be applied to poetry is debatable. Michael Riffaterre, almost alone, has attempted a generalized account of poetic description, and he has done so with the consistent thesis that description is a subset of poetic form, and as such bears only an incidental (though necessary) relation to what is described. To understand poetic description properly we must, he insists, resist description's apparent nature: it is "a type of discourse that sends the reader looking for signals of verisimilitude, symbols of accuracy."[6] The good reader looks instead for a relationship not between text and thing but between texts. But knowing what to look for does not necessarily eliminate the problems of the search, as a fascinating exchange between Riffaterre and Paul de Man shows. De Man's essay "Hypogram and Inscription," is dedicated to exploring the anxiety and uncertainty that remains in Riffaterre's seemingly decisive work. His basic understanding of the illusory relationship between description and reference is at the heart of the anxiety: in the last chapter of Riffaterre's *Semiotics of Poetry*, de Man says, "The ghost of referentiality, which has theoretically been exorcized in the model of the hypogram, does not seem to have been entirely laid to rest."[7] As evidence for an underlying uncertainty in otherwise confident readings, de Man cites Riffaterre's reading of a poem by Victor Hugo ("Ecrit sur la vitre d'une fenêtre flamande"), a reading designed to demonstrate that what "apparently returns to things, to signifieds" is actually "founded on a reference to the signifiers."[8] But, de Man claims, Riffaterre has misread as description a prosopopeia, which refers specifically to time: the poem describes a carillon in the course of an address, and "it is possible to identity without fail the *je* and the *tu* of line 1 as being time and mind."

The warning is clear. In recognizing that a description is not simply referential, we can lose powers of reference it may possess that are beyond description. In this case, because the description refers specifically to time, those powers are unusually significant:

> The relationship between the carillon and time should be of special interest to a semiotician, for it is analogous to the relationship between signifier and signified that constitutes the sign. The ringing of the bells (or the conventional tune that serves as the prelude to the actual chimes) is the material sign of an event (the passage of time) of which the phenomenality lacks certainty [. . .] The carillon's relationship to time has to be like the relationship of the mind to the senses: it is the sonorous face, the "masque aux yeux sonores" (Rilke) of cognition which, by metonymic substitution, links the sound of the bells to the face of the clock.[9]

One of the functions of description is to record non-visual aspects of the world, and *both* an overly referential reading and a reading overly resistant to reference will miss that function. Thus de Man's warning functions as something of an answer to Genette's problem of description and time; in a poetic context, we would best avoid thinking that there *is* a "story time" (to use Genette's phrase) to be represented. De Man's reflections about the hidden place of time in Hugo's poem are useful for reading Book 9 of *Paradise Lost*, in which people disagree about what something looks like as a way of disagreeing about how much time they have to deal with it. Time is essentially indescribable, and an attempt to include in description the particularly pervasive kind of time that exists in Eden only demonstrates an essential slowness of description, and of language itself.

Language in Book 9 seems slow; what I mean by this is that the discrepancy between the urgency of Eden and the untimeliness of Heaven is parallel to and largely responsible for a mode of rhetoric (limited to Book 9) that associates communication with immediacy and that responds to the human perception of mediatedness in Eden through a kind of inversion; mediatedness causes rhetoric to address the medium rather than the person being persuaded. There is no conception in Book 9 of rhetoric that can function through delay; delay in this part of the poem upends rhetoric. Inasmuch as this problem is related to persuasion, it can be thought of in terms of an issue raised by de Man, for whom persuasiveness is not a condition of all rhetoric but occupies a position within rhetoric, because language itself is a potential interruption or obstruction of persuasiveness. Discussing the relationship between philosophy and literature in Nietzsche, de Man summarizes the issue in terms of "the aporia between performative and constative language": "Considered as persuasion, rhetoric is performative but when considered as a system of tropes, it deconstructs its own performance."[10] Nietzsche is a particularly useful example for this anti-rhetorical function of trope because Nietzsche so frequently relies on trope in order to suggest new ways of thinking about existing philosophical problems. At the same time, his reliance on trope, however suggestive it might be, undercuts simple persuasiveness. What de Man is suggesting about trope is similar to what I am saying about description (which in light of the resistance to representation I find in it might best be thought of as trope anyway). Trope can intrude upon the rhetorical center and disrupt content, and description has the same potential. In both cases, *form*—the means and not the content of rhetoric—transforms the ideas within it, rather than responding to them. We see precisely this effect in Book 9: the effort to present an adequate description of Eden forces a reliance on a highly tropic language which necessarily undercuts persuasion. Indeed, though the book is full of rhetoric, real persuasion—argumentation that convinces—is notably absent. The anti-persuasive quality of the description of Eden in Book 9 undermines any potential rhetorical function.

This conception of an overflowing form is the best way to make sense of the bizarre rhetoric of Book 9, in which all arguments work against the person making the argument. Moments in *Paradise Lost* such as Adam's rhetorical reversal at the end of the separation scene reflect the self-deconstruction of rhetoric; Adam's need to describe Eden in a way that is convincing to Eve distracts him from his rhetorical purpose, leaving him unable to proceed. That disassociation between rhetoric and description is similar to the one that makes description create a locative time that works against the expected function of a place, so that Eden, whose purpose is the gradual development of human civilization, ends up with an urgent time, and instantaneous Heaven has a slow one. In other words, the inability of anyone to persuade anyone else and the tendency for everyone to persuade herself in Book 9 both stem from a problem of description: the timeliness of place. What we see in this book is a rhetoric that responds to an urgent Eden by attempting to slow itself down—through extensive description and trope. The de Manian self-deconstruction of a rhetoric that presents itself as trope is translated here into a rhetoric that succumbs to the discrepancy between the slowness of persuasion and the immediacy of description. Rhetoric is unconvincing here because it is *too late*.

"DISTANCE AND DISTASTE"

Milton's chief metaphor for the rhetorical problem that dominates Book 9 is *distance*. The opening of the book introduces distance as a new rhetorical mode, representing a profound shift from the dialectic of the long conversation between Adam and Raphael in Books 5 through 8. Milton begins Book 9 by describing the immediacy of the rhetorical mode of the previous books and contrasting it with the distance of the new mode. He opens by reminding the reader of the remarkable closeness between Heaven and Earth that allowed Adam's conversation with Raphael, who "With Man, as with his Friend, familiar us'd / To sit indulgent" (9.2–3). The addition of the adjective "familiar," close enough in meaning to "Friend," would be mere redundance before the Fall, but after it the repetition becomes the dirge of regret. In setting up the contrast between the close connection of this friendship and the separation caused by the Fall, Milton mimics the disruption of the Fall itself by invoking a similarly abrupt change in genre; the previous books, he tells us, were "talk" (9.1), while this one will be something else: "I now must change / Those notes to Tragic" (9.5–6). The line combines ideas of several genres; the use of the word "notes" is a familiar metaphor—poetry as music—but it is striking in this case because the line suggests blurring between genres on several levels anyway. The idea that a work can shift genres in the middle is already suggesting something unusually versatile about the concept of genre, but to call an epic "Tragic" is also to suggest leeway in the distinction between genres: at this point, Milton is saying, the epic is going to move further in the direction of drama than what has previously been established. In a study of genre, Genette blames Milton in part for what he calls the "improper attribution" of the distinction between epic, dramatic, and lyric poetry, quoting Milton's stern reference to "the laws" of those genres.[11] If Milton is unusually aware of the distinctions among genres, then his willingness to transcend that distinction is particularly relevant.

The openness to generic ambiguity is a signal of the shift in rhetoric: "talk" here means dialectic, and thus means an essentially mimetic form of poetry, in which the debate between Adam and Raphael has been presented for the reader's elucidation. But tragedy is something else: an imaginative rather than mimetic form—a form whose function is affective rather than didactic. Since Books 7 and 8 consist of conversation, however, and Book 9 also consists of conversation, the shift lies clearly not in the portrayal of the events but in the nature of the conversation; the shift in genre indicates a shift in rhetoric.[12]

Following his metaphor of sound ("Those notes") for the change in subject matter, Milton indeed introduces an entirely different sound—a polyptoton of prefixes resulting in both alliteration and assonance—for the lines that immediately follow, which are a summary of the events of Book 9:

>   foul distrust, and breach
> Disloyal on the part of Man, revolt,
> And disobedience: On the part of Heav'n

> Now alienated, distance and distaste,
> Anger and just rebuke . . . (9.6–10)

Still in a dirge, these lines give us a set of variations on the prefix "dis," arranged in a chiasmus. The parts of man and of heaven are parallel—both described with "dis-" adjectives—but the parallelism is reversed so that "distrust" and "disloyal" are at one end and "distance and distaste" at the other. Directly in the middle is the Fall itself, coded in the word "disobedience," a word identified in the first line of *Paradise Lost* as the poem's subject. The reference indicates that the shift here is a return to an earlier form: the mini-dialectic in the middle of the poem was the exception. The chiasmus suggests something static, since it arrives at its end with almost the same sound with which it started, but the terms listed are not equivalents; in fact, the phrase "Now alienated" (9) shows clearly that the latter half of the sequence is a response to the first half, and occurs temporally later. The comma after "revolt" (present in the 1674 edition) suggests that the revolt comes first and the disobedience after, and also emphasizes Milton's choice to characterize the Fall as a revolt rather than a succumbing to temptation. Particularly with that comma, the list of nouns implies a sequence of events, perhaps even a causative sequence. In that sense, the place of "distrust" (6), first in the list, is significant. Distrust is being related to distance; both are forms of disconnection in the once-amicable relationship between humanity and Heaven. But if distrust is the first of a sequence of events leading to and following the Fall, it implies that the relationship between Adam and Eve and God is not only affected by the Fall, but is part of the reason for the Fall; Adam's and Eve's distrust causes them to fall, and that act causes God's distaste. The lines are chiasmic not only in sound but in significance: the "distrust" is distrust by Man of Heaven, just as the "distaste" in line 9 is distaste of God toward Man. The Fall is surrounded by the problem of the disconnection between Eden and Heaven.

The alliterative list is particularly striking for what is not in it: death, which is what Adam has been told will be the result of disobedience; "Death" is also one of Milton's code-words for the Fall in the early part of the poem.[13] Distance, which is apparently the real punishment, is very different from death, because distance is already a factor in the relationship between humanity and Heaven, while death is entirely new. However close the friendship between Adam and Raphael may have been, Eden has always been distant from Heaven; Raphael's insistence on the incomprehensibility of Heaven reinforces that point. Heaven becomes alienated after the Fall, but that alienation is figured in terms of a disconnection that has always existed. As such, the diction inevitably reminds us of the distance that was such a problem in Books 7 and 8, and interferes with the idea of the Fall as a radical change.

Milton's expression of the result of the Fall as an intensification of something that already exists reinforces the chiasmus created by the alliterative arrangement. By portraying the result of the Fall as distance rather than death, Milton creates another analogy between prelapsarian and postlapsarian history. The chiasmus is created when the reader realizes that on either side of the Fall, she will find the same basic relationship between Man and God, with a difference primarily of degree. The Fall, the change in circumstances that has forced Milton's shift in genre, is not presented here as much of a change at all, since the location of the shift in genre extends before the Fall. Through the invocation of genre, Milton places extra emphasis on his formal use of language. But the forms themselves do not reflect the change as Milton describes it. Milton's tropes are at odds with his narrative, just as Adam's and Eve's descriptions undermine (as de Man would expect) their rhetoric. Eventually, such writerly concerns overwhelm any attempt to center the narrative predictably around the Fall, because of motivic relationships between descriptions of Eden before and after the Fall.

The chiasmic summary's implication of a relationship between Man's distrust of God before the Fall and God's distance from Man after the Fall strongly suggests that the major disruption in the poem should not be located at the moment of the Fall but before it. I argued in chapter 2 that distance—both the literal distance between Eden and Heaven and the figurative distance between Adam's intellectual capability and the realities of divine metaphysics—was a central issue in the conversation between Adam and Raphael in Books 7 and 8, before the Fall. In Book 9 the implications of that issue become clearer: the punishment for the Fall is distance, but distance exists before the Fall. The reader of *Paradise Lost* has already witnessed the problem of the distance between Heaven and Earth in the previous books, and in this one the reader is reminded that distrust, which is a denial of closeness and thus a form of distance, already exists at the time of the Fall; in the same line in which Milton tells us that distance is caused by the Fall, he tells us that the Fall is caused by distance. The paradox suggests that whatever Book 9 might be, it is not an account of the causes of the Fall.

Despite the shift toward drama, Milton emphasizes that the heroic mode still persists. His defense of the heroism of his subject, which is a defense of the appropriateness of this moment as the climax of an epic and also a defense of his chosen genre, encourages a reading that focuses on something other than causation, and indeed seems quite far from Milton's stated desire at the beginning of the poem to "justify" (1.25). His comparisons have much to do with tragedy and little with theodicy; he says of writing Book 9:

> Sad task, yet argument
> Not less but more heroic than the wrath
> Of stern *Achilles* on his Foe pursu'd
> Thrice Fugitive about *Troy* Wall; or rage
> Of *Turnus* for *Lavinia* disespous'd,
> Or *Neptune's* ire or *Juno's,* that so long
> Perplex'd the *Greek* and *Cytherea's* Son . . . (9.13–19)

On the theory that epic genre is centered around an epic hero, Stella Revard and others have read this passage to be a comment on the status of Adam.[14] That theory is mistaken: Milton is not discussing Adam here. The comparison is between, on the one hand, Milton's "argument," and on the other, a series of synonyms for anger: "wrath . . . rage . . . ire." His argument, clearly, concerns anger, and if so, then that anger must be God's; it is the "distance and distaste" of line 9. The subject that Milton is claiming to be suitable for epic, and thus the subject he is placing most centrally, is the anger of God, which is represented as the "distance" between God and Man. This central comparison suggests that Milton is more interested in the attendant processes of the Fall, both the "distrust" that causes it and the "distance" that results from it, than he is in the Fall itself, which, his comparison makes clear, is neither the subject of Book 9 nor that of the whole poem.

Furthermore, Milton's use of a strident comparative—"not less but more heroic" (14)—instead of a simple simile suggests that this comparison is a justification of the epic itself. Because the anger of God has such greater implications than the anger of the mythic heroes, that anger becomes, as a poetic subject, more heroic—more suitable for epic. The measure of the extent of that anger is its representation in the life of Man; what makes God's anger more heroic than Zeus's is that God's has greater significance for human history. However, Milton's representation of God's anger is "distance and distaste." Distance is mediation; God's relationship with Man, once direct, now cannot be. But distance is also Milton's characteristic term for the difficulty of creating a relationship between Eden and Heaven even before the Fall. The confluence of Milton's point about genre and his figuration of God's anger suggest that anger applies before the Fall. But if anger is what defines the heroic mode at play here, then that mode too extends before the Fall. The shift in genre here must be a metaphor, because there is no way to define that shift without extending it before the point at which

Milton places it. What is defined as characteristic of the epic in a moment of dynamism is also defined as something that has always been characteristic, and so that dynamism becomes static. Thus, critics' attempt to make Book 9 a classic narrative turning point obscures Milton's sense of time and of narrative structure.

In the opening of Book 9 Milton asks his reader to look in the events that follow not for temptation (Raphael's warning), but for distrust and revolt. In that context, it becomes clear that at every stage the Fall of Man is active rather than passive. In other words, the Fall itself is a form of distrust of God rather than of submission to Satan. In fact, in the three debates that make up much of the book, the debate over separation between Adam and Eve and the debates over the eating of the fruit between Satan and Eve and between Eve and Adam, the activity of the decision in each case is striking. Temptation would imply potential persuasion, but though there are debates, no one really persuades anyone of anything.[15] Indeed, in each case the ultimately persuasive point is provided by the character who first opposes it: Adam rejects Eve's arguments for both separation and eating the fruit but decides independently of those arguments to do exactly what Eve suggests, just as Eve's Fall is preceded immediately by her own monologue, not by any last arguments from the serpent. To go along with the opening summary's obfuscation of causation, Milton avoids making the persuasiveness of either Satan or Eve a cause of the Fall.

"WANTON GROWTH"

The inverted rhetoric of Book 9 is clearest and most significant in the separation scene, when Eve suggests she and Adam work in different places in the garden and Adam, after a long debate, reluctantly agrees. Critics have attached vast moral weight to this scene,[16] but I think the point of it is not as a dialectic in which Eve's stubbornness (or Adam's paranoia for that matter) is demonstrated as an anticipation of sin; the conversation is a human conflict resulting from an existing conflict built into the environment.[17] The curious reversal at the end of the separation scene, in which Adam suddenly abandons his rhetorical position and consents to the separation, in that sense, is not a moment of weakness but one in which a rhetorical and tropic trend that exists throughout Book 9, in which trope works against persuasion as Milton's opening chiasmus undermines his invocation of a shift in genre, infects Adam as well. Eve is arguing that Eden is too fast for conversation, and Adam that it is not. But he finds a way of arguing in favor of conversation that prevents conversation. The rhetorical form of his argument undercuts and reverses the point that he actually wants to make, to the extent that he finds himself agreeing to something that he thinks may lead to his destruction.

Eve's initial interest in the prospect of separation comes from her perception of a discrepancy between two kinds of time in Eden.[18] There is an urgency embodied in the landscape:

> *Adam*, well may we labor still to dress
> This Garden, still to tend Plant, Herb and Flow'r,
> Our pleasant task enjoin'd, but till more hands
> Aid us, the work under our labor grows,
> Luxurious by restraint; what we by day
> Lop overgrown, or prune, or prop, or bind,
> One night or two with wanton growth derides
> Tending to wild. (9.205–12)

Descriptiveness is the key to Eve's argument; the "wanton growth" of Eden overwhelms not just work but Eve's senses. The two halves of Eve's sentence present two different images of time. The repetition of the word "still" suggests that labor operates within a fundamentally dilatory time. "Still" has both of its meanings—continuation or iteration on the one hand and stasis on the other—in both lines 205 and 206. To "labor still" is to still be laboring but also to be laboring statically; this sense of time is echoed in the delay in the word "till" in line 207. The choppy iambics of "or prune, or prop, or bind" enforce the slowness and the repetitiveness of work; the alliterative Anglo-Saxon diction is almost pedestrian. The description of Eden is an extreme in the other direction. The word "derides" overflows into an enjambment whose abruptness is magnified by the difficulty of the sentence's syntax. We expect the relative clause ("what we by day . . .") to be the subject (perhaps, *what we lop, grows* . . .) but instead it turns out to be the object, and the subject, "One night or two," turns Eve's complaint from a description of the relationship between human labor and plants into one of the place of humanity in Eden itself. *Time* is the subject of the sentence, and time's function is to render human labor obsolete. As such, Eve's personification puts the blame not on fecundity but on time; time stands here for Eden's ability to affect humanity. The time-scale of her work, Eve complains, is simply not the same as that of Eden, and since Eden's time is so integral to Eden, labor and garden are necessarily at odds.

Significantly, Eve ascribes the discrepancy in time to the immediacy of her relationship with Adam:

> For while so near each other thus all day
> Our task we choose, what wonder if so near
> Looks intervene and smiles, or object new
> Casual discourse draw on, which intermits
> Our day's work brought to little, though begun
> Early, and th'hour of Supper comes unearn'd. (9.220–25)

As she repeated the word "still," Eve repeats "near," and indeed seems to be referencing her previous point about the sluggishness of labor in relation to the urgency of Eden; the suggestion here is that proximity makes the urgency of Eden worse, precisely because proximity entails a kind of immediacy, and immediacy slows things down. Eve's ambiguous use of "intervene" (literally "come between") illustrates the point: in the etymological sense, "looks intervene" between the two of them, but in the modern sense the intervention is with their work. Eve is suggesting, in other words, that the relationship between her and Adam depends on their mutual relationship with Eden itself. Her request is an attempt to address the discrepancy between urgency and delay built into that relationship.

Of course, the conversation is an instance of the proximity she is discussing. Furthermore, Eve's suggestion deals directly with the issue of time, connecting it to conversational proximity. In making the request for separation, she suggests patience and the avoidance of urgency:

> Thou therefore now advise
> Or hear what to my mind first thoughts present,
> Let us divide our labors . . . (9.213–15)

"Now advise" suggests a request for a process, not for an instant decision; "first thoughts" implies that Eve herself is prepared to reconsider, to have second thoughts. Even as she brings up the topic, Eve provides Adam with a rhetorical model for its discussion, a model that depends on a temporality opposite to Eden's hurriedness. The portrayal of the conversation that is to follow supports Eve's argument about the nature of her relationship with Adam: it is slow. Eve clearly accepts that such slowness can have a function, since here it is necessary for determining how to deal with the problems she has pointed out. However, for her own good, for Adam's, and for the garden's, she believes that slowness must be moderated in whatever way possible.[19]

Eve has introduced doubts about both the condition of rhetoric in the marriage as well as the nature of Eden itself. Adam's response is to deny both points. His defense of rhetoric comes in a very Adamic metaphor: the comparison of spiritual with physical pleasures. The divine command to tend the garden does not, he says,

> debar us when we need
> Refreshment, whether food, or talk between,
> Food of the mind, or this sweet intercourse
> Of looks and smiles, for smiles from Reason flow,
> To brute deni'd, and are of Love the food,
> Love not the lowest end of human life. (9.236–41)

For Adam, the "sweet intercourse" whose dilatoriness Eve objects to is not only positive but intrinsic if not definitive: he regards it as a sign of humanity and of the relationship itself.[20] He enforces this understanding by concentrating on "smiles," rather than conversation per se; that is, what matters to Adam is the form of marital conversation more than its content or immediate effects. The humanness of constant interaction not only justifies it but, for Adam, renders irrelevant Eve's concerns about how much time it takes. His rejection of her concern about the rate of landscaping is an even clearer objection to her terms:

> These paths and Bowers doubt not but our joint hands
> Will keep from Wilderness with ease, as wide
> As we need walk . . . (244–46)

Responding to Eve's pessimistic description, Adam offers his own entirely contrasting one. There is no trace of the lushness that troubled Eve in this prediction; "ease" replaces urgency. Again, Adam's argument depends on definition: what is easy, and all that is required, is keeping the garden a garden and not "Wilderness." The upshot of all of this interest in definition becomes clear a few lines later, in what Adam clearly regards as the last word on the subject:

> The Wife, where danger or dishonor lurks,
> Safest and seemliest by her Husband stays,
> Who guards her, or with her the worst endures. (267–69)

I must admit that I find Adam's use of normative definitions of husband and wife, in an era when there is only one of each, almost humorous. But for Adam it is his central point. Whereas Eve attempted to create a particular kind of rhetoric to deal with problems of place and time, Adam's rhetoric relies only on definition; what something is in its essence (says the namer of all things) is more important than its relationship with its environment.

For Eve, the individual's relationship with the environment defines its essence, and as the debate degenerates into quarrel, she ends her own last argument by stressing that point:

> Let us not then suspect our happy State
> Left so imperfet by the Maker wise,
> As not secure to single or combin'd.
> Frail is our happiness, if this be so,
> And *Eden* were no *Eden* thus expos'd. (337–41)

As Adam used the definition of humanity against separation, Eve uses the definition of Eden in favor of it. The argument that "Eden were no Eden" unless it is possible for Adam and Eve to defend themselves as independent entities defines Eden not only as a place of bliss but of a bliss not dependent on proximity. Her subjunctive is significant, because she believes that Eden *is* the Eden in her definition; it must be, since Eden's urgency means that proximity's dilatoriness requires separation in order to respond to that urgency and thus retain Edenic happiness.[21] She demonstrates simultaneously two different associations with Eden. One is normative—Eden is happy—and the other descriptive—Eden is overly lush. Trying hard to reconcile descriptive necessities with persuasion, Eve wants Adam to rethink the very nature of Eden; her frustration stems from his unwillingness even to consider the question. Her original point, that far from being the manifestation of bliss, Eden possesses intrinsic attributes that create problems for human happiness (or at least effectiveness), is enforced and strengthened; rather than relieve her doubts about Eden, Eve stresses, Adam has increased them by adding to them such an extreme account of risk. That proximity and immediacy are intrinsic goods is one thing, Eve seems to think, but to call them necessary for the avoidance of the Fall is to put an entirely new stricture on Edenic life, particularly since the urgency built into Eden, as Eve has already argued, makes proximity a problem.

Adam replies to Eve's last argument in favor of separation with the greatest emotion—"fervently" is Milton's word (literally *boiling;* 9.342); if his former replies represented "domestic *Adam*" (9.319), then this is Adam the moral warrior—and with premises on the grandest scale:

> O Woman, best are all things as the will
> Of God ordain'd them, his creating hand

Nothing imperfet or deficient left
Of all that he Created . . . (9.343–46)

This is a direct contradiction of Eve's statement that "*Eden* were no *Eden*" if Adam and Eve cannot be independent of one another; Adam's argument is that Eden is perfect because it is created to be perfect, not because of any of its attributes (clearly he does not consider his complaints about Eden in asking God for Eve in Book VIII to be the same thing). Of course, Eve's subjunctive meant that she herself was never questioning the perfection of Eden, but rather the implications of that perfection. Adam does not just disagree with her about the implications of perfection, though; he cuts off the line of inquiry. The statement amounts to an utter rejection of Eve's rhetoric; Adam wishes to make clear to her that not only do her arguments not persuade him but they merely serve to remind him that the opposite of what she says is true. The image Eve begins with, of crafting a space for the play and process of rhetoric out of the urgent air of Eden, is rejected so completely here as to leave little space for rhetoric at all; if Eden's perfection cannot be questioned, then the debate itself is invalid (and thus clearly not the kind of marital conversation that Adam thinks is so important). This distrust of rhetoric (particularly Eve's rhetoric) fits with Adam's distrust of reason (particularly, again, Eve's) a few lines later:

. . . Reason not impossibly may meet
Some specious object by the Foe suborn'd,
And fall into deception unaware . . . (360–62)

It seems at least plausible to hear Adam's doubt about Eve's reason as referring to the current debate; that is, far from convincing Adam with her argument for moral self-sufficiency, Eve's attempts at persuasion have left Adam with even more doubts about her ability to protect herself. Eve cannot doubt that the debate is over, since Adam has rejected not only Eve's argument but her ability to make arguments.

The debate is indeed over, but only because of Adam's astonishing reversal, which creates such problems for the ideas of rhetoric and of debate. It comes in the midst of his most damning criticism of Eve. Responding to her insistence that she is above temptation, Adam suggests again that her current position undermines that insistence, immediately before giving in to what he describes as an unchangeable inner self:

Wouldst thou approve thy constancy, approve
First thy obedience; th'other who can know,

> Not seeing thee attempted, who attest?
> But if thou think, trial unsought may find
> Us both securer than thus warn'd thou seem'st,
> Go; for thy stay, not free, absents thee more;
> Go in thy native innocence, rely
> On what thou hast of virtue, summon all,
> For God towards thee hath done his part, do thine. (9.367–75)

In the instant that Adam brings up the idea of obedience, suggesting that what Eve is doing in this scene is not merely arguing from incorrect premises but committing a basic moral mistake by not accepting his authority, he withdraws it through the abrupt turn to the idea of freedom. It is not hard to hear in these lines (particularly "what thou hast of virtue," which to modern ears sounds like condescension) considerable despair, and indeed the structure of the sentence seems to make the previous debate irrelevant: if Eve thinks it best, Adam says, she should leave without discussing it with him, without arriving at the truth through consensus. Adam does not even wait to gauge the effect of his last point, following it instead with this conditional in the present tense ("if thou think" [370])—the condition is what Eve thinks, as if there were no reason to expect (despite both spouses' continual praise of the pleasures of marital conversation) that what Adam says will have any effect on what Eve thinks. Obedience for Adam is opposed to rhetoric; obedience takes over when rhetoric has failed (and there is no doubt that it has failed here). But in Adam's opposition between obedience and rhetoric, conversation is rejected as well, so that the opposition destroys the idea of immediacy that is so important to Adam. If compelling Eve to be present makes her more absent, the suggestion is that proximity is not proximity without agreement. The line "thy stay, not free, absents thee more" uses the compression of its verb (a verb whose activeness elides the distinction between a decision that leads to absence and the effect of that decision[22]) to introduce the entirely new idea that Eve's decision to stay, if she does not agree with the justification, would amount to a detention. Neither Eve nor Adam has ever mentioned the idea that Adam was detaining Eve—to call her "not free" is to say that her stubbornness itself, her refusal not only to act as he does but to think as he does, constitutes enough of a rebellion that she may as well be physically rebellious. In order to be together in any sense, Adam feels, he and Eve must not only be physically proximate and conversationally in contact but must agree.

One could, no doubt, try to find a motivational or psychological reason for the reversal; since Adam needs agreement to feel proximity, maritally speaking he is not getting much out of this conversation, and is desperate for a reason to end it. More significantly, however, it is part of the larger rhetorical trend in Book 9, in which persuasion is beside the point and urgency prevents dialectic. Dialectically, Adam's reversal has little function. It ignores Eve's arguments; it is in no way a concession. Instead it raises an entirely new idea, that of freedom of choice, instantly turning the argument from a conversation about what should be done to a plea on Eve's part for Adam to allow her to leave. In the reversal, Adam misinterprets the conversation that has just been taking place. Eve has never made the plea that Adam ascribes to her, but that discrepancy is only one of a number of problems with the reversal. It seems to represent a turning away from Eve, and desire to end the conversation at any cost. As such, it also turns from the possibility of human connection. Adam does not persuade Eve, but persuades himself of something she never argued in the first place. In that moment he is completely cut off from her, neither listening to her nor speaking to her. The rhetoric of the reversal is indeed inverted in the etymological sense—turned inward. It is rhetoric addressed to the self.

"SOME ORATOR RENOWN'D"

Adam's understanding of human connection depends, in fact, on urgency, on the immediacy of contact. The force of his reversal, even if nothing were to happen as a result of it, would already suggest that the understanding of rhetoric that follows from that urgency is deeply problematic. Things do happen as a result of it; for my reading, the most significant thing that happens is that the separation leads to another debate, a debate in which the conflict between rhetoric and the intellectual determinations of Eden replays itself. Like the separation debate, Eve's debate with the serpent ends with the person convinced having the final word; Eve cannot be convinced until she convinces herself. In this case, however, part of the reason for that self-conviction is the serpent's (deceptive) identity as an animal; from Eve's point of view, the serpent's rhetoric comes out of the landscape itself, which is already a problem, since she associates rhetoric and landscape with two different kinds of time. To make matters worse, the serpent asks her to think of godliness, a state outside of urgency, as residing in the tree, and thus in Eden. Eve resolves these discrepancies by ignoring the serpent's linguistic rhetoric in favor of purely physical attributes (allowing her to continue perceiving him within Edenic time), and by reading the effects of the tree not as transcending Edenic limitations, as the serpent suggests, but as existing within those limitations; she reads any effects of eating of the tree as necessarily instantaneous and physical, as all of Eden is.

Even the narrator, in depicting the serpent's rhetoric, emphasizes its physicality. For the second time in the book (the defense of epic anger was the first), Milton describes the kinds of rhetoric at play in this section of the poem as classical. This time, the serpent is the subject, and the comparison is not to poetry but to oratory:

> As when of old some Orator renown'd
> In *Athens* or free *Rome,* where Eloquence
> Flourish'd, since mute, to some great cause addrest,
> Stood in himself collected, while each part,
> Motion, each act won audience ere the tongue,
> Sometimes in highth began, as no delay
> Of Preface brooking through his Zeal of Right.
> So standing, moving, or to highth upgrown
> The Tempter all impassion'd thus began. (9.670–78)

After the classical comparison, the reader might expect a description of "Eloquence" (670); that is, of the serpent's rhetorical abilities. Instead the emphasis is on the external characteristics, as it were, of classical orators: not only their gestures, but the importance to their effectiveness of the appearance of urgency, *as if* "no delay" could be emotionally tolerated (675). It is this last point in the comparison that most connects to the description of the serpent; lacking arms, his gestures are limited, but instead he draws himself "to highth upgrown" (677), imitating physically the trick of voice used by the old orators to convey urgency.

Milton concentrates on the physical aspects of the serpent's rhetorical style in part because that is the aspect Eve is most aware of. When the serpent first confronts her, Eve ignores the content of what he says (extreme flattery) to focus on the sheer fact of his speaking:

> What may this mean? Language of Man pronounc't
> By Tongue of Brute, and human sense exprest? (9.553–54)

The serpent's use of language and its "sense"—that is, not its significance but merely its coherence: the *fact* that it has sense—are what impress her; they may be the chief reason for her fall.[23] After the serpent's arguments, Eve returns to the serpent's ability to speak, still more important to her than what the serpent has said; she addresses the Tree of Knowledge:

> Great are thy Virtues, doubtless, best of Fruits,
> Though kept from Man, and worthy to be admir'd.
> Whose taste, too long forborne, at first assay

> Gave elocution to the mute, and taught
> The Tongue not made for Speech to speak thy praise. . . . (9.745–49)

Throughout her conversation with the serpent Eve focuses on its tongue, on the physicality of the serpent's speech. When she addresses the more sophisticated aspects of that speech, she does so, again, factually rather than analytically:

> . . . hee hath eat'n and lives,
> And knows, and speaks, and reasons, and discerns,
> Irrational till then. (9.764–66)

Eve focuses on effect rather than on transformation; her description is still external. The model she presents does not force her to alter her fundamental definitions; an irrational animal, after eating, reasons, but is still the same animal. The instantaneity and straightforwardness of the change fits within a definition that makes sense to her.

That definition, however, ignores the serpent's arguments. The serpent retains an understanding of an internal logic of Eden that Eve never mentions:

> That ye should be as Gods, since I as Man,
> Internal Man, is but proportion meet,
> I of brute human, yee of human Gods. (9.710–12)

The serpent's argument is based on an analogy between the respective differences between animals and man on the one hand and man and God on the other. Eve, thinking in terms of place, would hear this is as an analogy between Eden and heaven, and would not be likely to accept an equivalence between the two. Thus, it is not surprising that Eve does not comment on this argument. Adam and Eve can exist outside of Eden's limitations in a way that animal life does not; the concept of "Internal Man" challenges that distinction, but Eve does not regard it as necessary for her to accept that challenge in order to eat. Nor is she interested in the serpent's discussion of Eden's self-sufficiency. Of the idea of the divine origin of Eden, the serpent says:

> I question it, for this fair Earth I see,
> Warm'd by the Sun, producing every kind,
> Them [i.e., gods] nothing: If they all things, who enclos'd
> Knowledge of Good and Evil in this Tree . . . ? (9.720–23)

The serpent needs a description of Eden that allows for its productivity, which we already know is extraordinary; he produces such a description by including the Sun within the descriptive world. Making the Sun responsible for growth allows him to make the garden self-sufficient, and thus to leave Heaven out of the picture. For the serpent, to disassociate the Tree from Heaven, to suggest that its origin has nothing to do with God, is to remove it also from morality. Following the logic of origin (a logic that my discussion of *Areopagitica* in the Introduction shows that Milton does not endorse), Satan implies that if God is not responsible for the Tree, then he cannot govern its use. This is of course a typically Satanic idea; Satan of the internal hell associates place with the vast moral infrastructure of the universe. For someone who cannot leave hell even if he leaves Hell, place is equivalent to morality. By extension, the bonds that maintain Eden's balance between Heaven and Chaos define, for him, the moral status of anything within Eden. If he can convince Eve that those bonds do not exist or do not define the tree, he figures, she will find herself free to eat.

But Eve, under the spell of the timeliness of Eden, is more interested in effects than in the metaphysical status of Eden. The principal argument against eating that she considers depends upon her idea of the way time works in Eden:

> In the day we eat
> Of this fair Fruit, our doom is, we shall die. (9.762–63)

If the serpent were right that Eden had within it the potential of creation and of godliness then this understanding of the threat of eating would not make sense. Eve's assumption that punishment will occur "In the day" of transgression is based on her continuing sense that Eden functions in no other way but instantaneously. Since persuasive rhetoric itself exists outside of that instantaneity, and since the serpent's own rhetoric essentially argues against the definition of Eden that makes instantaneity necessary, Eve must ignore the content of the serpent's speech. The debate here is between two conceptions of place; Satan's is based on the question of the verifiability of creation, while Eve's is more purely empirical. Satan never wins this argument—Eve neither repeats his conception in her monologue before eating nor does she use it in talking to Adam later. Thus, the possibility for the Fall must exist *within* Eve's conception of Eden; it is not necessary to introduce a foreign concept of place in order for Eve to disobey.

My point here is not a moral one. Nothing of what I have argued prevents the serpent's deception from being the most immediate cause of the

Fall; on the contrary, Milton says that the serpent's "words replete with guile / Into her heart too easy entrance won" (733–34). Whether it is the content of the words or the fact of them that convinces Eve is something of a moot point, and the moral weight, clearly, lies in the "too easy entrance": Eve had the capacity to defend against the deception and did not. But by deflecting attention from rhetoric toward description, toward the physical existence and definition of the serpent, Milton makes the intellectual event of the Fall stem from a discrepancy between conceptions of Eden, not between conceptions of morality. That is, the sin of eating is there, but its prominence is not, because the sin is overshadowed by Eden itself, whose nature Milton figures as responsible for the Fall even though he knows and we know that it is not. At the same time, that rhetorical shadow intrudes also into the moral cause of the Fall. The conflict's results, at least, emerge in terms of time: Eve expects to die instantly or not at all, and instead she dies late. A late death is not an Edenic one; it belongs to a category Eve has not yet thought of.

One part of the Fall, then, is the failure to imagine delay, but that failure cannot be restricted to Eve. On the contrary, Eve seems to have access to Eden (or honesty about it) in a way that Adam does not. Eden does indeed seem to be hurried, however much Adam may suggest otherwise. Perhaps that fundamental disagreement is on Adam's mind during the third of Book 9's debates. In this debate, like the others, there is no persuasion—in fact, there is no real debate, since Adam's response to Eve's attempts to persuade him to eat is merely silence. Like the others as well, time is key. Eve uses time—her observation that she did not immediately die after eating—in her argument, and Adam uses time as well in his response, by pausing.

The debate is marked by a lack of communication. Eve's point that "bliss, as thou hast part, to me is bliss, / Tedious, unshar'd with thee" (9.879–80) is an idea that, rather than arguing against the original understanding of the Tree, ignores everything Adam has ever said on the subject in favor of Eve's perception of the immediate effect of eating. Adam's response to this solipsistic argument is to withdraw into himself, and at first he communicates nothing to Eve:

> *Adam*, soon as he heard
> The fatal Trespass done by *Eve*, amaz'd,
> Astonied stood and Blank, while horror chill
> Ran through his veins, and all his joints relax'd . . . (9.888–91)

At the moment that Adam hears of the Fall, all communication, even gestural communication, is cut off; whatever runs through his veins, his relaxed joints do not display it. But Adam's response is the first effect of the Fall to develop over time. Milton describes that effect from Adam's point of view, but what Eve sees, while she is speaking and afterward, is a pause. Adam's response is the first hint of the importance of delay, and indeed Milton stresses the length of the pause, even as Adam begins to recover from the shock:

> Speechless he stood and pale, till thus at length
> First to himself he inward silence broke. (9.894–95)

Silence is presented in degrees, broken gradually. "Inward silence" is the most complete rhetorical breakdown of all, but even when that silence is broken the outward silence remains. Milton, like his biblical sources, requires Adam to fall undeceived. That requirement accounts for the long silence, since it means that communication between characters on either side of the Fall cannot be complete, and certainly cannot be persuasive. The rhetorical gulf between Adam and Eve is represented as an unreliable echo, a distortion of sound. Adam's says that "if Death / Consort with thee, Death is to mee as Life" (9.953–54); Eve twists his words, telling him to expect "not Death, but Life / Augmented" (9.984–85). Like his rethinking of presence and absence in the separation scene, which is not persuasive because it is not directed toward Eve, Adam's redefinition of death as something that can occupy an identity with life goes nowhere; Eve's response returns to the antonymical status of death and life. Her dismissal is not unexpected, though, since Adam's question about death is based on an understanding of time and of the Fall that he has not even tried to communicate to her.

One effect of the extreme and explicit delay involved in Adam's response to Eve's fall is to refocus the communicative barrier between Adam and Eve within the problem of the disjunction of time. Adam's slow response necessarily forms a contrast to Nature's fast response, a contrast that ultimately suggests the relationship between description and rhetoric in the context of the Fall. The immediacy of the surroundings makes rhetoric obsolete, but humanity still depends on rhetoric, and Adam cannot possibly have the same kind of response that Nature has. Because of the existing association of Eden with an urgent time and Heaven with a delayed one, to place Adam's and Eve's now completely dysfunctional relationship in the context of that disjunction is also to think of it in terms of location. Location is the key to the shift in genre that Milton identifies at the beginning of Book 9; in the conversation between Adam and Raphael, the difficulty of describing Eden was part of the subject of a dialectical debate, whereas in the series of conversations leading up to the Fall,

Urgency and Delay in Eden 107

the difficulty of describing Eden becomes a context determining the very nature of conversation.

Paradise Lost itself is caught in the same problematical relationship between rhetoric and description. The poem describes a place getting ahead of the poem's image of it—poetic description of Eden is necessarily late, looking back from a hopelessly disconnected future. Any account of Adam's and Eve's attempts to respond to temptation and to sin should be viewed in the context of the futile poetic attempt to overcome the inherently mediated and delayed understanding of Eden. Thus, criticism's attempts to place the Fall in a moral context, whether along the lines of John Reichert's defense of Adam, Diane McColley's defense of Eve, or even Victoria Silver's reading of Eden in the context of the philosophy of the relationship between God and man,[24] will inevitably run into a profound obstacle: the problem of the poetic depiction of Eden.

"THE WAKEFUL BIRD"

I have said throughout this chapter that the urgency of Eden contrasts with the slowness of Heaven; the point needs some explanation and reinforcement. In Book 9 the distinction between locative forms of timeliness is clearest in its effect on rhetoric, but that distinction, particularly as it relates to the description of landscape, is a major theme in the narration of the entire poem. For the Miltonic narrator, the problem is that the poem as a whole is not trying, as Adam is, to work out a humble but still intellectually self-sufficient position within the conflict between Eden and Heaven, but to encompass that conflict enough to be able to incorporate it into the poem. At the point of the Fall, the disjunction between rhetoric and description appears as a crisis, but Book 9 is the climax of an ongoing dynamic. Throughout the poem as a whole, description maintains a very delicate balance with the rhetoric of Milton's explicit goal, a balance subject always to potential disruption. The attempt to unify the inherent conflict of description and rhetoric in the poem is particularly noticeable when Milton discusses the relationship between Earth and Heaven. In his greatest description of that relationship, the invocation to light in Book 3, the importance of descriptiveness to the poem—and its power for disruption—is clear. Once again, timeliness is an issue: Milton uses metaphors of a distinctively timed environment to express his own relationship with Heaven, though Heaven's untimeliness means that that relationship is characterized principally by delay and mediation. The metaphorical function of descriptiveness in these passages works against the poem's dependence on that mediation; the poem is opposed to description. In this way, the inability to see is a way to overcome the tendency of description toward a particular form of time, and allow the disjunction between the different forms present in the poem to appear in balance. Milton's blindness thus becomes the condition of immunity to environmental urgency, though that urgency is still contained through metaphor in Milton's descriptions.

Light is considered by most critics of the poem, however they interpret it, as necessarily singular. But the distinction between a blind descriptiveness that can account for both delay and urgency and a sighted descriptiveness constrained within an urgent environment means that light cannot have in the invocation the unity with which it is usually credited. The light of God transcends the problem of timeliness, while the light of seeing does not. Blindness *does* have a unified function, but what blind description references is necessarily a multiple light—a light divided between what blindness leaves out and that to which it is even more sensitive than sight. Thus, certain fundamental assumptions in critical responses to the invocation must be questioned. William Kerrigan's understanding of light has been influential; he describes light as the metaphor for Milton's wish for what his poem will achieve:

> As the holy light is absorbed and distributed in the body of the epic, Milton introjects, not just a specific tradition, but futurity itself. "Necessity and Chance" do not approach this unapproached light. It is not beholden to contingencies. It will make actual whatever pleases God, and God's desire lacks want. Considered in the opening lines without regard to any creation except its own, *light is the energy of wish-fulfillment unconditioned by a prior moment of satisfaction.*[25]

Kerrigan's exuberance comes from the unity that he perceives is given to the poem by the invocation; he says, "There is not a detail of *Paradise Lost*—not a river, a god, a simile, a word—that is not somehow the progeny of this light."[26] But his ambitious reading requires him to ignore the complexity of Milton's light. The invocation does display a unifying feature of the poem, but it is a unifying conflict. Light exemplifies a fundamental disjunction, but does not contain within it the resolution for that disjunction.

Light's importance for the process of writing means that the discrepancy in kinds of time we saw in Book 9 takes on a central role here as well. The metaphor for the relationship between modern man (as opposed to Adam) and Heaven is the metaphor of inspiration, a direct enough process in itself. But Milton's depiction of inspiration is qualified by an interest in delay, in mediacy, and in a metaphysically necessary obscurity. Thus the opening of

Urgency and Delay in Eden 109

Book 3 is the clearest instance of a problem that extends to the poem as a whole; the invocation contains an idea of God in which immediacy is neither possible nor desirable. There are two operative metaphors, one light, the other birdsong:

> . . . as the wakeful Bird
> Sings darkling, and in shadiest Covert hid
> Tunes her nocturnal Note. (3.38–40)

This is a description that avoids descriptiveness. The bird, its species unidentified (neither poetic tradition nor naturalism is enough for the phrase "nocturnal Note" to be an identification; many birds sing at night, and in fact the nightingale sings mostly in the late afternoon), is spoken of in the generic singular, and furthermore is dark and hidden, with the adverb "darkling" applied even to the song itself, as if one's hearing the song is affected by never seeing the bird. As a metaphor for inspiration, the figure becomes a celebration of difficulty, since inspiration is not determined by wholeness or purity but by the ability to hear despite the necessary obscurity of transmission—by its capacity to absorb and overcome complexity. As environment, the darkness, the hiddenness, and the quietness all suggest a lack of immediacy and proximity; this is clearly not the same kind of environment as the Edenic one whose lushness Eve finds troubling. That the image is, literally, late, a nocturnal image, adds to the sense of difficulty and obscurity.

In contrast to the difficulty of his inspiration, the visual world that the blind poet cannot see is described specifically:

> Thus with the Year
> Seasons return, but not to me returns
> Day, or the sweet approach of Ev'n or Morn,
> Or sight of vernal bloom, or Summer's Rose,
> Or flocks, or herds, or human face divine;
> But cloud instead, and ever-during dark
> Surrounds me . . . (3.40–46)

The plural of "Seasons," "flocks," and "herds" suggests innumerable specific objects, each identified separately and clearly, in the world that is lost to the blind inspired poet. Time also is ordered and distinguishable in the world of sight, and without boundaries in blindness. The suggestion is that the poet's blindness forces him to ignore a world of everyday distinctiveness and temporal regularity in favor of one that is transcendent, but also obscure and without clear time. The distinction in time, as it matters to Eve in Book 9, matters here—blindness removes the poet from a natural time, the sequence of seasons, and places him in a different kind of time associated with inspiration, whose obscurity suggests that it does not have the same immediacy as time does to the sighted. Milton's description of his blindness as "cloud" is significant (45); his internal sight is still described as an environment, but one that is entirely different from the environment of the natural world. Blindness blocks out natural time.

In keeping with the obscurity of that vision, the central figures in the vision, as the invocation to light makes clear, are never entirely distinct. Milton makes an analogy between God and light which is then refined and qualified in order to point toward the kind of imagination which, though less well represented by Milton's analogy, is in fact closer to the truth. This refinement contains the explanation for the distinction in the invocation between clear external light and diffuse internal light: though bold, vision is not immediate. The refinement is a reminder for patience: the meaning of an idea is not fixed until its context is complete.

Light is the metaphor Milton provides for that mediation. Tellingly, the narrator describes light itself in terms that are shifting and contradictory. The form is of a dialectic: the first person, the narrator, wants something in particular of the second person, light, and because what the narrator wants is poetic inspiration, he asks for it in such a way that the rhetoric of the asking includes the evidence of his getting it. The dialectic is closed, one might say: it sets up a problem and resolves it at the same time. But even as the rhetoric of the invocation suggests the completion of the dialectic, it also casts doubt on the formal identity of the second person figure, since light is several things here.

Light's most important function is as conduit to God, but from the first sentence of Book 3 Milton shows at least two different relationships between God and light, and the division between those relationships will make it much less clear from where exactly the inspiration for which light is a metaphor is coming:

> Hail holy Light, offspring of Heav'n first-born,
> Or of th'Eternal Coeternal beam
> May I express thee unblam'd? since God is Light,
> And never but in unapproached Light
> Dwelt from Eternity, dwelt then in thee
> Bright effluence of bright essence increate. (3.1–6)

Urgency and Delay in Eden 111

Light is both the first creation of God and God himself. However, the question about blame, which is the main idea of the entire sentence ("May I express thee unblam'd?" [3]), is connected to light only inasmuch as light is God; *that* light is the one that is "unapproached" and unapproachable, and the possible blame attached to talking about light as God's first creation comes from the metonymy of light as God: "since God is light," the narrator says, he must wonder whether talking about light at all, even as "offspring of Heav'n first-born" is acceptable. Milton does not mean physical light, exactly, by either of these kinds of light; that is, we can assume a further distinction between the light of the opening of Genesis and the light of the Sun, the light that is denied by the narrator's blindness (more on this below). But he carefully avoids the distinction I am making between created light (the light of the opening of Genesis), which is real in itself even if not solar, and increate light, which is metonymical and stands in for God. He avoids this distinction for two reasons, I think: to show that words for metaphysical entities are made uncertain by the limitations of an inherently metaphorical language, and to insist that despite that uncertainty the use of these words carries considerable moral weight.

The trouble is that the nature of light in Genesis is not very clear. On the first day God creates light, appreciates it, and separates it from night (Gen. 1:3–5). This light seems to *be* day, and thus would fill the physical space of day equally, as the day itself does. However, on the fourth day God creates the sun, moon, and stars, and places them "in the firmament of the heaven to give light upon the earth," the sun during the day, the moon and the stars at night (Gen. 1:17). Clearly the light that shines on the earth during the day is different from the light that is the day; the former is present more in some cases than other cases (depending on the brightness of the day or the darkness of a shadow) and apparently did not exist until the fourth day, while the latter light, the day itself, is present in sunshine or in shadow, and exists from the Beginning. The light that the Gospel of John discusses, the "life" that is "the light of men" (John 1:4), is clearly a third kind of light, since it exists regardless of day and night. Though John does not give his light temporality, Milton would presumably think of it as existing even before the light created on the first day (like the Word).

In the description of creation in Book VII, Raphael makes sure that his description will be consistent by accounting, from the beginning, for the presence of light without sun:

> Let there be light, said God, and forthwith Light
> Ethereal, first of things, quintessence pure
> Sprung from the Deep, and from her Native East
> To journey through the airy gloom began,

> Spher'd in a radiant Cloud, for yet the Sun
> Was not; shee in a cloudy Tabernacle
> Sojourn'd the while. (VII.242–48)

This description is far more precise than anything in Book III, and in fact has rather the opposite effect. Light here clearly does not mean inspiration or God or any of those things, presumably because Raphael wishes to make sure that Adam can follow his narrative. The passage is also very clear about points of origin—light moves from East to West, and also radiates to the world from its cloud. On the other hand, "Sojourn'd" is static; in that sense this light is already behaving like the light Milton associates with the seasons, the light he cannot see: a light that changes cyclically but not fundamentally. Time here, too, is clarified; light is identified as "first of things," a signal that time in fact has already been created, and sequence is now imaginable. Raphael's hint at a future, "for yet the Sun / Was not" (246–7), enforces the sequence. Light in creation is clearly not the same as the light of the invocation in Book 3; the former is ordered, exists in time, and operates within a narrative motion, while the latter is outside of time and mediated through inspiration.

Milton introduces a new kind of light when he brings up his "flight / Through utter and through middle darkness" (3.15–16). This graduated light cannot be the same light that Milton addresses with these lines:

> Before the Heavens thou wert, and at the voice
> Of God, as with a Mantle didst invest
> The rising world of waters dark and deep,
> Won from the void and formless infinite. (3.9–12)

Here dark and light have a binary relationship; where one exists the other does not. There is no possibility of "middle darkness" in this light, the light of the first day.

Both of these instances of light occur between two direct addresses. Line 9 addresses the first day's light as "thou," but the discussion of darkness and of "*Chaos* and *Eternal Night*" implies distance from that second person figure. Milton acknowledges the distance through the climax of the narrator's return trip:

> . . . thee I revisit safe,
> And feel thy sovran vital Lamp; but thou
> Revisit'st not these eyes, that roll in vain
> To find thy piercing ray, and find no dawn . . . (3.21–24)

Because what cannot enter his eyes is still a form of light, Milton can refer to it in the same vocative that he has been using all along, even though this light is not the same as the other lights. His vocative is inclusive. The light that is denied to the blind narrator, addressed in the second person here, is different from the light that God created on the first day. It is not to be disregarded, however; the blind man's loss is real and even significant for the kinds of knowledge he is discussing, which is why he complains of "wisdom at one entrance quite shut out" (3.50).

Because both solar and divine light matter, and because he uses the second person to refer to both, the meaning of the end of the invocation is somewhat more difficult than it first appears:

> So much the rather thou Celestial Light
> Shine inward, and the mind through all her powers
> Irradiate, there plant eyes, all mist from thence
> Purge and disperse, that I may see and tell
> Of things invisible to mortal sight. (3.51–54)

It sounds as if the narrator is addressing "thou Celestial Light" as reiteration, a reminder of the immediacy of the invocation's plea. But the earlier "thou / Revisit'st not these eyes" complicates this meaning, since the light of the Sun, the light Milton cannot see, is external, and this one works internally. Of course, "Celestial" itself could have two meanings: heavenly light sounds like either the light of the first day or even John's Light, but all light is celestial in that it comes from the sky, as Hughes seems to acknowledge in his note on Milton's interest in "the 'lucid essence' of God as mysteriously related to the physical light of the sun on the one hand and to the human mind on the other . . ."[27] Even in this sentence, then, Milton is including several very different ways of thinking about the relationship between the narrator of divine events and his inspiration. "There plant eyes" is a metaphor, of course: a metaphor about the mysteriousness of the human ability to narrate things beyond human understanding. "Things invisible to mortal sight" is literal: the metaphor in this clause is only the implied idea of a sight that can see invisible things, but the things themselves, the events of his story, Milton means literally. "Celestial Light" is both literal and metaphorical: Milton wants both the idea that inspiration is similar to light and thus can be thought of as light, and that God actually manifests himself *in* light.

Earlier I suggested that Eve's idea that one can counter the urgency of Eden with a kind of rhetorical deliberateness runs up against Adam's own attachment to an immediacy which is as urgent about place as Eden is urgent about time. The invocation to light comes after the first two books of *Paradise Lost,* a description of Satan in Hell, emblematic in every respect of confusion and darkness. When we first read the line, "Hail Holy light, Offspring of Heav'n firstborn," we are expecting an antidote to the obscurity of the first two books, like Eve's antidote for urgency; light is direct, and light is first of all things, and those two attributes ought to dispel the complexity and temporal and spatial remove of the beginning of the poem. But as the invocation goes on, and light divides into different things addressed at different moments by the same word and the same second-person pronoun, the antidote gives way to still more confusion.

It is not a coincidence that, in a poem in which environment is such a problem (as Nature and Eden are a problem in Book 9), Milton's choice of the metaphor for inspiration is an environmental conceit: an inner landscape in which the celestial Sun shines. Like his characters, Milton's readers at first expect environment to be direct, but later find it indirect and unclear. Long before Adam's discomfort with Eve's attempt to understand the nature of time and connection in Eden, Milton has indicated his embrace of an even more fundamental mediatedness—through the avoidance of directness—in his definition of inspiration. Book 3 suggests that *Paradise Lost* itself is *late,* that it willingly sees itself as written on the other end of a profound barrier of time, of space, and of the unimaginable discrepancy between human understanding and divine reality. The urgency of Eden—its instantaneous reaction to the Fall and its overwhelming lushness—is a stark contrast to the sense of mediation in the invocation to light. It is no wonder then that Adam and Eve are unable to create a rhetoric that both accounts for that urgency and allows for a genuine connection. Their rhetorical efforts are only a part of a larger rhetorical structure, a structure that has already established a preference for mediatedness over directness, delay over urgency.

In this sense the rhetorical breakdown in the separation scene, a breakdown that can be seen as leading directly to Fall, has its route not in a moral circumstance but in a yet larger rhetorical one. But the greater rhetorical problem—the impossibility of description in the context of a disjunction of timeliness—has its own roots in doubts within Milton's fundamental project. His goal is to use a poetry that is at once descriptive and narrative, at once georgic and epic, to transcend a break in time so complete that descriptiveness itself is distorted by the process. A relationship between Earth and Heaven, whether in the prelapsarian time of the separation scene or the postlapsarian time of the writing of *Paradise Lost,* is always disrupted.

Chapter Four
Collapse and Consolation: The Postlapsarian Environment

In the previous chapter, we saw that the relationship between the Fall and Eden is not so much about Eden's status as prelapsarian bliss as it is about Eden's function as a place. Contingency on its physical relationship with humanity—heating, echoing, needing pruning, *appearing* as sky, field, plants, and animals—prevents Eden from functioning as an abstract state of being. Instead, again and again Eden turns out to be a surrounding, a location. Even after the Fall, as this chapter will demonstrate, Eden continues to function more as a landscape—first disrupted, then closed off, then destroyed—than it does as its more abstract form: the state of prelapsarian innocence and bliss. The question is still *where:* what has become of Eden after the Fall? But this question also demands a new historicizing of Eden—a rethinking of Eden in light of the Fall. In that sense, the question is: can the Fall be separated from Eden? This question is on Adam's mind after the Fall, but it is overwhelmed by a simpler desire—the desire to retreat into Eden, to divest himself of responsibility by becoming indistinguishable from his surroundings. However, he cannot separate Eden as refuge from Eden as the location of his troubled history. This chapter will investigate the relationship between the desire to be in Eden or a part of Eden and the description of Eden, focusing on Adam rather than Eve, since Adam's soliloquy of despair is the central intellectual statement of the problem of postlapsarian Eden. Faced with the memory of an Eden whose definition was unclear, Adam cannot define the new Eden he and Eve have created, and so cannot place himself in it. As the prelapsarian Eden was blissful, but still created anxiety, the fallen Eden is restrictive, but seems to contain "loopholes"—the word is Milton's (9.1110)—through which a surprising degree of environmental connection is possible. Still, the desirability of that connection, which is tainted by its association with the Fall, is questionable.

The consistency of Adam's awareness of his environment throughout and on either side of his despair is notable, but the more important lesson is that even in his lowest moments, Adam's primary concern is with the logic of his relationship to his surroundings, not with loss or regret or death in themselves. The basic model through which Adam understands virtually everything that happens is the situation of humanity located in Eden; in the dark time after the Fall and before his reconciliation with Eve, Adam reads even sin and death within that model. The problem is that Eden is not simply a particular environment; it carries implied expectations with which Adam and Eve consistently struggle. As I discussed in the previous chapter, in Book 9 Adam and Eve are both as much concerned with the *idea* that Eden is a place of bliss as they are with its actual ability to foster (or distract from) their happiness; the difficulty of achieving that idea in the real world only makes it more necessary to think of Eden as a place rather than as a state. Similarly, after the Fall Adam only notes the alarmingly real changes to the landscape in terms of what he thinks they mean (what, in Milton's term, the air of Eden "represent[s]" [10.849]), and is more concerned with more difficult questions such as the location of death or sin. By the time of his reconciliation with Eve, Adam seems willing even to take those changes as a form of consolation.

In order to understand the significance of place immediately after the Fall, it will be necessary to read Book 10 significantly differently from the approach critics have taken in the past. Because Adam is in despair (a sin), and because his logic bears a noticeable similarity to some of Satan's casuistry from earlier in the poem, critics have assumed that the logic of his thinking after the Fall and before his reconciliation with Eve is merely a moral trap. The most compelling argument against this assumption is the sheer consistency of Adam's tendency to turn to his surroundings in order to understand himself. The importance of the turn to place on either side of the Fall implies that it carries meaning in itself, regardless of the context in which it appears. I wish to understand the turn to the surroundings in itself, and thus, despite the danger of indulging Adam's despair, I will enter into the details of his rather tortured logic, even though that will require creating some similar interpretive mazes of my own. But the function of place in Book 10 extends beyond Adam's logic; the literary handling of place as it appears in the narrator's descriptions of Adam's relationship to his surroundings and particularly in Adam's own thought matters enormously for the way Milton redefines the nature of the fallen world. The rhetorical choices Adam makes in describing his surroundings are Milton's introduction to the entire history of the fallen world, and to ignore them is to lose the incipient stage of what is, for Milton, the actual context of *Paradise Lost*.

If disconnection with environment caused Adam anxiety before the Fall, after it his anxiety centers around the threat of collapse. In his moments of despair and regret after eating from the Tree, Adam for the first time considers the possibility of no longer being located, of losing environment altogether. But his concerns about the collapse of Eden have an unexpected relationship to his earlier anxieties about disconnection; after the Fall, collapse becomes both an apprehension and a desire. The soliloquy is dense and casuistic, and its logic has been subject to dismissal by critics. But, even within that twisted logical structure, the soliloquy can still achieve *descriptive* integrity. Adam's intent, such as it is, is sophistic—a desperate attempt to outmaneuver the logic of his sin and punishment—but that intent does not mean that Adam's figurative choices provide only an example of what not to do. On the contrary, it is within figuration that the consistency of Adam's perspective is preserved. The de Manian reminder that trope undercuts rhetorical goals applies as much here as it does to Adam's and Eve's arguments in Book 9, since even if Adam's rhetorical goals really are bad, he must still pursue them within whatever tropic possibilities are generally available—trope exists essentially outside of his moral circumstances. To put this in psychological rather than rhetorical terms, though the Fall changes the way Adam thinks and behaves, it does not change the way he sees, and so his relationship with his surroundings is to a large extent preserved.

Still, there is a significant change in Adam's goal in regard to his landscape. The earlier desire to understand place gives way to a desire to retreat into place. A trope suggested by Adam's interest in connection with environment is synecdoche; he wishes to think of himself as a part of a whole rather than as a person located in a place.[1] As we will see, the trope is used specifically at important moments in Adam's despair, but it also appears behind much of his interest in environment in general. Adam's goal (and sometimes his problem) is continuity between himself and the environment; his anxiety (and very occasionally his salvation) is discontinuity. Synecdoche provides meaning, but also suggests collapse. It is associated both with prelapsarian Eden and with death.

"INTO THE THICKEST WOOD"

Because of the persistent questions about the function of Book 10 in the poem as a whole, it is difficult to discern what the canonical reading of the book might be.[2] Milton critics have frequently read Adam's despair in Books 9 and 10 as a linear process in which Adam gradually prepares himself, through the intervention of divine reason over bestial irrationality, to recover his relationship with God and with Eve, through forgiveness and humility, and to prepare for his life in the fallen world. A common understanding of the soliloquy is expressed succinctly by John Reichert, who claims that Eve's "sweet converse and love recover him from the depths of despair, anger, pride, and resentment into which he has fallen."[3] Reichert regards as obvious and not needing comment that Adam's despair is completely distinct from the pious self recovered by the end of the poem. Two versions of this idea exist, depending on whether a critic sees the passage as part of the process of Adam's redemption or as simply a demonstration of his unredeemed state. Either way the process is linear; it is a path from despair through resignation to redemption or from despair through aporia to redemption, but both views assume that whatever insights Adam's soliloquy manages are purely temporary in effect. Taking the gradual redemption approach, Leonard Mustazza argues that the soliloquy is crucial both for Adam's use of "language on himself in much the same way that Satan uses words on himself in his soliloquies" and for the progress Adam makes within it: "with the aid of God's grace, Adam unlike Satan, here begins the journey toward true repentance, which must include full acceptance of his guilt."[4] Stanley Fish's reading is directly contrary to Mustazza's, since for Fish, "the process is hopelessly circular . . . The way out is there, but not through reason, which conspires, like rhetoric, to prevent the mind from looking beyond the artificial coherence of a limited system."[5] What these two readings have in common is that they assume that Adam's observations and realizations in his despair are something that, sooner or later, need to be repudiated. The speech can seem helpfully progressive to one critic and hopelessly static to another precisely because the issues it statically pursues are true to the nature of the fallen Eden; the speech is a despairing *version* of a process of thought that occupies Adam during his best and worst moments alike.

One problem with this linear reading is that it treats Adam's despair as simply part of the machinery of his transformation into a fallen but religious man, and assumes that the expression of that despair is intended by Milton to show Adam's position within that transformation. But there is no evidence that Adam's gradual acceptance of his fate represents a metamorphosis in his relationship with, or understanding of, Eden. Adam has never before experienced the Fall or anything like its aftermath, but his reaction to it is still his; that is, Adam reacts to the Fall as the Edenic Adam would react.[6] He is still concerned with the insufficient reach of a relativistic account of the relationship between Earth and Heaven, and he still desires a connection with the landscape which must necessarily be incomplete (the concerns and desires I explored in chapters 2 and 3). Furthermore, in his later contrition, rather than eschewing his despairing representations of Eden, he incorporates them into his consolation. Indeed, as Adam points out himself in the soliloquy, the problems with his despair are the inescapability of his fears and the impossibility of his desires, not the underlying thinking that informs those fears and desires. The overall theme remains incomplete connection to the surroundings, just as it was in Adam's wonder at his birth, in his arguments with God and Raphael, and in his fear over Eve's rebelliousness, and as it is finally in his despair and his eventual resolution.

The twin species of environmental collapse—universal continuity and universal disconnection—prevent a straightforwardly moralistic account of Adam's despair. Because Adam's desires and fears are both figured as forms of collapse, the fallen environment becomes simultaneously the most unbearable aspect of Adam's fallen situation and the consolation that makes that situation bearable. Adam presents his own account of his despair, which begins with a fundamentally ambivalent attitude toward environment beginning very shortly after the Fall. In these first, confused moments, environment primarily represents a hiding place: one that offers a form of consolation through the simplicity of the possibility of being part of the woods, and offers a refuge from divine wrath through its figuration as shelter. Adam sees his association with Eden as a way of avoiding moral responsibility. At the same time, the postlapsarian environment can never escape an association with the Fall itself, of which the violence and storminess of the new Eden is a constant reminder. That association, however, exists within the same effects that Adam is able to find consoling or sheltering. What Adam calls savagery, the loss of humanity through immersion in the landscape, is a way of avoiding the Fall and also, through its worldliness, a reminder of the Fall.

From the start, the cataclysmic collapse of environment is ambiguous, presented as both a perfect refuge and a terrifying separation. At the end of Book 9, Adam interprets his newfound fear of God as one in which environment stands in for the unbearable while potentially making it bearable. Discussing with Eve the presence of sin in the face, he turns to his new dread of the face of God, and to the woods as shelter:

> How shall I behold the face
> Henceforth of God or Angel, erst with joy
> And rapture so oft beheld? those heav'nly shapes
> Will dazzle now this earthly, with thir blaze

> Insufferably bright. O might I here
> In solitude live savage, in some glade
> Obscur'd, where highest Woods impenetrable
> To Star or Sun-light, spread thir umbrage broad,
> And brown as Evening: Cover me ye Pines,
> Ye Cedars, with innumerable boughs
> Hide me, where I may never see them more. (9.1080–90)

It is not immediately clear to what the dislocated "them" in line 1090 refers; it could be "Star or Sun-light" (1087) or "God or Angel" (1081). It could also be both, since both are referred to in the same terms, as a light that the woods will block. The ambiguity is particularly significant since, though he imagines himself as hiding in the woods, Adam does not fear that God and the Angels will see him but that he will see them, that he will be blinded by their brightness. If hiding from God is not preventing oneself from being seen but preventing oneself from seeing, then the focus of Adam's fantasy moves from his relationship with God per se to his relationship with God as part of his environment—as something whose effect is external, not moral or existential. The fantasy clarifies the change Adam is discussing; when he says "those heav'nly shapes / will dazzle now this earthly" (1083), the force of "now" is that after the fall the meaning of "earthly" has changed. Earthliness once included a receptiveness (if often a puzzled receptiveness) to the divine; now, because of Adam's personal estrangement from heaven, the earth itself is alienated as well. By turning to the woods for protection, Adam desires only the completion of that change: the change brought to its logical conclusion. He is not, after all, imagining that the woods can somehow prevent him from being judged for his sin, but only that they will take him into their obscurity. The desire for darkness explains Adam's desire to "live savage"; the word "savage" takes here its etymological meaning: "of the woods." Savagery indicates here his desire for darkness as a reaction to his despair, not as an attempt to lessen the impact of his crime or the extent of his punishment. Savagery represents part of the closing-in of the surroundings, and, though it is connected to the fall through its bestiality and chaos, savagery still has the power of consolation.

The word "savage" stands in for the complexity of Adam's position. Savagery is dangerous; there is a very real threat of Adam's losing all moral direction, a threat he recognizes. On the other hand, Adam's desire for perfect synecdoche, to be entered into the woods without possibility of distinguishing himself from them, is also an amoral fantasy. Thus, the need for moral absolution and the anxiety of further moral degradation are both subsumed into a desire for a unity with the environment that would make any moral identity impossible. Adam hopes to hide himself even from the light of God, the light that "shineth in darkness" (John 1.5). Thus, he imagines a radically different kind of shelter, which can shelter him completely.

Though Adam's interest in savagery is temporary, Milton suggests in these lines that landscape can stand in for the prelapsarian pastoral relationship between humanity and Eden, and at the same time for fallen bestiality. Connection to environment is both the ideal from which Adam and Eve have fallen and the completeness they still, even in their sin, desire. Indeed, even as Adam and Eve worry about confronting God and the Angels, the Miltonic narrator suggests a kind of endorsement of the hiding Adam has in mind. Looking for leaves to cover themselves, Adam and Eve stumble on an inclusive pastoral environment similar to Adam's fantasy:

>   . . . both together went
> Into the thickest Wood, there soon they chose
> The Figtree, not that kind for Fruit renown'd,
> But such as to this day to *Indians* known
> In *Malabar* or *Deccan* spreads her Arms
> Branching so broad and long, that in the ground
> The bended Twigs take root, and Daughters grow
> About the Mother Tree, a Pillar'd shade
> High overarch't, and echoing walks between;
> There oft the *Indian* Herdsman shunning heat
> Shelters in cool, and tends his pasturing Herds
> At Loopholes cut through thickest shade . . . (9.1099–1110)

This is a different Eden even from the over-exuberant garden Eve struggled to contain earlier in Book 9. *That* Eden was still a garden, still a provider; it just provided too much. This one is not a garden at all, as Milton emphasizes with his fig tree specification: "not that kind for Fruit renown'd" (1101). Because Eden is wild, no longer cultivated, its relationship with the earth is different. The fig tree returns to the earth ("Twigs take root" [1105]) and thus becomes an environment itself, not just a tree. This metamorphosis creates a new synecdoche: to call the second bends of the branches "Daughters" is to represent a part of the tree as a whole, distinct tree in itself, recalling both Adam's creation from the earth of Eden and Eve's from Adam's body. That is, the new trees' separation from the old is emphasized even as they are all described not only as the same tree, but as a unified space, figured as a classical building or colonnade—a "Pillar'd shade" (1106). Furthermore, that environment is described as specifically pastoral, the home of the herdsman, and as precisely the kind of shelter that Adam imagines can block even the light of God. Here, pastoral—the genre of the created landscape—signifies the breadth and power of the range of hiddenness Milton associates with the tree. The tree's purpose in this instance is hiding—covering for the body. Its ultimate, larger, later purpose is shelter—separating (in ways that can be mediated by "Loopholes" [1110]) the herds from the heat. Connecting those two purposes is an assemblage of kinds of hiding—the tree hides its limits, re-rooting itself to create an obscure border between one tree and another. It hides its organicism, disguising itself as man-made shelter. Like Adam's imagined environments, these hiding-places go two ways at once; they provide shelter, but by hiding themselves they also represent a form of disconnection.

Perhaps most significantly, the tree hides from Milton's imagined English readership; it is known "to *Indians*" (1102), not to westerners. The reference is designed not to point toward a particular interpretation but rather to avoid easy categorization; to mediate the interpretation of the tree through a knowledge identified as someone else's. Balachandra Rajan, responding to a tradition that considers the tree straightforwardly infernal and its shepherd inhabitants simplistically primitive, points out that the tree moves in many directions at once; that it *is* infernal and pagan but that it is Christian and pastoral at the same time. This "contesting interpretation" leads to a comment on the moral significance of Milton's language:

> Milton's lines in their dense entanglements work powerfully to persuade us that appropriation is not simply a matter of channeling the properties of the tree to infernal uses. The tree is reinvented by the perspective in which it is installed.[7]

Rajan's observation is particularly germane given the moment at which the description occurs. Despair makes nature seem darker, more obscure, more impenetrable—literally and figuratively. But Milton's descriptions do not allow themselves to be subsumed within that mode. In the moment of his despair Adam desires a kind of hiddenness he associates with nature, but that the desire is a desperate one does not mean that nature can not, in general, hide. In other words, though his understanding of nature in this moment occurs in the context of despair, it is a mistake to call that understanding a despairing one in itself; like the bad books of *Areopagitica* which, "to a discreet and judicious Reader serve in many respects to discover, to confute, to forewarn, and to illustrate," the origin of Adam's insight does not finally determine its meaning or its usefulness.[8]

Just as the tree, as Rajan argues, prevents us from relying on too narrow an ideological perspective in interpreting the poem, it also prevents too narrow an emotional perspective: it is not possible to identify the moral context of this moment solely through Adam's despair. In that sense, the image's pastoral overtones work in both directions. The image presents a version of Adam's association of nature and shelter while undercutting it, since Adam's pastoral (as we have seen in previous chapters and will see again in his despairing invocation of echo below) is explicitly Edenic; to imagine a fallen pastoral is already to move beyond Adam's perspective. But what emerges in that imagination is still hiddenness locating regret and desire in the same place. If there are two available pastorals referenced here—the prelapsarian pastoral (the figurative shepherd in an accepting landscape) or the postlapsarian pastoral (the literal herdsman in the landscape of labor)—the figuration of place in this image never belongs completely to either one. That ambiguity stems from the equally ambiguous savagery that Adam seeks—a savagery that is both the culmination of the Fall and the return (through an immersion into nature) to Eden.

The fig-tree's morally ambivalent pastoral returns several times in the late books. This theme has primarily to do with the question of the unity of the perspective with which the surroundings are viewed, a feature of the synecdochic understanding of landscape. In chapter 1 we saw that pastoral is often about the seamlessness of perspective, the way that every part of the landscape can be involved in a single project, usually the reflection of the pastoral lover's inner states. Pastoral is invoked after the fall in part because that seamlessness of perspective has become anxious; as we will see later in this chapter, some disunity of perception, coming from the chaos of the postlapsarian landscape itself, is necessary in order to imagine a future in the fallen world. That disunity, however, stems directly from the Fall, as Adam and Eve both know. So while pastoral is nostalgic for a once-blissful seamlessness, it always has the potential to invoke the Fall, both through its worldliness and also through its interest in the unity of environment. In his soliloquy in Book 10, Adam continually has these two aspects of a pastoral environment in mind.

"THIR NATURAL CENTER"

Within the logic of Adam's thinking in Book 10, the culmination of the Fall—represented in Adam's embrace of the collapse of the world—and the quest for a renewed Edenic existence are compatible. It is in part this paradoxical reasoning that has led critics to assume that Adam's thinking in this section—particularly in his long soliloquy—is not to be taken seriously. But the result of that assumption is that the passage has not really been read. I propose that, rather than dismissing Adam's logic, we enter into it and see what its patterns and structures are. That approach raises a number of problems—moral problems that other critics have pointed out, but also interpretive problems caused by the sheer density and opacity of the language—but it will also make clear why these passages are included and what their function is in the overall poem. I believe that *Paradise Lost* is far too efficiently planned out to allow one part to exist solely that the reader might learn not to read it; as tortured as Adam's logic is in Book 10, it has, I think, lingering lessons about the nature of the Fall, of Eden, and of the human condition in the postlapsarian world.

The continuity Adam both desires and fears is comparable to that de Man associates with synecdoche, through his analysis of symbol.[9] Synecdoche, however, is a rather slippery figure; it posits a relationship between two things, part and whole, by questioning the distinction between them, and thus questioning in turn their individual identities.[10] The relationship between humanity and Eden is tenuous; if ultimately the attempt to interpret it synecdochically fails, then so too does an important part of Adam's sense of himself. Without an environment he can describe through synecdoche, Adam is given one fewer tool for understanding his condition, and after the Fall he becomes that much more alone and alienated. In his despair after the Fall, Adam's desire for synecdoche comes in a variety of forms; at times, Adam wishes for a kind of simple shelter, to be taken in as a part of the natural world in order that it might shield him from God and from his own sin. At others, he desires a synecdochic relationship with Eden as a concept—the emblem of prelapsarian bliss—more than as a place. Finally he expresses the desire to be subsumed entirely into his surroundings, and to become, in death, a part indistinguishable from the whole. The predominance of this trope at the end of *Paradise Lost* is a key to Adam's response to the Fall, which is an attempt to hold off the threat of collapse by re-figuring it—by creating competing figurations in which collapse is deflected into something else. More significantly, the use of synecdoche in Book 10 is part of a larger pattern within the epic, in which figurations of place mark the elements of the poem least interpretable within the limits of theodicy.

The desire to rethink collapse through trope is closely related to Adam's longstanding complex attitude toward his surroundings: his reluctance to accept his lack of knowledge of physics and astronomy in Book 8; his difficulty in making sense of Eve's complaints about Eden's lushness in Book 9. But Adam's desires imply more than one basis of anxiety. Synecdoche's interest in making the subject a subset of something larger suggests the possibility of a collapse in which the subject is no longer distinct. In fact, Adam's synecdochic Eden invites two different kinds of collapse: one in which the relationship is completed and the part becomes indistinguishable from the whole, and one in which the relationship is replaced by complete disconnection. Either way, the relationship between part and whole no longer exists—the opposite of Adam's desire for synecdoche. In my study of Adam's soliloquy I find that, as Adam points out in a crucial, frankly interpretative moment in the midst of his despair, his desire for a collapse into identity and his fear of a collapse into alienation have too much in common; both mean the end of environment.

However, the extent and complexity of Milton's interest in the desperate's perspective on his surroundings suggests that despair does not finally determine the meaning of these environments. Though created in sin, the fallen landscape, I will show, exists outside of sin, and to create a simple interpretive opposition between a virtuous and sinful (or, for that matter, unfallen and fallen) understanding of Eden and the world is futile. In this way, the sense that Adam has in despair of his surroundings is a necessary starting-place for any understanding of Milton's postlapsarian environment.

Adam's soliloquy has been described as circular in logical structure,[11] but though it returns to the themes it began with, it is not without development. He begins and ends with a desire for shelter and to be hidden, and an association of that desire with his physical surroundings in Eden, but in between Adam discovers a great deal about the nature of his situation, and those discoveries, despite their provenance of despair, carry over into his continuing search for consolation. The soliloquy is essentially a labored exploration of the partitive relationship of man to environment. Beginning with his favorite idea, of himself as a synecdoche for his surroundings, he attempts to foster a nostalgic conception of an Eden that can absorb him into itself. But his nostalgia is inevitably defeated by the anxiety of the converse of that conception: that Eden's collapse around him either destroys him or, worse, leaves him out. Adam experiments with replacing the idea of himself as a part of Eden with his centrality in Eden, reasoning that Eden is created around him, an idea enforced by his sin as much as by the memory of his past glory. But though human sin as the cause of Eden's climate change seems to support Adam's centrality, death's lack of autonomy turns out to be a challenge to that centrality, and Adam is left with no way to distinguish between the form of environmental collapse he wants and the one that terrifies him. What is most remarkable about the soliloquy, however, is that Adam recognizes this problem. More self-aware than Satan, Adam acknowledges the circularity of his despair as such: the circular form of all despairing thought.

Before the soliloquy begins, Milton establishes a specifically environmental context for Adam's thinking. The transformation of Eden turns it into a kind of place that presents a challenge to the very idea of a unified perspective of surroundings. Milton describes in blunt terms the concrete effects of the fall, but creates for those effects a context of doubt within a specific perspective: the human understanding (or misunderstanding) of environment. He prefaces the description by placing it within a doctrinal debate rather than under the narrator's authority:

> Some say he bid his Angels turn askance
> The Poles of Earth twice ten degrees and more
> From the sun's angle . . . (10.668–69)
>   . . . Some say the Sun
> Was bid turn Reins from th'Equinoctial Road
> Like distant breadth to *Taurus* . . . (10.671–72)

Here Milton evokes perspectives deliberately distant from Adam's, creating doubt by emphasizing the difference between them. But the debate functions only to draw attention to his shift back to Adam's perspective, since just as doubt introduces the description of the material effects of the fall, the inherent limit placed upon Adam's perception by the Fall concludes it:

> Beast now with Beast gan war, and Fowl with Fowl,
> And Fish with Fish; to graze the Herb all leaving,
> Devour'd each other; nor stood much in awe
> Of Man, but fled him, or with count'nance grim
> Glared on him passing: these were from without
> The growing miseries, which *Adam* saw
> Already in part, though hid in gloomiest shade,
> To sorrow abandon'd, but worse felt within . . . (10.710–17)

This time, the continuity of environment as an extension of the self—which Adam found incomplete when he asked God for Eve—now confounds him with its completeness. The animals demonstrate the reach of the Fall in two ways, by turning against one another and by not acknowledging Adam as the center of their existence. Still, by ignoring him the animals enforce—in a different way—Adam's position as the center, both because it is his sin that has caused this state of affairs and, more significantly, because Milton carefully describes this breakdown in environmental unity as something arranged around Adam. These are "The growing miseries" which, seen "from without" (714–15), are not only metaphorically parallel, not only emotionally parallel, but metaphysically parallel to the greater miseries that Adam feels "within" (717).[12] Milton carefully divorces the changes to Adam's surroundings from history, placing them first in the context of authorial doubt and last and most importantly in the context of Adam's perspective, and thus defining them as a subset of Adam's attempt to understand the nature of a fallen Earth. Thus the narration itself reinforces Adam's own sense of the limitations of his perception.

Because of this distinct perspective, Milton's locative metaphor for Adam's despair, "in a troubl'd Sea of passion tost" (10.718), takes on particular force. Having just made a direct comparison between the misery outside of Adam and that inside, Milton figuratively conflates the two, describing interior pain in exterior terms. The figure is immediately picked up by Adam, who reads the relationship between his own despair and the collapsing world around him to indicate not just a causal relationship but a possible identity. So anxious before the Fall about the lack of a complete connection between himself and his environment, Adam is now more anxious about the parallels between the two. But the overriding interest in the connection is consistent, and unites the development of Adam's character over the epic. Furthermore, we will see that the soliloquy's account of the surroundings, in which the collapse of the environment is welcomed as an escape or defense from the Fall while feared as a form of death, reinvents itself through Adam's own comment on his logic.

The soliloquy is not just a reinforcement of Adam's perspective; it represents a functional attempt to come to terms with Adam's place in the fallen world. In one of the densest passages in this part of the poem, Adam attempts to render into language the peculiarity of his position after the Fall. His *place,* literal and figurative, is figured by the synecdoche representing Adam's desire for environmental connection, which appears in a series of genitives—compressed prepositional constructions—providing a flexible relationship between self and environment. Adam plots his own transformation in the context of the transformation of Eden:

> O miserable of happy! is this the end
> Of this new glorious World, and mee so late
> The Glory of that Glory, who now become
> Accurst of blessed . . . (10.720–23)

This introduction to Adam's long soliloquy of despair suggests, from its first highly ambiguous interjection, an understanding of Adam's situation which is at once sophisticated and very confused. The genitive "miserable of happy" suggests several kinds of relationships simultaneously, and, significantly, brings together a sense of change (happy has given way to miserable) and a sense of location (miserable is a part of happy, i.e. Eden). The entire passage is governed by this same degree of ambiguity, but there is a logical structure to it all the same. Read in order, it is hopelessly confused; read backwards, its meaning becomes clear. Line 720 is without any referential definition: "miserable" could be a substantive adjective referring directly to Adam or the adjective itself referring to his state or that of the world; "happy," according to the status of "miserable" could be Eden or his former self. The ambiguity is heightened by an ensuing complex synecdoche. "This," still in line 720, makes "miserable," whether it is Adam himself or the current status, identical with "World" in 721: an identity reinforced by the repetition of "Glory" in the next line: Adam is refusing to make a distinction between the former glory and current misery that is his environment and the former glory and current misery that is himself; whole and part are expressed with the same words.

The passage is condensed; the ideas of curse and blessing, happiness and misery, and glory and (implied) shame are jumbled together, united by a simple pseudo-parallelism created by the repetition of the word "of": Adam's genitives trace the uneven outlines of his understanding of the Fall. The passage is emblematic both of the stakes of reading Adam's logic—it is the only account he gives of the postlapsarian human condition—and of the difficulty doing so. The opening interjection is entirely cryptic; it has no subject and no tense, so that though at first glance it appears to contrast Adam's current misery with an earlier happiness, the rest of the passage alters that appearance. The sequence, and the statement at its start, only makes sense, as I said, read in reverse—in the context of the whole passage, the opening statement reveals itself as a partitive genitive, not a temporal shift. The clearest exposition is the last genitive of the passage, "Accurst of blessed," a description of change involving a stark, nonreciprocal inequality: blessedness has entirely given way to accursedness. The description clearly points back to the emphatic pronoun "mee" in line 721, but the genitive before this one—"The Glory of that Glory"—suggests that such accursedness cannot end with the self, because for Adam to identify himself as "The Glory of that Glory" is a genitive representing synecdoche; Adam thinks of himself as both a part of Eden and as identified with Eden, so that his "of" is actually ambiguous, implying simultaneously location and essence. That genitive explains the one previous ("the end / Of this new glorious World"); it is because Adam *is* the glory of Eden that the "glorious World" has ended. The chaos around him, which, the narrator has just noted, "*Adam* saw" (10.715), is evidence of his centrality; it is thus retrospectively evidence of his importance to whatever

Eden once was. Adam is not only concerned with change here; he is also concerned with what perseveres through the Fall, which is the extent to which he cannot be independent of Eden. His despair is not simply the despair of loss; it includes an anxiety about what happens when loss joins with the continuing interdependence between humanity and its surroundings. Seen together in this way, these three latter genitives show that the first, "miserable of happy," is not the same temporal change indicated by the "become" at line 722 below. The lack of a verb in this opening interjection allows it to represent at once the change from happy to miserable and the suggestion that miserable is a part of happy: that is, while "miserable" is Adam's current state, "happy" here is both Adam's former state and Eden itself. Grammatically, "of happy" is a genitive of source, indicating transformation, and a partitive genitive indicating location (the chorographic genitive) as well as the traditional genitive sense of the divided whole. The despair of the interjection, then, is an astonishment at the change from one state to another and also at the paradox of an Edenic misery.

The passage goes from very vague to very specific, from "miserable of happy," which could mean anything, to "accurst of blessed," which *must* mean Adam. It moves from a self that is indistinguishable from its environment to a self that cannot escape the moral distinctiveness gained through sin. As my previous chapter discussed, both Adam and Eve define Eden in essence as the place of bliss, but since Adam is identified with Eden, and Adam is miserable, then a paradoxical synecdoche is created in which Adam tries to identify himself as a part of a whole whose essence denies his participation. Even as this passage is caught up in the logical labyrinth of Adam's despair, its interest in Adam's centrality in Eden, in the extent to which the universe is organized around him, reaches beyond that despair. The genitives represent both Adam's desire—figured here as nostalgia for his past glory—to be a part of Eden, and his anxiety that he cannot be separated from the fallen, collapsing Eden. This pairing represents a cycle present throughout the soliloquy: nostalgia leads Adam to emphasize his centrality in Eden, but that centrality after the Fall suggests a disruption in his relationship with his surroundings. Even if the pattern is cyclical, however, he is clearly moving past his initial desire for simple shelter towards something more sophisticated and less tangible.

That something is a kind of shelter that can be escape at the same time—shelter conceived as a release from the world: a release from place altogether. Even Adam's concerns about his cursedness—the heart of what appears to be the *moral* logic of his despair—are in fact not moral but locative. It is Adam's locative anxiety, his fear that his own misdeeds must (as they will) corrupt his environment as well as himself, that makes him so worried about the lack of limits of his accursedness. As he remembers being the glory of Eden's glory, he wishes that he could separate himself into a distinct moral entity; he could even bear God's wrath, he says, unbearable though it is, if his self didn't spill out into his surroundings:

> hide me from the face
> Of God, whom to behold was then my highth
> Of happiness: yet well, if here would end
> The misery, I deserv'd it, and would
> My own deservings; but this will not serve;
> All that I eat or drink, or shall beget,
> Is propagated curse. (10.723–28)

In asking to hide "from the face / Of God," (723–24) Adam echoes his earlier desire, at 9.1090, for the same thing, but this time the imperative is not addressed to his environment, but to something much less tangible (the implicit subject is the "miserable" of line 720 above). The problem, however, is still locative: Adam is now thinking of his environment not in terms of the desire to be taken in by it, but in terms of the anxiety that it cannot be separated from him. In Book 9, the fig tree became shelter by not being food; here, food refuses to be distinct from humanity and from human sin, since everything eaten is "curse." Adam is losing his sense of place as the source of everything, and thus, in wishing that "here would end / The misery," Adam's "here" is despairingly vague. Specifically, it appears to mean the memory of the happiness of beholding God, which cannot in itself be misery; "here" seems to refer to the prospect of beholding God now, when such an act would no longer be happiness. The argument is that Adam could bear the pain of facing God only if he knew that the pain in itself was his punishment. That notion brings "here" back to its natural meaning, location: the connection between the remembered "highth of happiness" and the current despair is that when Adam held that happiness he was the glory of Eden's glory. Because of his special locative position in the past, the position as center of Eden, which allowed facing God to hold such happiness for him, he must in the present eat and propagate his own curses.

The idea of Adam's locatedness, and of his centrality both in and to Eden in particular, is both the most poignant aspect of Adam's memory of happiness and at the root of his greatest fears. Because Adam's centrality makes his sin worse, his nostalgia for his old relationship with Eden leads directly to his anxiety about environmental collapse. Faced with that fear,

Adam attempts to remove the question of unity from his goal: with the simple idea of his embeddedness in Eden as his only premise, he reasons his way toward an understanding of his situation and a solution to his despair. His logical basis is the idea of locative centrality. Adam's first important parallel is between his centrality in Eden and the historical centrality of his sin, which he already anticipates. The image of himself as the moral center of a world that no longer acknowledges his authority extends to his vision of a human future in which the centrality of his sin overwhelms his function as father of all. He says of the blame of future men:

> All from mee
> Shall with a fierce reflux on me redound,
> On mee as on thir natural centre light
> Heavy, though in thir place. (10.738–41)

"All" (738) refers to the "curses" that Adam fears propagation will multiply; the inference is that fault is located, that it exists in the universe as a place does. But the organization he refers to is the organization of prelapsarian Eden, in which Adam was both the literal and figurative center. In this case he is the "natural centre" of all curses because he assumes that it is in their nature to organize themselves around him, not only because he is their origin but because he sees himself as center of all.

So the assertion of locative centrality, followed by its inevitable qualification and rethinking, provides part of the soliloquy's logical structure. The Fall forces Adam to challenge that notion of centrality, since he cannot bear the function he imagines for himself, either the center around which the world collapses or left outside of a world collapsing without him. Adam makes that challenge by questioning his centrality directly, by attempting to reinterpret his location as that of an accidental inhabitant rather than the center around which the environment is organized. This shift is demonstrated by a change in trope: Adam turns from synecdoche, which figures his own connected place in the world, to apostrophe, which by its conversational nature suggests separation. Apostrophizing God as a way of turning toward a more appropriate center, he emphasizes both his worldliness and his location as mere location, not as synecdoche:

> Did I request thee, Maker, from my Clay
> To mould me Man, did I solicit thee
> From darkness to promote me, or here place
> In this delicious Garden? (10.743–46)

The reinterpretation, as Adam admits quickly, is a failure. The problem is that Adam has never believed that he was placed in the Garden, but always that he was, or at least should be, part of the Garden. The form of this objection reveals that he retains the notion of himself as a part of Eden. In a soliloquy obsessed with the relationship between Adam and his immediate and future surroundings, this turn to God, to something outside of them, is an abrupt change. But it reveals itself as only a partial turn, first because it is still concerned with environment, here rethinking creation as a mediation in the relationship between Adam and Eden, and second because it is clearly marked as apostrophe (rather than direct address): Adam is still hiding even as he addresses God. Anxious to be in darkness, he refers apostrophically to God's removing him from darkness as if he were already back in it.

This moment demonstrates the extent to which Adam's logical problems are not so much the problems of despair as the rhetorical problems of trope. Part of the problem with apostrophe as a trope, Jonathan Culler mentions, is that it "may complicate or disrupt the circuit of communication, raising questions about who is the addressee . . ."[13] Such disruption is precisely Adam's intended effect here; he wants to imitate prayer to allow for the force and boldness of his complaint, but not actually to be heard. It is not Adam's logic in itself that prevents him from negotiating a different relationship to Eden, but the simple impossibility of achieving such an end through argumentation. The problem of describing his surroundings—a problem, as we have seen, that he struggled with as much before the Fall as after—is itself an obstacle of his desires.

Adam's response to his own question reveals that this address is designed to preserve his hiding-space rather than to qualify it. The invocation of God leads—through Adam's continued qualification and questioning of his centrality—directly to an apostrophe of self:

> inexplicable
> Thy Justice seems; yet to say truth, too late
> I thus contest; then should have been refus'd
> Those terms whatever, when they were propos'd:
> Thou didst accept them; wilt thou enjoy the good,
> Then cavil the conditions? (10.759–64)

Including second-person pronouns with different antecedents in the same sentence ("Thy" in 760 is God; "thou" in 763 is Adam) is even more abrupt than the turn toward God above; the chaotic grammar indicates that this apostrophe is no more than an attempt to shift the focus of Adam's synecdoche—here representing Eden—from location to state of being. Eden becomes in this analysis "the good"; that is, Adam is talking about the idea of Eden, the Eden that defines bliss, not the corruptible place. Thus, while Adam assaults his own questioning of the conditions of the "good" he enjoys, his self-condemnation is undermined by the collision between his contradictory notions of what Eden is. So this turn does not represent, as some critics have argued, the beginning of a progress toward redemption; it is merely one more failed attempt to come to turns with his position in the world.[14] Furthermore, the self-objection amounts to a return to the earlier idea of his centrality. Adam is not clay placed in a Garden, he is an Edenic being, and his attempt to separate himself from Eden, to say that its pleasures were an accidental result of his being there, is no more successful than is his attempt in this sudden apostrophe to separate himself from himself. The "Justice" he at first calls "inexplicable" (759–60) turns out to be logical to him; it is a byproduct of his relationship with his surroundings. Again, the question of centrality provides structure to the overall soliloquy—after positing and then questioning it, Adam begins to look for centrality through other means.

Unable to escape the logic of his past relationship with Eden, he tries to refigure his future relationship. Adam has been struggling for some time with what exactly death is; now it occurs to him that it may represent a shift in his relationship with his surroundings. Although he is willing to concede the basic change in Eden brought about by the Fall, he continues to think of his own status in terms of place. Even death is a place, and even death can contain Adam's desire for synecdoche. Adam's first thought on the subject, a welcome one, is that the shift will be from the center of a garden to an inextricable part of a larger whole:

> How gladly would I meet
> Mortality my sentence, and be Earth
> Insensible, how glad would lay me down
> As in my Mother's lap! (10.775–78)

In wishing to "be Earth" (776), Adam reaches simultaneously toward two questionable understandings of the nature of his situation.[15] He is still desiring the completeness of his increasingly torturous connection to environment; he is hoping that death means that all the barriers between himself and Eden disappear into a simple identity. On the other hand, the basis for Adam's logic of the complete connection of death is that death removes the problem of location—a dead person, he hopes, is a part of his environment *as opposed* to being placed in it. Picking up on this logical leap, Adam worries that death is itself located:

> . . . then in the Grave,
> Or in some dismal place, who knows
> But I shall die a living Death? (10.786–88)

There could be no greater difference than that between being "in the Grave" and *being Earth*. To "be Earth" is to no longer need to imagine oneself surrounded by an environment; the "in" is notably missing. Adam's modifier of that state is "Insensible" (777), because he hopes that in death the senses are no longer necessary, because their function of placing the self in its surroundings is no longer relevant. But if that function is still relevant, death becomes Adam's greatest fear rather than his greatest desire, because the environment would be taken up by death just as his current environment has been taken up by sin. In other words, as a complete connection with environment, death turns out to be unsatisfactory, since that connection would depend on human locatedness working in the same way even after death. Faced with that problem, Adam rethinks the desire for the complete identification between subject and environment, and location ("*in* the Grave"), as opposed to equivalency, returns. We should read "in some dismal place," then, with the stress on "place" rather than "dismal"—it is imagining death located that terrifies him.

Indeed, the unsatisfactory resolution of the question of the location of death forces Adam to reconsider his earlier idea of the locatedness of fault, and thus return once again to the question of his centrality. Here, anxious still about propagation, he hopes that his blamefulness can relieve his progeny of their place in the punishment. But an environmental logic convinces him otherwise:

> first and last
> On mee, mee only, as the source and spring
> Of all corruption, all the blame lights due;
> So might the wrath. Fond wish! couldst thou support
> That burden heavier than the Earth to bear,
> Than all the World much heavier, though divided
> With that bad Woman? (10.831–37)

Adam's distinction is between blame, which he has already said and says again here is located, and wrath, which apparently is not. His explanation actually points to two reasons for this difference: the immediate one is that because the wrath of God is not something a single person could possibly absorb, considering the possibility, whether as desire or fear, is futile. But

Adam's interest in planetary weight as the metaphor for the way wrath acts upon a person points back to a slightly earlier argument about the necessary limitations of death. In that earlier argument, God, Adam says, cannot possibly make death infinite while man remains finite, because:

> that were to extend
> His Sentence beyond dust and Nature's Law,
> By which all Causes else according still
> To the reception of thir matter act,
> Not to th'extent of thir own Sphere. (10.804–08)

The consistency of the metaphor suggests that even as the argument itself shifts, trope can reveal the categories and processes of Adam's thinking. Adam's argument here is that death's properties cannot be understood in terms of death itself, but must be thought of only through death's actions upon other things. It is an important turning point in the soliloquy, since the question of the limits of death forces Adam to wonder about a new question: to what extent the Fall can govern everything in the Universe. He seems convinced that some grand unity governs death, but he does not know whether it is the unity of morality (a unity in which everything is a punishment for sin) or the unity of environment (everything is governed by the tenuous relationship between self and surroundings). Adam comes to the conclusion that death must act as things in nature act: in other words, that the unity of environment trumps that of morality. The conclusion represents the triumph of the logic of place.

Adam's question about death is a version of his struggle with a problem John Rogers identifies as central to the poem: the conflict between an "identification of God with nature"—in which God's decrees work through natural law—and the idea of an omnipotent, punitive God; Milton "holds tight to the idea of God's absolute freedom and omnipotence even as he forwards the premise of the irrevocable laws of nature."[16] Those laws are a part of "Milton's story of the interdependence of human freedom and divine constraint."[17] Rogers points out that this individualism through naturalism is eventually challenged by Michael's "relentless delineation of an authoritarian philosophy of organization that nearly overwhelms the poem's attempt to engender a discourse of liberal individualism."[18] His "nearly" is significant; for Rogers liberalism wins out.

For Adam, however, the question is epistemological; he wonders here, as he often wondered before the Fall, whether his own resources are sufficient to make sense of his situation. If death is a divine punishment existing essentially outside of nature, then none of Adam's efforts at logic will come to anything, but if death exists within nature then Adam's rhetorical project in the soliloquy is vindicated. Adam clearly comes to the latter conclusion, which is crucial for the ultimate implications of his dialectic of despair; his immediate quest, for refuge, proves futile, but the soliloquy has an important function for Adam's postlapsarian life. By establishing that his punishment falls within natural law, Adam's logic convinces him that he can play an intellectual role in determining his own future, but also that his prelapsarian struggle with his environment continues. Both of these themes will be central to his eventual consolation and reconciliation with Eve.

On the other hand, Adam's sense of the inexorability of nature, within the poem as a whole, echoes a larger context: it may remind us of the image from the *Georgics* we saw in chapter 1 of an oarsman rowing against the stream—"everything by fate rushes toward the worse." In Vergil's metaphor, man's knowledge of his own status and agency in the world are both contested by an overwhelming nature, and it is that knowledge that concession to "Nature's law" questions.[19] Adam's imagination of sin, which represents itself in the sinner as gravity and which is punished through nature and through landscape, never ceases to be locative. In the narrow sense, we would say that Adam never stops thinking of his problem as the loss of Eden, but more broadly he never stops thinking of it as the question of the condition of being surrounded. There are two questions here—whether death will act on him according to natural laws, and distinctly whether the burden of God's wrath, figured through weight, is unbearable. But both questions are a version of the desire for an environment that can take him in.

Adam comes to no definite conclusion about any of these questions, but the process leads him to one very certain conclusion: that it is not working. Summing up all that has come before, his wish for death either as escape from locatedness or as absorption of the full punishment of his sin as a kind of absolution for his surroundings, and his anxiety about death's location or the limitlessness of punishment, Adam expresses all in terms of his separation from environment:

> Thus what thou desir'st,
> And what thou fear'st, alike destroys all hope
> Of refuge . . . (10.837–39)

Adam remembers here his original desire, which was not to avoid or lessen punishment on himself and others but, simply and instinctively, for shelter. But after all of his recalculations of his situation he cannot once again turn to the idea of hiding in the woods, because, as he recognizes, the desire cancels itself out. Ultimately, Adam's desires and fears mean the same thing: the collapse of environment. The desire to enter into environment wholly, to "be Earth" (776), would mean a collapse of environment through identity; an environment cannot be said to surround something if it cannot be separated from it. But the fear of deathless death—whether or not it is made impossible by the Newtonian principle Adam cites ("Nature's law")—is equally a collapse of environment, because it represents the end of any connection with the environment and the final loss of Eden.

Adam's desire for the collapse of environment, his desire for something that would "destroy all hope of refuge" is significant—it indicates that he does not, in his despair, seek a way out, does not seek redemption, but instead seeks the culmination of that despair, the logical telos of the despair. On its own this would indicate that Adam, as Fish accuses him, is stuck in the logic of his despair and thus of his sin, and that this entire soliloquy is merely a kind of temporary rhetorical exercise which will be abandoned when Adam is contrite, conciliated, and ultimately redeemed. But Adam's acknowledgment that his desire and his fear have the same end complicates that reading. This realization gives Adam all the tools that he needs to escape from the logical cycle that always leads back to catastrophe; he still does not escape because he recognizes that what he is observing is not local but is part of the nature of fallen desire. The soliloquy, then, is not circular; it moves through the assertion and then qualification of Adam's centrality and finally toward an actual theory. The theory is a desperately pessimistic one, in which hope itself is questioned, but it is still different from what Adam started with.

One thing that Adam has accomplished over the course of his long internal debate is a reinterpretation of "refuge." Originally, he sought "shelter," and meant it literally: a way simply to hide. His attempts to reason his way into some version of that hiding place have now convinced him that the Fall cuts off the possibility of refuge, because it leaves him with a desire for a kind of completeness that leads elsewhere. Adam's sense of shelter evolves from a hiding place to an escape from a locatively over-determined existence, an evolution that informs his realization about desire. There is no escape from location, even in death. Adam never comes up with an idea of death that is not either a desired refuge or a terrifying collapse of environment, nor can he imagine a relationship between himself and the lost Eden that is anything more stable than the impossible quest for shelter. In that sense, Adam's return to the idea of refuge is not the culmination of what he has been saying throughout the soliloquy but an exception to it; he adopts at this moment an earlier idea. The statement in which Adam summarizes what he has said does not seem to take into account everything the soliloquy contains. In itself, however, it reinterprets the soliloquy. Adam's discovery of destruction at the heart of his own desires suggests that the collapse of environment provides consolation for the very catastrophe that causes it, to the point that the collapse of environment can be figured as environment itself. Both forms have in common a certain self-destructiveness and a sense of an irrevocable amorality; the relationship between the two contradicts the long-running assumption in Milton criticism that Adam's observations at the height of his despair are somehow replaced by a later revision of his thinking. Critics have given great weight to the interpretive finality of Adam's despair, believing that the sinning nature of the emotion governs the output. As I said in discussing the flexibility of meaning in regard to origin in Milton in my introduction, I am not convinced that Milton is ever interested in such a simple relationship between the intent of discourse and its meaning. But in Book 10 in particular such reverence for origin is misplaced, both because of the continuities in Adam's responses to his surroundings before and after the fall and because of the continuum that characterizes his despair itself. After all, as Book 10 proceeds it becomes clear that the despairing desire for environmental collapse must be understood and rendered into a less immediately self-destructive form before the "loopholes" become available. Despair counts in the end, and the alleviation of Adam's despair, in that sense, is a matter of degree, not of kind.

Fish's influential reading considers the soliloquy solely as evidence of Adam's internal state, but I believe it has a distinct interpretive resonance. Adam has been desiring destruction throughout the soliloquy, but at the end, addressing himself as if acting as a detached interpreter, he points out that he has been desiring destruction. Adam's acknowledgment of the futility of his quest for shelter is the culmination of a soliloquy that has demonstrated the close relationship between that quest and the Fall itself. His self-awareness makes less convincing the assumption that the conclusions of the soliloquy are products of sin, since the point turns out to be the unity of perception within a fallen landscape. This self-awareness separates Adam from Satan, who is also concerned about the unity of the fallen world in his own despairing soliloquy on Mt. Niphates: "Which way I fly is Hell; myself am Hell" (4.75). Escape from despair is not possible if everything surrounding must be viewed through the Fall itself.

We see from the soliloquy that there is nothing interpretively simple or direct in the function of place in despair. Environment makes itself constantly present through its mediation of Adam's understanding of his condition, but in a way that is profoundly ambivalent. Adam knows that Eden is the best resource for making sense of his situation, but he cannot tell how to make use of that resource. His difficulty translates into an interpretive difficulty for critics. The interpretive function of place is revealed by Adam's concern with it, but that function can never be separated from Adam's thinking, and his despair colors our own attempts to understand the nature of postlapsarian Eden. One cause of this critical difficulty is that the logic of the soliloquy lingers after Adam's supposed recovery from despair. In the next section I will argue that, though Adam returns from the worst of his despair, in the process of that return he still relies on environment for a similar mediation. Furthermore, Adam still finds that environment just as ambivalent, though he begins to be able to acknowledge its ambivalence with less anxiety. Even as despair diminishes and the emotional context of environment's role changes, the contradictions about place evident in the soliloquy will remain.

"THWART FLAME"

By the end of Adam's soliloquy, the escape from despair through some self-saving process of thought has been eliminated, and it does not reappear throughout Adam's reconciliation with Eve and his acceptance of the Fall and its punishment. No longer trying to avoid despair does not, however, mean the end of despair. The logic of his soliloquy convinces Adam that he must seek a relationship with the landscape other than shelter, but he is still left with the need to account for the landscape's reflection of the Fall. The solution to that problem that he discovers surprises him: the fallen landscape is capable of creating a kind of relationship with humanity that the Edenic landscape was not. While the georgic inexorability of the fallen landscape alienates it from mankind, its restlessness—its interest in trouble—potentially allows for a freedom from the unity of perspective. Strikingly, Adam's most enthusiastic embrace of destruction (in his description of fire) comes *after* his realization that his despair causes him to desire destruction. The desire continues, but in a different form.

To make sense of Adam's new kind of desire for destruction I must return to his anxiety about the form of death. Adam considers two ways of imagining death, one in which he will "be Earth" and the other a "living Death" within the grave. The question hinges on the relationship between the synecdoche of landscape and perception; the problem is that sensibility seems to be required for the connection with landscape that Adam desires, and yet connection with a fallen landscape—a landscape that includes death—would seem to require that he *be* dead. But death without sensibility defeats the purpose, while the idea of sensibility in death is necessarily troubling (that idea "must give us pause," as Hamlet says). Adam's contemplation of death leads him to give up on his analysis altogether, because he begins to suspect that to desire a more complete connection with a fallen landscape is necessarily to invite death (even though death will not help); the resources he needs are not available within the perspective of the living, mortal human being. One issue is that human perspective is fallible (and if it was fallible in Book 8 when Adam and Raphael were arguing about the nature of the created universe, it is a lot more so now), another that human perspective is limited to the situation; the changes in Eden mean that Adam's senses receive different stimuli, suggesting that his connection to Eden must be mediated by these superficial appearances. Thus the contingency of the idea of Eden on its actual physical manifestations turns out once again to be a challenge to the synecdochic continuity of perception Adam desires. His perception is still necessarily unified, however, because he continues to see Eden as a single entity requiring a single interpretation.

In the context of Adam's attempt to rethink his relationship to Eden, perception and interpretation are essentially equivalent. What prevents Adam from thinking his way out of Eden is its constant and continuous presence to his senses. There is a unity to Adam's understanding of his location connected to the unity of his perception. The new despair the end of the soliloquy reveals is one obsessed with the senses. As a pair of contrasting codas to this soliloquy, Milton presents two differing understandings of Adam's locative condition, one in his own voice; one in Adam's. The first is an image of an environment that is certainly not shelter but that is, in its own way, sympathetic. The image is one of a direct and multiplying correlation between Adam's inner and outer situations:

> Thus *Adam* to himself lamented loud
> Through the still Night, not now, as ere man fell,
> Wholesome and cool and mild, but with black Air
> Accompanied, with damps and dreadful gloom,
> Which to his evil Conscience represented
> All things with double terror: On the ground
> Outstretcht he lay, on the cold ground . . . (10.845–51)

This description is very much from Adam's point of view, and the "double terror" with which everything is represented (850) applies to the image itself. The "damps and dreadful gloom" of the night (849) not only participate in the doubling of terror; it is the terror of them that is doubled. In other words, the image of Adam lying "on the cold ground" (851), whose coldness indicates the lack of the desired shelter, is an image in fact of his centrality in Eden and of Eden's dependence on him. No division can ultimately be made between the conscience to which the environment is represented and the fallen landscape that so represents them. In this image, Adam is as much a part of the surroundings as ever.

He may even be more a part of his surroundings than before, since the image of a "black Air" (847), in control of Adam's "evil Conscience" (849), suggests a stricture on thought. But Adam, with his newfound understanding of the catastrophic teleology of desire, seems to have access to the paradoxical idea that a prison which represents itself directly through environment is still his own creation. It is not clear in this passage where Adam's conscience ends and the environment whose perception his conscience determines begins; the "evil" is located in both, or rather as inherent in the connection between the two. Throughout the end of this soliloquy, even in this moment of highest despair, he is confronted by and struggling with the change in the relationship between his own mind and his surroundings. Responding to the simultaneity and similarity of changes in each, Adam is left without a means of distinguishing between his own perception and what he perceives.

Adam's predicament—the limitations of perception—can be understood through an issue Nietzsche explores in several works of his aphoristic period. Concerned about the hubris of human confidence in perspective, Nietzsche calls the unity of perception a prison, though for him it is important that the struggle is not understood—he thinks of man as blindly in the control of his perceptions of his surroundings:

> . . . it is by these horizons, within which each of us encloses his senses as if behind prison walls, that we *measure* the world, we say that this is near and that far, this is big and that small, this is hard and that soft: this measuring we call sensation—and it is all of it an error! . . . The habits of our sense have woven us into lies and deception of sensation: these again are the basis of all our judgments and 'knowledge'—there is absolutely no escape, no backway or bypath into the *real world!*[20]

When Nietzsche notes the impossibility of an "escape . . . into the *real world*" (the emphasis is his), he is in effect claiming that the function of perception is metonymy rather than synecdoche; that is, the only relationship between the things that we think we see and what is really there is that we decide to call the latter by the former's name. This is not mere radical skepticism; for one thing, it is a specifically rhetorical model of the crisis of perception, since the question is how we "measure" the world—what we *say* is near and far, big and small. Our senses, Nietzsche says, lie to us *because* we attempt to use them as a means of description: as measurement. But tropically, too, this model is distinct from skepticism, since Nietzsche wishes to enforce, through the metaphor of the prison, the alienation of the universe. Our desire to measure, to make sense of our surroundings, is hubris that must be punished, not merely a futile attempt to know the unknowable.

Nietzsche's main point is the impossibility of subversion; in fact, in the Nietzschean model, the prisoner is *content* to measure the world through the limitations of his perception, but it is precisely this limitation that informs Adam's despair. In this sense, his predicament resembles Nietzsche's account of the desperation with which alternatives to the unity of one's perspective can be contemplated:

> We cannot look around our corner: it is a hopeless curiosity to know what other kinds of intellects and perspectives there *might* be . . . the world has once again become infinite to us: insofar as we cannot reject the possibility *that it includes infinite interpretations.*[21]

That sense of infinity, Nietzsche says, might lead us toward deification but is equally likely to make us think of the satanic. I bring this idea up, despite the anachronism, because I want to emphasize the power of the "double terror" Adam feels when confronting Eden collapsing around him. Exploring his own perspective of that collapse, as he does at the end of the soliloquy, will only lead him into Nietzsche's prison; he must somehow logically reinstate a location distinct from his perception of it in order to survive.

If Adam wants to be part of his environment, then perception can at times seem like the solution (since it is in fact Adam's only source of connection with the environment), but at other times it can seem like the problem (since perception is limited to perspective). Death is desirable because it frees one from the prison of perception, but that freedom does not in fact result in a greater connection with the environment. This dependence on perception is the key to the importance of description in Book 10—it is Adam's description of his surroundings that defines the effects of the Fall, because there is no way for Adam to describe Eden as separate from himself. Thus, as much as despair leads Adam to try to change the way Eden is described, there is a continuity to that description that (contrary to all moralistic readings of the soliloquy) has nothing to do with despair.

Adam's response to the predicament the Miltonic narrator describes is nostalgia: in this moment, he recalls (probably mistakenly) a prelapsarian Eden with a totally different interpretation of his own status within his surroundings. Adam imagines a relationship between himself and his environment in which his own agency allowed his perception to have some role in determining the nature of Eden itself: a memory of the Eden created around him and for him. Milton gives Adam one last word before this extended passage ends, with which Adam creates what is on the surface an entirely different account of his current situation; one of a relationship with his surroundings which has not just changed but has ended:

> O Woods, O Fountains, Hillocks, Dales and Bow'rs,
> With other echo late I taught your Shades
> To answer, and resound far other Song. (10.860–62)

The passage is as frankly pastoral as any in *Paradise Lost;* it is practically a quotation from the first *Eclogue* ("resonare doces . . . silvam"—see chapter 1, in which these lines are quoted and discussed at length). Adam seems to be commenting on his own soliloquy here, the new song of which his former echoing calls were the "other Song" (862). As a comment on his current situation it is a peculiarly aestheticized one: what was once a terrified desire for shelter is now reinterpreted as a wistful remembrance of bucolic song.[22] But the key is the power of that song, which "taught" the woods to echo (861—a translation of Vergil's "doces"), giving Adam authority over, literally, the air of Eden. Adam's pastoral fantasy is the inverse of Milton's preceding description; in both, Adam and his environment are inextricably linked, but in Adam's memory, his perception of Eden is determined by Eden's response to his voice, while in the postlapsarian present, his perception is determined by his "evil Conscience"—his inability to conceive or to recreate an Eden without the Fall. However abrupt it may seem, Adam's reference to song follows from his realization that his desire for completeness will not lead to shelter. His nostalgia is for a desire that fits into a different relationship between himself and Eden, and what he laments now is the loss of that desire itself. In Eden he did not have the complete connection with environment that he wanted (as the pastoral connection is never fully complete), but at least he had the capability of hoping for that connection. Now he cannot even make an attempt for the connection, since his fallen desires lead him to something else.

These consecutive passages—Milton's description of Adam's inseparability from Eden and Adam's lament for a lost Edenic eclogue—indicate two contrasting ways of understanding the presence of the Fall in the postlapsarian landscape. Like Satan's Hell, Adam's Fall takes over his surroundings, and prevents him from distinguishing them from himself. On the other hand, Eden still reminds him of a prelapsarian connection (or at least a prelapsarian desire) in which environmental synecdoche was a good thing. Eden refuses to shelter Adam from the Fall, but what prevents it from doing so is the synecdoche in which Adam, as the central part of Eden's totality, creates its barrenness. Thus Adam is foiled by the same relationship that led him to look to Eden for shelter in the first place; his centrality in Eden prevents his refuge. What is left at the end of Adam's soliloquy of despair, then, is a new kind of despair that is more settled, less anxious, because it has no hope of shelter.

The lack of shelter, the "cold ground," becomes a stopping-place; whatever comes next, it must be in that environmental context. Lying on the ground, feeling its hostility, Adam begins the reconstruction of his relationship with environment. Arguing to Eve against suicide, Adam invokes God's kindness in the midst of the changes to the landscape:

> . . . lest Cold
> Or Heat should injure us, his timely care
> Hath unbesought provided, and his hands
> Cloth'd us unworthy, pitying while he judg'd . . . (10.1056–60)

When Adam and Eve sought the fig-tree in the forest, they were associating clothing with shelter, an association endorsed by Milton's pastoral description of the tree. Now Adam imagines a relationship with the environment that acknowledges its fallen destructiveness but does not seek shelter per se, since clothing here works within the cold or hot landscape instead of freeing Adam and Eve from it.[23] The suggestion is that, to put it crudely, humanity and God are teaming up against nature. The danger of the fallen landscape is acknowledged and accepted, but Adam suggests that it can be avoided.

As Adam extends the logic of clothing, however, the teamwork breaks down, and the destructiveness of the fallen landscape becomes itself a kind of consolation. He begins with the same sense of sheltering oneself from landscape but finds his own descriptions pulling him away from that idea. Adam hopes that God will

> teach us further by what means to shun
> Th'inclement Seasons, Rain, Ice, Hail and Snow,
> Which now the Sky with various Face begins
> To show us in this Mountain, while the Winds
> Blow moist and keen, shattering the graceful locks
> Of these fair spreading Trees; which bids us seek
> Some better shroud, some better warmth to cherish
> Our Limbs benumb'd, ere this diurnal Star

> Leave cold the Night, how we his gather'd beams
> Reflected, may with matter sere foment,
> Or by collision of two bodies grind
> The Air attrite to Fire, as late the Clouds
> Justling or pusht with Winds rude in thir shock
> Tine the slant Lightning, whose thwart flame driv'n down
> Kindles the gummy bark of Fir or Pine,
> And sends a comfortable heat from far,
> Which might supply the Sun . . . (10.1062–78)

Weather is dangerous and alienating, but its danger provides opportunities for new divine lessons and new technologies, and its alienation suggests a new kind of relationship between humanity and its surroundings. In these passages in book 10—in their sheer success—we see that the reality of the experience of the Fall in Eden is more complex than has generally been thought.[24] What is so striking about the end of Book 10 is that Adam successfully figures out a way to exist in a postlapsarian Eden, before Michael tells him he cannot. Adam's personification of the sky emphasizes its separation from humanity and from himself, and its "various Face" the fundamental discontinuity the Fall brings to the landscape. But the discontinuity is in its way beneficial. He is no longer thinking of bad weather as a direct reflection of his sin; on the contrary, his personification accepts that weather has nothing to do with him; even its destructiveness, "shattering the graceful locks" of the trees (1067), seems in this description to be simply part of the nature of the landscape, and not some poetic justice. With the winds personified injurious and the trees personified injured, the landscape is presented as if in conflict with itself, not with humanity, and that conflict turns out to be the best thing about it.

Adam's newfound acceptance of the landscape's separation from humanity thus culminates in the most enthusiastic endorsement yet of the destructiveness of the fallen environment. Adam introduces his description of fire as "some better warmth" (1068), but his personification is one of conflict; winds push clouds, clouds are shocked, and clouds destroy those gracefully personified trees of a few lines back. Adam's description of fire, caused by "collision" either among the clouds or on earth (1072), is an emblem of Adam's newest observation of the fallen landscape: that conflict creates good and bad at once. This is the same landscape whose "damps and dreadful gloom" terrified Adam. But, Milton stresses, the *meaning* has changed. In Adam's despair, the "black Air" "represented / All things with double terror" (849–50); that is, the air's unsettledness not only surrounded things, it became what presented those things to Adam's perception, preventing Adam from seeing things in any other context. That presentation has not been replaced in this description, but it has been appended. The description itself has in its "rude shock," its "slant" and "thwart" fire, the same harsh concentration of consonances that signaled Adam's unease about the landscape earlier. But now the idea of "comfortable heat" (1077) is added to the description, an addition allowed by conflict within environment. When the representation of environment was unified (as gloom), Adam was in a prison of his surroundings; disunity is escape. Still, the disunity is achieved through analogy between human and landscape; Adam and Eve's rubbed sticks are tiny models of nature's grand collisions. Because both forms of friction create fire, there is an implied synecdoche, in which the tropic association between the sticks and the clouds means that the sticks really are on the same scale as the clouds, since they can create the same function. The trope magnifies the human role, too, and gives the stick-rubbers the influence over their surroundings that they have been seeking. Fire is the resolution of the desire for a pastoral relationship with the surroundings; Adam and Eve can teach the woods by burning them.

Adam seems to be negotiating a new kind of relationship between the internal understanding and the external environment, in which the way the landscape appears to perception does not wholly determine its meaning for the understanding. The violence and unsettledness of the new landscape, once so disturbing to Adam, can be a form of freedom in itself, but only at the expense of the unity of perception; in that sense, the violence of nature is a solution to Nietzsche's prison of the senses. To imagine that the very aspects of environment created by the Fall can be used to defend against the Fall, to defend against other versions of those same aspects, is to resist the internalization of landscape. But Adam is still personifying landscape, and thus still resisting its separation from humanity. The twin devices work together; nature's disunity and alienation allow Adam to understand it in analogy with himself, as he did before the Fall, and thus as consolation for the collapse that alienates it. Consolation is thus achieved rhetorically. Adam reverses his previous descriptions of the relationship between subject and surroundings, *emphasizing* the scale of the environment and the scale of the destruction in order to suggest a possible means of escape from the prison of location. By entering into the hugeness of fire, Adam and Eve can transcend their tenuous position within the fallen Eden.

Whether Michael eventually provides another form of consolation does not concern me here, nor does the possibility that Adam and Eve's reconciliation provides its own comfort from the fall. My contention is that, within Book 10, the freedom generated by the unpredictability and destructiveness of environment is the readiest consolation available for the postlapsarian state. It is a necessarily unstable consolation, and one will not find much evidence of it in the last two books of the poem. The consoling power of destructiveness, however, serves as evidence of the overall importance of environment, rather than sin or death, in the definition of the fallen condition. Destruction provides a relationship between practical, metaphysical, emotional, and rhetorical aspects of place. The figurations of sin, the Fall, death, and punishment vary widely in Book 10, but there is a consistency to the figuration of Eden that suggests that, even in despair, the understanding of Eden can be a clue toward a plausible postlapsarian existence.

"THE DUNGEON OF THYSELF"

Figurations of place in Milton demonstrate how caught up Milton's metaphysics of place is in the problems of trope. In moments of despair—that is, in those moments when the Fall is most present—Milton refers often to a tension between the despairing person's alienation from his environment and the potential connection between the despairing subject and the fallen landscape. The final moral status of this pattern is difficult to determine in *Paradise Lost* 10; it seems closely associated with death, and possibly even with Satan. The pattern is instructive, however, because it points to the uncertainty and ambiguity of the fallen relationship with the surroundings. As often as one is tempted to say that despair isolates the subject from environment, Milton never allows that level of simplicity. On the contrary, a figurative description of place that suggests a synecdoche between subject and surroundings becomes most prominent in the context of despair. Landscape that is purely rhetorical allows us to see how this kind of synecdoche works—as a way to bring the power of description into an internal figuration. This inward landscape is the culmination of Adam's discovery of description's ability to console: the collapse of the self can be made less unbearable by changing the scale of description, and figuring the desperate subject as a collapsing landscape.

The use of place to figure despair is a theme in both *Samson Agonistes* and *Paradise Regained*, and I will address that theme briefly here. I do so in part to demonstrate both that the problem of place I have described in *Paradise Lost* is useful for understanding certain cruxes in the other two poems (even if a full consideration of the question will have to wait for another time). But I also mean to reinforce the point I have made a number of times, that *Paradise Lost* is informed more by Milton's interest in the poetic problem of describing the Fall than in the moral context of the Fall itself, by showing the importance of the same poetic problem in his other work. I will not address the thorny problem of the dating of the two poems published in 1671; on the contrary, I think they show that the struggle in which I have found Milton engaged persists throughout the latter half of his poetic career, and perhaps through all of it.

In *Samson Agonistes*, Samson's imprisonment and blindness work together to cut him off from environment. But though he laments his current isolation, Samson does not have Adam's nostalgia for a past connection with environment; his nostalgia is primarily for his life "when in strength / All mortals I excell'd" (522–23), not his freedom or his eyesight. It is in contemplating his present misfortune, rather, that Samson discusses his surroundings. His metaphor for blindness is locative; he says that he is

> exil'd from light;
> As in the land of darkness yet in light,
> To live a life half dead, a living death,
> And buried; but O yet more miserable!
> Myself my Sepulcher, a moving Grave . . . (*SA* 98–102)

Samson explores two levels of despair in this passage; both are expressed through the inner landscape of the blind man. When Adam contemplated death in Book 10, he thought that the "living death" might be the worst thing possible, and Samson's blindness reinterprets and clarifies the status of that situation in the landscape. The life of this unfinished death is the awareness of the landscape that is still there: Samson's awareness that he is still "in light" (99). The darkness that separates that light from Samson is at first akin to the experience of death, but for Samson unlike Adam, something is "yet more miserable": to be oneself the collapsed environment that makes one's life a living death. Samson's "moving Grave" (102) is Adam's synecdoche in reverse; the whole is reduced to the part. The question of what environment represents is central to this idea, because the landscape of the blind man, the "land of darkness" (99), can represent nothing but death, even though it is not death. Just as Adam was afraid that death meant, rather than the elimination of perception, the reduction of perception to an unbearable unity, Samson perceives a similar unity and considers it to *be* death. Once again, catastrophe must be figured in such a way as to render it thinkable, by re-figuring the subject back into the collapsed landscape. "Myself my Sepulcher" is really a consolation—as bad as that metonymy sounds, it is not as bad as the image of the self *in* the sepulcher but isolated.

Samson rejects his first metaphor—"land of darkness"—because it still admits the possibility of a landscape, but his final metaphor of the sepulcher does as well, except that in this case the landscape does not extend beyond Samson's body. He defines his misery through his surroundings, which are as a grave or a coffin, but which are also identical to himself. The Chorus picks up the same tension in attempting to define Samson's condition. From outside, his "land of darkness" looks to them not like death but like prison. The Chorus, which has not heard the monologue in which Samson calls himself a "moving Grave" (102), offers a metonymy of Samson's physical location for the condition of his blindness:

> Thou art become (O worst imprisonment!)
> The Dungeon of Thyself; thy Soul
> (Which Men enjoying sight oft without cause complain)
> Imprison'd now indeed,
> In real darkness of the body dwells . . . (155–59)

Something of the Chorus's typical shallowness is in these lines, particularly in their parenthesis against "Men enjoying sight" ; even if Samson could see, he would certainly still have cause for complaint.[25] Their translation of Samson's despair is at best inaccurate and indeed, as at least one critic has argued, may be partially responsible for his abandoning it.[26] But their reduction of the metaphor into a single genitive phrase, "The Dungeon of Thyself," creates a compressed logic similar to Adam's "Miserable of Happy," implying a relationship of ownership and of identity simultaneously. The Chorus has reversed Adam's synecdochic relationship between self and environment; the environment here is the part of the self, not the other way around. But Samson and the Chorus, attempting to define his alienation from landscape through his emotional and physical situation, are forced to do so locatively.

Samson and the Chorus remain at odds, and when, changing his mind from an earlier position, he eventually decides to appear before the Philistian crowds, that change (unlike the various monologues of decision in *Paradise Lost*) is entirely internal:[27]

> Be of good courage, I begin to feel
> Some rousing motions in me which dispose
> To something extraordinary my thoughts.
> I with this Messenger will go along . . . (1381–4)

The "rousing motions" in Samson seem out of place in the dungeon of himself described by the chorus; the image suggests an internal self which can be an escape from surroundings and not merely an extension and reminder of surroundings. But the contrast brings to mind the chorus's stark metaphor. Though Samson addresses the chorus directly, his description of his internal change both shuts them out and repudiates their understanding of his character. That the new feeling Samson is experiencing may lead to his death is clear to him (this may be, he tells the chorus, "The last of me" [1426]). But the death he confronts in this moment is not the locative death that he imagined when he was figuring himself as a "moving Grave"; the actual expectation of death is completely different from death used as a way of understanding the condition of despair. Death's figurative function, though crucial for understanding the fallen condition, is distinct from the potential to die.

As these two different deaths in *Samson Agonistes* might suggest, it may be more useful to conclude that the calamitous landscape Samson and Adam invoke is distinct from death as an actual event. The figuration of collapse, a distinct poetic entity in itself and related to the various kinds of interaction between subject and surroundings that we have seen throughout this book, functions as a way to introduce place into a discussion of death. But discussing death in the context of place necessarily pulls the figure away from the mere cessation of life and towards environmental collapse. This is evidence that the figuration of collapse of the surroundings has priority in Milton's poems even to death itself—not in philosophical terms, but in terms of the construction of the poetry. It is a tool that he can use for different purposes in different situations, but at the same time the figure carries with it its own drama, demonstrating Milton's constant awareness of the challenge of description. *Paradise Regained* contains particularly extreme examples of this challenge, since description in that poem—particularly descriptive figuration—is associated chiefly with Satan, and yet carries with it the same resonance of the continual conflict between a sheltering and a distant environment we have seen in *Samson* and in *Paradise Lost*. The Satanic context informs Milton's descriptions, but does not dominate them.

The independence—and even, I think, sympathetic bent—of description and figuration in Satan's speeches explains something that has long troubled me about *Paradise Regained*. Critical debates over the poem have been dominated by two schools; one that does not think much of the poem, and the other that assumes its principal interest lies in the temptation and resistance of Jesus, and the reader's sympathetic participation in both. Thus, Milton's depiction of the temptation, as John Shawcross says, is a tool of salvation:

> The effect of Satan . . . is to compel a reader to the necessity of seeking understanding of God and God's way through revelation and relationship.

Thus seen, Satan becomes a kind of emancipator for God by prospering good in humankind's relationship with God as the only counteraction to evil.[28]

The problem with this idea is that Satan would have to be much more rhetorically effective than he is in order to show that God is "the only counteraction to evil"; on the contrary, his temptations are easily picked apart, so that logic and analytic reading can themselves function as counteraction to evil. Shawcross's reading, it seems to me, requires the poem to be thought of as a failure (though he insists it is a success). Furthermore, Jesus seems even more invulnerable to Satan's rhetoric than Miltonists have been; the drama of *Paradise Regained* is ultimately claimed more than it is present. But another drama—a more effective one, in my view—surrounds the depiction of Satan, because it is in the images that inform both his own speech and Milton's descriptions of his position that the conflicts of the poem emerge.

Samson's interest in the landscape of death comes up again in this poem. The Satan of *Paradise Regained*, without being concerned about death as such, expresses a similar form of this tension about the despairing landscape in one of his most straightforward moments. Jesus asks Satan why he is so eager to see Jesus' glory, since "my promotion is thy destruction?" (3.202). Again, the landscape is turned inward, and in this case Milton emphasizes the correspondence, rare in this poem, between Satan's words and his real internal state:

> . . . the Tempter inly rackt replied.
> Let that come when it comes; all hope is lost
> Of my reception into grace; what worse?
> For where no hope is left, is left no fear;
> If there be worse, the expectation more
> Of worse torments me than the feeling can.
> I would be at the worst; worst is my Port,
> My harbor and my ultimate repose,
> The end I would attain, my final good. (*PR* 3.203–12)

The forcefulness and sincerity of this passage have sometimes been praised.[29] Despite Satan's sincerity, however, his metaphors do not match up well with his logic, so that it seems that destruction is desirable to Satan for two distinct reasons. His argument about the "expectation . . . Of worse" is casuistical (207–8); there is no reason for Satan's confidence that he understands what it will be like to experience "worse." But the desire for destruction as a "harbor" (211) suggests something else, clarified by Satan's expression (just after he has said that "all hope is lost" [204]) of a last hope, that when Jesus is elevated, he will

> stand between me and thy Father's ire
> (Whose ire I dread more than the fire of Hell)
> A shelter and a kind of shading cool
> Interposition, as a summer's cloud. (3.219–22)

Satan's contradictory images, the restful harbor of the worst and Jesus as a shelter from God's anger, combine to show his idea of his final destruction. Whatever he might say about the end of hope and the end of fear, he cannot in fact imagine any situation that does not have the potential of getting worse but is not in some basic locative way protected. Satan believes that the loss of hope is a protection in itself, but it does not turn out to be enough for him; even the protection of destruction must be figured as shelter, as a protection that takes the form of a new and better environment. As Satan desires the collapse of his world, he imagines that collapse as refuge. "Port" in line 210 at first *means* "final good" (212); the metaphor need not have a very strong sense of place. However, as Satan continues to consider the situation, the figuration intensifies, and "port" comes in retrospect to mean a sheltering environment. For Satan, the figurative consolation of environment evolves into a more profoundly locative version.

However, Satan's use of this kind of figuration does not mean that this is a specifically satanic mode of discourse. In fact, just as Satan imagines Jesus as a potential part of his environment, Milton imagines Satan as a part of Jesus's. Prefacing Satan's final temptation, Milton elides whatever motivations Satan has had all along in favor of a simile in which he is a georgic landscape in himself:[30]

> Or as a swarm of flies in vintage time,
> About the wine-press where sweet must is pour'd,
> Beat off, returns as oft with humming sound;
> Or surging waves against a solid rock,
> Though all to shivers dash't, th'assault renew,
> Vain batt'ry, and in froth or bubbles end;
> So Satan, whom repulse upon repulse
> Met ever, and to shameful silence brought,
> Yet gives not o'er though desperate of success,
> And his vain importunity pursues. (4.15–24)

This image has fundamentally the same logic as the harbor Satan imagines in his future. It is busily active, but its activity is static; its futility protects it from change. Like Satan's "summer's cloud" (3.222), the simile is of a collapse in the form of refuge. The collapse is clearest in the simile of waves, which are "dash't" and reborn simultaneously and continuously (18). Milton images Satan in the same environment in which Satan projects his own future, which, because it is found after the end of the world (from Satan's point of view), is a world without end. Even the complex logic of regret and revenge that informed Satan in *Paradise Lost*—and a version of which existed in the opening books of *Paradise Regained*—is gone here. Without hope, he is no longer distinguishable from a landscape that destroys not out of ill will but only because it is in its nature to do so. Ultimately, this is how Milton imagines the fallen landscape, and indeed how he imagines the Fall, since he is willing here to make a figurative identity between Satan and the version of nature his temptations have wrought.

Critics have generally regarded the Satan of *Paradise Regained* as quite different from that of *Paradise Lost*, particularly since the famous charisma that so many generations of readers have found attractive in the epic seems to be missing in the other version of the character.[31] At the same time, the canonical reading of *Paradise Regained* regards Satan's temptations of Jesus as possessing genuine drama; even if we are not as taken with Satan's rhetoric, the logic seems to go, Milton still expects us to assume that Jesus is susceptible to it. I find that idea unmaintainable in the face of the poem's structure. In *Paradise Lost*, Satan's rhetoric (as I argued in the previous chapter) is not very effective, but his deception is, and Eve is taken in by it. In *Paradise Regained* his rhetoric is even less effective, as he almost admits to Jesus in Book 3 and as Milton acknowledges to us with the fly metaphor quoted above. Furthermore, there is no deception. Thus I find it difficult to imagine that Milton expects us to believe that there is any actual potential for Jesus to concede; if he does, with as little cause to be persuaded as Jesus is given, we must conclude (and some readers have) that this is not a very good poem. If we admire *Paradise Regained*, we must also recognize that Milton makes clear from very near the beginning that Jesus is essentially impervious to Satan's attempts, and that Satan himself has understood this by Book 3, and is still trying only because, like the flies that return again and again though beaten off each time, it is in his nature. *Paradise Regained* is not a poem about temptation, not a poem about deception, and certainly not a poem about persuasion. It is about the nature of Satan—to try and to fail—and the nature of Jesus—to be tried and to prevail. More importantly, its own narrative problems work to highlight the difficulties of contemplating such a conflict, so that Milton sets up the brief epic as a problem poem. The poetic side of the problem of making narrative out of these events he associates with georgic and the poetics of unceasing labor.

The nature of the potential collapsed landscape in Milton demonstrates that the complex relationship I have studied throughout this project between humanity and environment is not determined by some happenstance of Adam's and Eve's intellectual makeup. There is no best way to understand Eden that Adam and Eve have somehow missed. Eden itself, both in its prelapsarian and postlapsarian states, invites contradictory interpretations; the process of making sense of Eden as environment is necessarily inconsistent. Even after the Fall, what seems like a misprision created by despair can be the only way to begin an account of the condition of humanity in a fallen world. In that sense, an account of Eden must *follow* from an account of the collapse of Eden. Adam must put his own history into the landscape in order to make sense of the landscape. Milton, too, writing about Eden after its collapse, is in a similar position. Whether he is discussing prelapsarian Eden or postlapsarian Eden, his recreation of Eden must still account for Eden's collapse, which is inseparable from its relationship with human subjects, Edenic or modern. I began this book with a reading of the last passage of *Paradise Lost,* the description of Eden's destruction. That passage is placed at the end of the poem, but the reader knows that it is coming, that she is looking back at Eden through its collapse. In fact, what unifies the poem, bringing together its descriptions of Heaven and Hell, of prelapsarian and postlapsarian Eden, is the necessity of Eden's end.

The collapse of the surroundings, then, is not charged with any particular moral force. Adam may be sinning while he considers the ramifications of collapse, but that does not mean that doing so is itself a sin, since the consideration of collapse is necessary in order to make sense of the relationship between prelapsarian and postlapsarian place. Similarly, though Satan is being resisted by both Jesus and the reader when he describes the desirability of the end of the world, the description itself cannot be interpreted only through our resistance to it; its relationship to Samson's thoughts about death shows that Satan, despite the obvious necessity that we reject his logic, is still one of the many mouthpieces through which Milton explores the poetics of death—indeed, the poetics of any species of collapse, of which Adam, Samson, Satan, and clearly Milton himself see death as a subset—that is prerequisite to writing either a poem about the Fall or a poem about salvation. The drama of the struggle with collapse, it turns out, pales next to that of the struggle of describing it.

Conclusion

This book is not so much a reading of *Paradise Lost*—it considers, after all, only about a third of the poem—as it is a detailed account of the obstacles to a reading of *Paradise Lost*. The description of place stands out among Milton's multiplicitous concerns because the sheer difficulty of reading the poem is most apparent when that aspect of the poem is considered. Place functions as an emblem of difficulty; the reader shares in the sheer challenge of locating oneself in the universe that Adam discovers in Book 8. Imagining the surroundings is an inherently doubtful enterprise, for where they begin and end and what relationship there is between the immediate and the distant are questions beyond the capacities of human imagination. As the distance of the stars requires Adam to imagine "Speed to describe whose swiftness number fails," the hugeness of place and the imprecision of location outstrip the capabilities of language.

But the challenge of imagining place does not merely make the interpretation of the poem more difficult; it changes the kind of interpretation *Paradise Lost* requires. The complex literary history of Renaissance Vergilianism I describe in the first chapter of this book shows that Milton belongs to a tradition in which place serves a number of functions at once, which are held together only by the continuity of poetic form. Thus, place functions in the poem to destabilize any interpretation that is attempted from a strictly theological point of view. The act of description is so crucial to the interpretation of place in *Paradise Lost* and so intertwined with poetic history that place effectively reinscribes the poem's status as an epic in the classical tradition, at the expense of its explicit theological premise.

Understanding the poetics of place in the poem creates new foci for interpretation. Traditionally, readings that acknowledge Milton's apparently heretical thinking at the end of his career focus on Satan, and to a lesser extent (as in a crucial chapter of Empson's *Milton's God*) on Eve. As we have seen, however, the figure most concerned with the problem of making sense of the relationship between self and surroundings is Adam, and one of the chief lessons of this book is that we must rethink Adam's role in the drama of the poem. One of the dominant images of the latter half of *Paradise Lost* is of Adam as the center of Eden literally and figuratively, and any attempt to understand Eden should begin with Adam's attempts to do so, and thus with his failures to do so. Those attempts unite the poem, their consistent logic unites this book, and most importantly they provide a key to understanding the way the poem works, because Adam stands in for the reader's attempt to understand place equally before and after the Fall. His intellectual struggles with the nature of his surroundings are not fundamentally altered by the Fall, and the story of Eden as Adam understands it is a story in which the Fall is only one concern out of many, and more importantly does *not* represent a fundamental change in the operations of the poem's universe. That story is Milton's as well; the image he repeats several times in the poem of the poet needing to be transported beyond his worldly location in order to write the poem is an image of the difficulty of understanding itself, not of the status of postlapsarian life.

This model for understanding the poem suggests a new focus for Milton studies. The principal topic of debate within the field in recent years has been between those who argue for the overall consistency of Milton's beliefs and rhetorical strategies and Milton critics occupied by the poetics of contradiction. The contradictions I am exploring here are to be found not in scriptural exegesis but in descriptive setting, off to the side both literally and figuratively. But I believe I have demonstrated here that in Milton what matters most is what is most easily overlooked. Indeed, I would apply that model of interpretation to poetry in general. If reading Milton for his poetics rather than his religious thought inevitably discovers contradiction, then that is part of the danger of reading, but also one of the reasons to pursue it. Paul de Man argues in his late essay "The Return to Philology," a defense of theory in response to a polemic against the Yale School by Walter Jackson Bate, that what disturbs the critical establishment about deconstruction is the subversiveness (the word is de Man's) that comes out of reading itself.[1] "The turn to theory," de Man says, "occurred as a return to philology, to an examination of the structure of language prior to the meaning it produces."[2] Because of the sheer scale of Milton's argument, and his own ambition as a poet and as a thinker in poetry, the theoretical turn has never quite shaken (even several decades later) the desire of Miltonists to know what exactly Milton thought about God, man, the angels, and the Fall; nor has the New Historicism that followed had the same effect on Milton studies it has had on the rest of scholarship about Renaissance literature, because the historicist approach has merely shifted the terms of the old question of whether it was possible for a mid-seventeenth century Puritan to have thought the things some of us see in the poem. Most Milton criticism continues to sidestep questions of interpretation in favor of questions of intellectual and religious history.

The interpretation of the poem, however, does not have to be isolated from the circumstances of its composition. Barbara Lewalski's recent *Life* shows a poet with a great many interests, many of them (as evidenced by his love of Italy and Italians despite his distrust of Catholicism) deeply contradictory. Milton's life suggests, rather than the *discordia concors* that is a frequent model for understanding Miltonic contradiction, an acceptance of discord and a willingness to follow the model of Plato, who (Milton points out in *Areopagitica*) recommended that even Aristophanes should be read. The contradictoriness of Milton's politics, too, is still only slowly coming to light. William Kolbrener's admonition that Milton is not as Whiggish as was once thought is well taken, but does not fully describe his complex relationship to the emerging liberalism and republicanism in which he was closely involved and influential.

The chief biographical question as far as this book is concerned is the interpretive significance of Milton's interest in the Vergilian *rota:* the place of the classical genres in the model poetic career and in his own. The question is an extraordinarily complex one, as I have shown in these pages, because Milton's understanding of genre is fluid and contingent upon poetic goals distinct from his classical poetic ambitions, and because he reinterprets Vergil at the same time as he imitates and emulates him. Just as Dante revivifies Vergil in the service of literary goals that are simultaneously competitive within the Vergilian tradition and entirely new, Milton must constantly reimagine his predecessor in order to take his own desired place in the epic canon. Like Dante's in the *Inferno,* however, Milton's relationship with Vergil does not exist merely on an intellectual plane; it is conducted through the development of his poetic technique. Thus, better understandings of Milton's approach to genre, his relationship with the Vergilian canon, and the forms, concerns, and tensions of Miltonic poetics all depend on the simple act of reading.

Notes

NOTES TO THE INTRODUCTION

1. All quotations from Milton's poetry are from Merritt Y. Hughes, ed., *The Complete Poems and Major Prose of John Milton* (New York: Macmillan, 1957), cited by poem, book, and line number; all quotations from Milton's prose are from Don Wolfe, ed., *The Complete Prose Works of John Milton*, in eight volumes (New Haven: Yale UP, 1953–1980), abbreviated *YCP* and cited by volume and page number.
2. See Anthony Low's *The Georgic Revolution* (Princeton: Princeton UP, 1985) for a useful definition of the georgic mode as it is invoked outside of the georgic genre. Low says of this passage, "Milton evokes a timeless picture of georgic man in a bleak evening landscape, but he complicates the sorrow by introducing a return home from labor. For labor ends at nightfall, at death, and finally, as the covenant of the floor reminds us, at the end of time, when man will return to paradise once more" (Low, 311). I will discuss Milton's use of georgic extensively in chapter 1.
3. Interest in the space of the Universe "as absolute and more particularly as infinite," Casey argues, led to a disregard for the specificity of place—"the specialness of place, above all its inherent 'power'"—in the period (*The Fate of Place: A Philosophical History* [Berkeley: U California P, 1997], 133–34). Of course, poetry's concern with precisely that specificity thus creates a distancing from the philosophical trends of the time. For this reason, some critics (as I discuss in chapter 1 below) have concluded that Renaissance use of classically influenced description of place is merely a superficial technique of construction. One of the principal arguments of this book will be that, on the contrary, classical place, and in particular Vergilian place, wields a powerful if often unacknowledged influence in the period, in large part because similar ideas of place *are* lacking in Renaissance thought.
4. See Silver's *Imperfect Sense: The Predicament of Milton's Irony* (Princeton: Princeton UP, 2001), 283–346.

5. For a reading that does some of what I am not doing, see Ken Hiltner's *Milton and Ecology* (Cambridge: Cambridge UP, 2003). Hiltner's argument that Milton really was concerned with deforestation and the like may well be right, but I find his first sentence telling: "Place is of profound environmental importance." I surely misunderstand this, but it sounds tautological, and it demonstrates a danger to which I am sensitive of the word 'environment,' which frequently means something other than environs. I do not intend the term in the common modern sense, and in fact environment as I invoke it can mean something man-made or indeed heaven and hell, which exist outside of nature.
6. This relationship between earthly and less earthly environment makes it impossible to rely on recent ecocriticsm for an account of Miltonic place. As Jonathan Bate puts it, ecocriticsm is "an acknowledgment of the rights of nature—the land, the ocean, the polluted air, the endangered species . . ." (Bate, *The Song of the Earth* [Cambridge: Harvard UP, 2000], 72). According to Bate's formulation, ecocriticism's interest is not in place per se but in place as a subset of nature; my argument about *Paradise Lost* is that environment functions first and foremost in its capacity as the subject's surroundings (whether natural or unnatural), and therefore not as a representation of nature.
7. Achinstein, *Milton and the Revolutionary Reader* (Princeton: Princeton UP, 1994), 199.
8. Swaim, *Before and After the Fall: Contrasting Modes in Paradise Lost* (Amherst: U Massachusetts P, 1986), ix.
9. Fish, *How Milton Works* (Cambridge: Belknap P of Harvard UP, 2001), 191.
10. Empson, *Milton's God* (Revised Edition, London: Chatto and Windus, 1965), 11.
11. Silver, 8; 259–261.
12. Teskey, *Delirious Milton: The Fate of the Poet in Modernity* (Cambridge: Harvard UP, 2006), 7.
13. Kolbrener, *Milton's Warring Angels: A Study of Critical Engagements* (Cambridge: Cambridge UP, 1997), 49; Rogers, *The Matter of Revolution: Science, Poetry and Politics in the Age of Milton* (Ithaca: Cornell UP, 1996), 112.
14. Rajan, *The Form of the Unfinished: English Poetics from Spenser to Pound* (Princeton: Princeton UP, 1985), 111.
15. Peter C. Herman, in a recent study of what he calls "incertitude" in *Paradise Lost* which is comparable in its arguments about criticism to this book, though vastly different in approach, argues that even critics interested in contradiction still assume that those contradictions are ultimately resolved (Herman, *Destabilizing Milton:* Paradise Lost *and the Poetics of Incertitude* [New York: Palgrave Macmillan, 2005]). This assumption is true of many critics, but Rajan's study seems particularly clear evidence that the idea of unresolvable contradiction in

Milton has existed for some time, though I would also point to the first chapter of Empson's *Milton's God*, which makes clear that Empson is not seeking ultimately to resolve the ambiguities he discovers.
16. Rajan, *Paradise Lost and the Seventeenth Century Reader* (1947; Ann Arbor: U Michigan P, 1967), 22.
17. Rajan, *The Form of the Unfinished*, 94.
18. Fish, *How Milton Works*, 195.
19. Fish, *How Milton Works*, 190.
20. In an entirely different approach from mine, David Gay too sees this passage as having room for the variability of reception. He argues that this passage "evokes the Eucharist with its fracturing and distributing of the broken body and blood of Christ" and thus connects "the conscience of the reader, the reformation of the nation, and the text of scripture" (Gay, *The Endless Kingdom: Milton's Scriptural Society* [Newark: U Delaware P, 2002], 35). There is no reason to think, as Fish does, that the exuberance of Milton's metaphor for books means that the metaphor disregards the role of the reader. To praise origin is not necessarily to ignore process.
21. David Loewenstein makes a similar point another way in pointing out *Areopagitica*'s "resilient capacity to embrace social conflict as the essential element of the historical process" (Loewenstein, *Milton and the Drama of History: Historical Vision, Iconoclasm, and the Literary Imagination* [Cambridge: Cambridge UP, 1990], 49). If the conflict itself is necessary, then Milton's interest in endorsing disagreement is justified. Even for Loewenstein though, a motion is necessary: the continuing roll of history pushed along by such conflicts.
22. Stephen Burt argues that Milton's interest in "open-minded Athens" (Burt, "'To the Unknown God': St. Paul and Athens in Milton's Areopagitica." [*Milton Quarterly* 32, no. 1 (1998):23-31], 31) and in particular in the open-ended theological debate that went on there during Paul's visit, is an important part of Milton's argument for the centrality of free discussion in religion. For Burt, Milton attempts to use Paul as support for a platform in which "neither the state nor anybody else could be considered to know true religion: true Christians were by definition still 'seeking' . . ." (28). His contention that for Milton the obligation of the state toward Christians was in large part "to get out of their way" is probably an overstatement (28), but he is correct that Milton believed that Paul could quote a pagan not because he had converted the pagan idea but because he did not need to, since the truth is large enough to admit multiple sources. For Kolbrener, enthusiastic pluralists like Burt represent a crucial but one-sided aspect of *Areopagitica;* a more complete reading, he argues, is one in which

> . . . radical liberty and public authority are simultaneously asserted; the conception of agency that emerges in the tract is at once constrained

> by, and constructed through, the language of civic republicanism. (Kolbrener, 26–27)

This idea of a concept that appears through the assertion of two things at once suggests again a kind of motion: understanding results from conceiving of the relationship between author and reader as indirect, bouncing, in this case, off two contradictory but simultaneously valid sets of ideas.

23. Guss, "'Enlightenment as Process: Milton and Habermas" (*PMLA* 106 [1991], 1156-69), 1159.
24. Fish, *Surprised By Sin* (1967; Second Edition, Cambridge: Harvard UP, 1997), 347.
25. Fish, *Surprised by Sin*, 328.
26. One of the most aggressive voices in the resistance to Fish belongs to John Rumrich, for whom Fish's Milton is an unrecognizably dogmatic and narrow-minded caricature of the poet. Rumrich observes that the reader's genuine interest in the machinery of evil in the early part of the poem does not necessarily mean that he has to abandon that interest in order to be saved by the end. As long as the interest is partial, and predicated on what commonality there might be, the reader maintains without difficulty or contradiction his difference from Satan:

   > . . . as readers begin Paradise Lost they repeatedly find themselves surrounded by senselessness. If we sympathize with Satan, we do so because like us, though for different reasons, he is dazed and confused. Against the contemporary understanding of Milton's authorial persona as prescriptive and authoritarian, I therefore propose an alternative possibility, that at least in its first books, Paradise Lost inspires in readers a Christian negative capability (Rumrich, *Milton Unbound* [Cambridge: Cambridge UP, 1996], 22).

   Ultimately, I find Rumrich's "Christian negative capability" too vague. I agree that sympathy with Satan is not something to be ashamed of, and that it results in part from uncertainty. But Rumrich like Fish makes the mistake of thinking that the uncertainty can go away or be replaced by something else; as my reading will show, it is an important part of the poem from beginning to end.

NOTES TO CHAPTER ONE

1. Genette, *Palimpsests: Literature in the Second Degree* (1982), trans. Channa Newman and Claude Doubinsky (Lincoln: U Nebraska P, 1997), 83.
2. I use the term "landscape" here in its modern sense: the line between civilization and the wilderness that is what is seen when looking toward nature. Milton's use of the word in a more-or-less pastoral context in "L'Allegro" is

one of the earliest in English, and the precise meaning of the term was very much in flux at the time. John Barrell observes that the evolution of the term from a strictly visual meaning to a more general one took place somewhere between this first use and the mid-eighteenth century (Barrell, *The Idea of Landscape and the Sense of Place, 1730-1840: An Approach to the Poetry of John Clare* [Cambridge: Cambridge UP, 1972], 1–2). The evident newness and uncertainty of the word should be recalled in reading this book—I do not think all of these poets regard the idea of landscape (whether or not the word is available to them) in the same way.

3. Alpers, *What is Pastoral?* (Chicago: U Chicago P, 1996), 27.
4. Fitter, *Poetry, Space, Landscape: Toward a New Theory* (Cambridge: Cambridge UP, 1995), 2.
5. Rosemary Kegl makes an analogous argument to Fitter's about the implications of the figure of Marvell's Mower. For Kegl, Marvell's portrayal of agrarian labor "promotes an economic structure which exploits wage laborers" (Kegl, "'Joyning my Labour to My Pain': The Politics of Labor in Marvell's Mower Poems" [*Soliciting Interpretation: Literary Theory and Seventeenth-Century English Poetry*, ed. Elizabeth D. Harvey and Katherine Eisaman Maus (Chicago: U of Chicago P, 1990), 89-118], 89), in part because the portrayal is so fundamentally unrealistic—in fact, she points out, because mowing was a seasonal activity being a mower could not be seen as the same kind of occupation as being a shepherd (96). For Kegl, the inaccuracy of Marvell's depiction highlights his portrayal of agrarian life. I would argue the opposite, that Marvell's clear lack of interest in actual labor indicates that labor here is a metaphorical construction having more to do with Vergil than it has to do with the life of an English farmhand.
6. Patterson, *Pastoral and Ideology: Vergil to Valéry* (Berkeley: U California P, 1987), 134.
7. Joseph Lowenstein, looking for instances of Echo in *Comus,* finds this anxiety, though he sees it as reflecting poorly on the Lady, who asks Echo to locate her brothers ("O if thou have / Hid them in some flow'ry Cave, / Tell me but where" [238–240]):

> . . . she shows her naive wit by an effort to *invoke* the orienting Echo, calling on the uncalled for. Bookish and musical, she makes the mistake of thinking that she can compel the response of that Echo who restores or relocates us in the woods (Loewenstein, *Responsive Readings: Versions of Echo in Pastoral, Epic, and the Jonsonian Masque* [New Haven: Yale UP, 1984], 136).

Loewenstein associates this failure with Adam's new relationship with repetition (through the Law) after the Fall (144), but it reminds me just as much of the struggles Adam has with landscape, if not explicitly with echo, in Book VIII, before the Fall. Loewenstein conceives of the difficulty of connecting with landscape as postlapsarian, but I will show in later chapters that the connection is just as difficult before the Fall.

8. Watkins, *The Specter of Dido: Spenser and Vergilian Epic* (New Haven: Yale UP, 1995), 6; Tudeau-Clayton, *Jonson, Shakespeare, and Early Modern Virgil* (Cambridge: Cambridge UP, 1998), 21–43. Rebecca Helfer ("The Death of the 'New Poete': Virgilian Ruin and Ciceronian Recollection in Spenser's *The Shepheardes Calender*" [*Renaissance Quarterly* 56 (2003)], 723-756) and David Scott Wilson-Okamura ("Virgilian Models of Colonization in Shakespeare's Tempest." [*ELH* 70 (2003)], 709-737) make similar arguments for the fluidity of Vergil's influence in the period.

9. Patterson, 133–162; Low, *The Georgic Revolution;* Tylus, "Spenser, Virgil, and the Politics of Poetic Labor" (*ELH* 55 [1988]), 53-77. Both Low and Tylus present evidence for the unusual versatility of the georgic mode, which does not seem to constitute a genre in itself in the period as much as it intervenes in other genres. Paul Alpers summarizes the issue as a religious one:

> "In Virgil's works, pastoral and georgic are distinct: in the latter, nature's uncertainties and harshness are more prominent, because it is conceived as the habitation of farmers. In the Renaissance the two types merge in various ways, largely because in Christian thought ideas of humility are connected with the curse of labor." (Alpers, 28)

10. Sukanta Chaudhuri observes that Renaissance pastoral is "curiously precarious in its imaginative identity" (Chaudhuri, *Renaissance Pastoral and its English Developments* [Oxford: Clarendon, 1989], 6)—that is, that the specificity and uniformity of pastoral's subject matter does not lend it the interpretive confidence one might expect. I would like to suggest that rather than a phenomenon introduced during the difficult linguistic and cultural translation of Vergil, that precariousness results from a reinterpretation of a similar (but less pronounced) discontinuity in Vergil.

11. Patterson argues that "an ideology of landownership and land use" merges with issues of political representation and class in the seventeenth century, so that "the cultural history of pastoral becomes truly inseparable from georgic" (Patterson, 134). She is right to point to an overlap between the two, but I think "inseparable" is too strong. In reconsidering the relationship between the two genres, I find a lingering importance of the separation between the two—because a pastoral innocence and refuge is still desirable—and at the same time several ways in which the genres overlap.

12. A recent article by Judith Owens complains that critics of the poem have focused on its "syncretic powers" at the expense of its historical, and particularly political, context (Owens, "The Poetics of Accommodation in Spenser's 'Epithalamion'" [*Studies in English Literature* 40 (2000), 41–62], 41). Owens does not speculate on why this might be the case, but it seems

reasonable to assume that the poem has invited consideration of its "express harmonies" (Owens's phrase) because its structure so overwhelmingly emphasizes them. In fact, the poem's insistence on its continuity, like one who proclaims his innocence too loudly, should perhaps encourage us to look closer for possible discordances.

13. All quotations from Spenser are drawn from *The Yale Edition of the Shorter Poems of Edmund Spenser*, ed. William A. Oram (New Haven: Yale UP, 1989).
14. All quotations from the *Georgics* are taken from *Georgics*, Vol. 1: Books 1–2 and Vol.2: Books 3–4, ed. Richard F. Thomas (Cambridge: Cambridge UP, 1988).
15. All the translations in this chapter are my own.
16. The *Georgics* contains moments of optimistic appreciation for agrarian labor and very dark treatments of both human society and nature itself; there is considerable debate among Latinists about how those two aspects play out. While acknowledging the critical tradition reading the poems as rather pessimistic, Llewelyn Morgan suggests that it is only in its proper historical context that the "'upbeat,' propagandistic import" she reads in the poem is clearest (Morgan, *Patterns of Redemption in Virgil's Georgics* [Cambridge: Cambridge UP, 1999], 13). However, propaganda is always subject to rethinking according to different agendas, and Andrew Wallace suggests that a "despair at the possibility of founding a technique for putting poetry to use" in the *Georgics* was somewhat suppressed by Renaissance humanists who were "deeply invested in the promise of such a project" (Wallace, "Placement, Gender, Pedagogy: Virgil's Fourth Georgic in Print." [*Renaissance Quarterly* 56 (2003): 377–407], 404). By arguing for the propagandistic use of the poem, Wallace suggests implicitly that its *original* propagandistic function is not necessarily prioritized by Renaissance readers, though they knew of the poem's history. In any case, it seems reasonable to assume that the ultimate stance of the poem—optimism or pessimism—was as unclear in the Renaissance as it is now.
17. Because labor is offered as the only way for man to reinforce his position as the center of the landscape, the constant potential for failure threatens always to undermine that position. For a reading of the importance of failure to the *Georgics*, see Christopher Nappa, "Fire and Human Error in Vergil's Second *Georgic*" (*American Journal of Philology* 124 [2003], 39–56).
18. For an entirely different reading of this passage (and its implications for Renaissance poetry), see Kevis Goodman, "'Wasted Labor'? Milton's Eve, the Poet's Work, and the Challenge of Sympathy" (*ELH* 64 [1997], 415–446). Goodman sees the crucial word in the passage not as "rapit" but as "labor"—the idea that introduces it (specifically, the frustrating toil of sowing seeds). Thus, she separates the idea behind the simile from the descriptiveness of the simile itself: "*Labor* is . . . not defined in terms of any particular kind of pursuit (for example, agriculture rather than poetry); it is

a more general word for the force spent and burden sustained in any pursuit or *ars* (skill)" (Goodman, 421). I do not think I have ruled out this possibility; my assertion that it is in the nature of georgic landscape in particular to make man's burden greater means rather that the simile is working on two levels at once—both through analogy and through description. That double function, however, is part of what makes landscape in Vergil such a difficult topic to grasp: description is never merely description.

19. One could of course see it the other way—that it is a passage about man's weakness, a possibility Michael Putnam seems to preserve: " . . . there seems to be a point beyond which further control of nature is impossible. Merely to maintain the *status quo* against her negative pressures requires all man's powers." (Putnam, *Virgil's Poem of the Earth: Studies in the Georgics* [Princeton: Princeton UP, 1979], 39). However, Vergil's reference to *fate* suggests to me a fundamental quality of nature, and thus the balance of power between man and nature is not something that, by applying additional strength, man could alter.

20. Land grants for soldiers were a Roman tradition culminating in a disastrous massive confiscation and redistribution in 42 B.C. Eleanor Winsor Leach, departing from a critical tradition focusing on that particular year, argues that the *Eclogues* comment on the land-distribution tradition as a whole; see Leach, *Vergil's Eclogues: Landscapes of Experience* (Ithaca: Cornell UP, 1974),130–133.

21. All quotations from the *Eclogues* are taken from *Eclogues*, ed. Robert Coleman (Cambridge: Cambridge UP, 1977).

22. Echo in pastoral indicates approval, a kind of applause of nature, and as such inevitably invokes *divine* approval, as Hollander makes clear: "Generally, the pastoral echo is a version of the Olympian sounds of confirmation, taken down from the rocky heights . . ." (*The Figure of Echo: A Mode of Allusion in Milton and After* [Berkeley: U California P, 1981], 14–15).

23. Eleanor Winsor Leach identifies two of these projects, political and intertextual, within the same interpretive idea: "Through its images of nature and its cognizance of historical forces, [*Eclogue* 1] shows the impossibility of maintaining an old [Theocritean] pastoral ideal in a new world" (Leach, 113). Putting the issue in more general terms, Annabel Patterson suggests that the interpretive difficulty of these opening lines of the first *Eclogue* can define the entire pastoral tradition: "Roman readers faced, even in these first five lines, a challenge that has remained intensely audible" (Patterson, 1).

24. David Ferry, the noted translator, renders "mirata," "stupefactae," and "mutata" all with the same English word: "spellbound" (Ferry, *The Eclogues of Virgil* [New York: Farrar, Straus, and Giroux, 1999], 61). The insistence on the uniformity of the three reactions suggests that Ferry (as one would expect him to) is emphasizing the distinctively pastoral continuity of landscape. My point is that both Ferry's less anxious reading and mine

are available; the question for my purposes is which of them any particular Renaissance poet seems likelier to prefer.
25. This sense of withholding figures heavily in Renaissance treatments of Vergilian landscapes. I will discuss similar ideas in relation to Marvell's mower poems below, but similar as well is the discrepancy Adam objects to at *Paradise Lost* 8.391–93 when he notes that the animals rejoice in each other in Adam's vicinity, without him, even as he commands them (see chapter 2 for a discussion of this passage). The human perception of continuity in the environment seems to lead to an anticipation or desire for human participation in that continuity (and a sense that human superiority, fragile in Vergil anyway, is not sufficient).
26. Silver, "The Obscure Script of Regicide: Ambivalence and Little Girls in Marvell's Pastorals" [*ELH* 68 (2001)], 29–55, 46.
27. All quotations from Marvell are taken from Marvell, *The Complete Poems*, ed. Elizabeth Story Donno (London: Penguin, 1972).
28. The subject of the last sentence of this quotation is actually "arbusta," meaning trees or, really, grove (the word is grammatically plural but used with a suggestion of the singular)—that is, "the grove resonates with the raucous cicadas." However, the word "mecum" ("alone with me," loosely) puts stress on the cicadas, something the English language has no way of doing without awkwardness if the grammar is translated literally. Thus, like several translators before me, I have made the cicadas the subject. Either way the stress is on the landscape—Corydon cannot be the subject.
29. As Robert Coleman puts it, by complaining about sunburn in the shade Corydon "is perhaps putting on the agony a little" (*Eclogues,* 2.13n).
30. For Judith Haber, the entire poem is concerned with the discrepancy between an ideal environment and one in which connections are harder to make. The key to the subject's desire for connection with the landscape is a kind of emotional similarity:

> . . . in a poem that—like all of Marvell's poems—identifies distance from external reality with displacement, the mere fact that "innocence" is symbolic is evidence of separation from it; and what it symbolizes, of course, is that separation itself—the Fall. Separation thus becomes both the means of connection, and the point at which connection is made. (Haber, *Pastoral and the Poetics of Self-Contradiction* [Cambridge: Cambridge UP, 1994], 101–02)

The interest in innocence pulls the reading in a different direction from mine, but it represents further evidence that disconnection's constant proximity to connection is a central problem here.
31. The introduction of the Mower himself is gradual in "Glowworms"—first the landscape is presented, then an indistinct nation in the second stanza, then a plural "mowers" (10), than finally, resoundingly, "I" in the last line.

The relationship between the singular Mower and the plural mowers is parallel and akin to the problematical relationship between subject and landscape. Of course, the absence of pastoral laborers other than Damon is part of what makes these poems such unusual pastoral. Paul Hammond, commenting on the difficulty and surprise of the rare invocations of the Mower's larger community, calls the "us" in the last line of "The Mower Against Gardens" "an ideal unattainable plural, a human community free from original sin and dwelling with the gods"(Hammond, "Marvell's Pronouns" [*Essays in Criticism* 53 (2003), 219–234] 225).

32. In an interesting reading, Susan Snyder argues that it is the alteration in him caused by Juliana that enables Damon to make this comparison: "Because the speaker is now aware of other, less innocent portents the comets might bear, he can use the great events of a highly evolved society as a foil for nature's lowly simplicity" (Snyder, *Pastoral Process: Spenser, Marvell, Milton* [Stanford: Stanford UP, 1998], 61).

33. Alpers seeks a middle ground between reading the glowworms as heavily portentous and reading their minor clairvoyance as a courtly condescension. The image, he says, "represents a natural phenomenon and a human activity that are not only normal and benign, but complete unto themselves . . . its implications are not grasped by extending its significance into the world of wars and princes . . . but by assimilating to itself all forms of death and suggesting that they are fundamentally the same" (Alpers, 55). I agree with Alpers about the way the Mower thinks the glowworms *ought* to integrate themselves into the agrarian world, but the stanza still represents a failure he ascribes to them (even if it is really his own fault).

34. *Second World and Green World: Studies in Renaissance Fiction-Making* (Berkeley: U California P, 1988), 281.

35. *Some Versions of Pastoral* (1935; London: Penguin, 1995), 119.

36. *Using Biography* (Cambridge: Harvard UP, 1984), 15.

37. Because the doubling of the two poems extends to a doubling within them, I must disagree with Marshall Grossman's simpler assignment of the relationship between the two and Vergilian genre; for Grossman, "The relationship of 'L'Allegro' to 'Il Penseroso' is that of one who celebrates the cultivator of the soil to the cultivator of the soul or of the georgic to the epic poet" (Grossman, "The Fruits of One's Labor in Miltonic Practice and Marxian Theory" [*ELH* 59 (1992), 77–105], 88). Grossman's reading of georgic elements within L'Allegro is insightful and compelling, but the presence of those elements in one poem does not preclude their presence in the other, and I believe there to be ample evidence of a more complex generic dynamic between the two.

38. Segal, *Orpheus: The Myth of the Poet* [Baltimore: John Hopkins UP, 1989], 42.

39. I believe that georgic passages in *Paradise Lost* support the idea that Milton's understanding of the *Georgics* is essentially pessimistic. Others disagree of course; see, for example, Stella Revard for an entirely different reading of the

presence of the landscape of the *Georgics* in *Paradise Lost*. I think she overlooks passages like those I quote when she says, for example: "Throughout the *Georgics* Vergil shows how man prospers when he governs his life by the diurnal and seasonal rhythms that govern nature" ("Vergil's Georgics and Paradise Lost: Nature and Human Nature in a Landscape" [*Vergil at 2000*, ed. John D. Bernard (New York: AMS, 1986)], 262). At times Vergil shows how man can prosper from observing these rhythms, but at other times (the description of Spring quoted above, for example) the rhythms are shown in such a way to exclude man utterly, so that like the man rowing upstream, the farmer is at a loss in the face of a landscape he cannot account for.

40. As Martin Dawes argues, all of "Lycidas" may be understood as a qualified and possibly failed attempt to escape the elegy's own heavy Orphic overtones ("An Orphic Lament for Orphic Lament: 'Lycidas' and the Persistence of Orphic Desire," *Milton Quarterly* 38 [2004], 188–98).

41. See, for example, Barry Weller, "The Epic as Pastoral: Milton, Marvell, and the Plurality of Genre" (*New Literary History* 30 [1999], 143–157), 143–145; and Anthony Low's *The Georgic Revolution* (310ff.).

NOTES TO CHAPTER TWO

1. Fish's 1967 book *Surprised by Sin* (Second Edition, Cambridge: Harvard UP, 1997) provides a reading of the passage clarified and further developed, but essentially unchanged, in his more recent *How Milton Works* (Cambridge: Belknap P of Harvard UP, 2001). Schwartz's *Remembering and Repeating: On Milton's Theology and Poetics* (Chicago: U Chicago P, 1993) focuses more on Raphael's discussion of those heavenly actions in which Adam can participate, such as praise, but still regards the warning as the interpretive center of the conversation.

2. Marshall Grossman seems to assume that the problem of imagination applies only to heaven. Grossman comments on the difficulty of describing Heaven: "When Milton intends to relate 'things invisible to mortal sight,' he faces a specific and language-bound problem. He conflates two visions—one temporal, empirical, mimetic; the other eternal, revelatory. These visions are double, but each is projected into the single linear discourse of a poetic narrative" (*"Authors to Themselves": Milton and the Revelation of History* [Cambridge: Cambridge UP, 1987], 178). This discrepancy may be part of the problem, but the difficulty of place extends to Earth as well as to Heaven.

3. For Fish Book 8 is the clearest point in a pedagogical exercise governing the whole poem: "The point is that in Milton's universe interpretive labors of a world-constituting kind are performed by everyone, and these labors begin by constituting or conceiving God, after which everything else follows. In book VIII of *Paradise Lost*, Adam learns from Raphael exactly how

it is done" (*How Milton Works*, 518). Various permutations of the reading that the warning is there but does not work are possible; Shoaf believes that Raphael has given Adam adequate reason not to fall but that "Raphael's lesson is forgotten, unheeded . . ." (Shoaf, *Milton, Poet of Duality* [New Haven: Yale UP, 1985], 151). If the lesson is "forgotten," it follows that it must have been heard and made sense. In other words both of these critics regard the problems with Raphael's warning as somehow external to it, an assumption I consider to be undermined by Raphael's anxieties.

4. After the Fall, according to Readings, and after Michael's already somewhat revisionist reading of postlapsarian history, Eden as such becomes accessible only indirectly through a sort of self-history: "The immediate truth of Eden is disbarred, and has been transferred into the realm of subjective historical speculation, whence it may arise as the idea or concept of Eden" (Readings, "'An Age Too Late': Milton and the Time of Literary History" [*Exemplaria* 4 (1992): 455–468], 460). I will argue here that the problems created by postlapsarian Eden actually extend beyond Readings's question of history, and indeed extend beyond the problem of Eden itself. As we will see, generalized anxiety about the description of place reaches its apex in the description of Eden but does not necessarily originate there. However, Readings' warnings about the difficulty of the historicism of a poem that more or less invented literary history are important to the rather ahistorical idea of Miltonic place I am suggesting here.

5. Empson, *Milton's God*, 11.

6. Fish, *How Milton Works*, 527.

7. A.J.A Waldock, for example, says that Raphael's speech toward the end of Book 8 is a sign of Milton's growing uncertainty, and that in delivering God's and Milton's message "Raphael does his work rather clumsily and gives us little confidence that his props will hold" (*Paradise Lost and its Critics* [Cambridge: Cambridge UP, 1964], 52). Fish mentions parenthetically that Raphael is "imparting a warning he knows will go unheeded" (Fish, *Surprised by Sin*, 192). Waldock's claim, though strong, is probably an accurate depiction of a reader who expects that Raphael has the power to prevent the Fall and is waiting for him to do it. Fish, however, simplifies Raphael's position; even if Raphael knows his warning will fail, he has every reason to think that Adam will pay attention to it, and as my reading of Book 8 below shows, Adam takes the warning seriously enough to make distinctions between those parts that make sense to him and those that do not. Adam, at least, is determined not to let Raphael's shortcomings cause him to fall.

8. Schwartz, arguing that a central concern of the poem is the proximity of chaos to creation, assumes that Raphael's uncertainty while describing creation reflects Milton's own concerns about the problem of the description itself: "To say that Milton's creation is imperilled even as he describes it is not to say enough; it is *especially* when Milton thematizes creation, both the

divine cosmic one and his own, that the danger is most acute" (Schwartz, 61). Schwartz stresses the relationship between God's creation and Milton's because her argument depends on the idea that Milton perceives his poem as freeing creation from chaos in a way similar to God's own function. Similar relationships between Milton's and God's respective projects occur elsewhere in the criticism as well; central to Angela Esterhammer's argument, for example, is the idea that "Raphael addresses Adam and Eve at the same time that the poet addresses the reader" (Esterhammer, *Creating States: Studies in the Performative Language of John Milton and William Blake* [Toronto: U of Toronto P, 1994], 114); like Schwartz, she would assume that whatever ironies are present in Raphael's speech, they do not prevent Milton from speaking through him in delivering an account of creation.

9. Fish, *How Milton Works*, 63.
10. Danielson points out Adam's intellectual accomplishment in deducing, "from his own existence and from the wonders of creation that he beheld round about him," the necessity of God's existence (Danielson, *Milton's Good God: A Study in Literary Theodicy* [Cambridge: Cambridge UP, 1982], 121). Raphael's discouragement of this kind of thinking has little support; Danielson approves of Adam's ambitious imagination, and God does as well.
11. Charles Eric Reeves finds a similar problem but locates it within the literary depiction of Raphael: an "apparent incompatibility of his ontological and narrative presence," caused by his rhetorical and moral dilemma resulting from the foreknowledge of the Fall (Reeves, "'Lest Wilfully Transgressing': Raphael's Narration and Knowledge in Paradise Lost" [*Milton Studies* 34 (1997), 83-98], 93). Reeves devotes considerable attention to the possibility that Raphael has heard God's prediction of human sin, but since Raphael stresses to such a degree the difficulty of Adam's understanding of any heavenly event, the incompatibility would seem to exist regardless of whether Raphael knows about the Fall.
12. Schwartz argues that angelic song solves the paradox of human knowledge: "Knowledge born of a will to dominate an objectified creation 'out there' leads to the return of chaos; knowledge which celebrates creations furthers the continual process of creation. This is why the battle between kinds of knowledge is waged in such proximity to the creation narratives; it is also why legitimate expressions of the creation—ones that are unblamed—are framed as song of praise" (Schwartz, 41). I think she is right about the unity of the relationship between chaos and creation in Milton's thought, in God's, and in Raphael's, but that unity is why "legitimate expressions of the creation" are tinged with the same anxiety about Adam's ability to imagine Heaven that we find in his attempts to imagine, as it were, secularly. If creation were in itself the solution to the problem of knowledge, then Adam *would* be able to participate in angelic praise, but as it turns out there is no part of Heaven that he can have access to without risk.

13. As Victoria Silver explains, the angels' mediation is made necessary by God's unintelligibility, which is of an entirely different sort than the mere invisibility of the angels themselves. Thus the immediacy that Raphael reports can actually be seen as a distinction between their understanding of God and their reaction to God. Silver emphasizes that "although Raphael conveys to Adam how the angels experienced the world's creation, the sense of simultaneity he mentions isn't the effect of their intuitive (as against discursive) intellects, moving as it were in tandem with the divine mind." Indeed, this is not a simultaneity of coincident moments in time, but one outside of time: ". . . exempt from the conditions of space, time, and appearance to which the human and angelic are more and less bound in the poem . . ." (Silver, *Imperfect Sense: The Predicament of Milton's Irony* [Princeton: Princeton UP, 2001], 290). Still, Silver's observation explains the possibility of the mixing of the timeless and time-bound in Raphael's report of creation, but not its function—why, in a narrative in large part about the timelessness of creation, does Raphael stress angelic song, which does not fit in to that timelessness?
14. Theodor Adorno has in mind something like this supplanting of one idea with a related but larger-scale idea when he calls the *Abgesang*, the 'B' in an AAB form, "the fulfillment of a musical context by something fundamentally new" (Adorno, *Mahler: A Musical Physiognomy*, trans. Edmund Jephcott [Chicago: U of Chicago P, 1992], 42). The most significant thing about AAB form for Adorno is that unlike most musical forms it is not "closed": it ends on a new idea rather than returning to an old one.
15. The *OED*, however, lists no such usage of "sing." The closest it gets is an object of the verb as either an event narrated by the song or a thing described.
16. Coming at the problem from the question of the epistemology of evil, Tanner argues that the distinctions Raphael makes by "explicitly contrasting Adam's discursive knowledge to his own angelic intuitive knowledge" apply to the created world as well as to Heaven: "Adam's intuitive knowledge about the world is incomplete" (Tanner, *Anxiety in Eden: A Kierkegaardian Reading of* Paradise Lost [Oxford: Oxford UP, 1992], 83). The distinction is only exacerbated by the problem of description, because for Raphael and Adam both the location of praise with a place means that it must be mediated by description.
17. A directly analogous example to "soft on the flow'ry herb" is the narrator's description of Adam waking Eve: "Her hand soft touching" (5.17). "Soft" modifies "touching" as an adverb, but also suggests a modification of "hand" (as an adjective); the line contains both Eve's beauty and Adam's gentleness.
18. Hartman calls the image of the sun at the center of Adam's description "startling" and "extreme" (Hartman, "Adam on the Grass with Balsamum," [*Beyond Formalism: Literary Essays 1958–1970* (New Haven: Yale UP, 1970), 124–150], 124–25): the directness and physicality of the relationship between

Adam and nature it describes seems out of place, particularly in response to Raphael's austere image of creation.

19. Fish explains the presence of seemingly postlapsarian aspects in Eden before the fall as risk: "the 'raw material' of the Edenic character exists in potential, and can go either way . . ." (*How Milton Works*, 532). This reading does not, however, explain the disconnection from landscape Adam feels (or the disconnection from Heaven Raphael enforces): I find not only the potential causes of the fall, but the actual effects of the fall in prelapsarian Eden.

20. As William Flesch puts it, both Adam and Raphael "speak in the vocabulary of a possible scarcity" (Flesch, *Generosity and the Limits of Authority: Shakespeare, Herbert, Milton* [Ithaca: Cornell UP, 1992], 227).

21. For Flesch, the issue here is economics: "As in his conversation with Raphael [about astronomy], and as in his talk with Eve about the children who will soon share in all this plenty, Adam expresses a sense of proportion that is finally utilitarian. All this wealth must have some use" (Flesch, 228). Flesch thinks that this logic is part of a general dynamic throughout this part of the poem, but I would argue that in all of these instances Adam here is returning to the kind of logic he believes God has approved during his request for Eve.

22. Michael Allen makes a similar point about the distinct kinds of education Raphael and God pursue; for Allen, "Raphael is far from a perfect exponent of Milton's pedagogy" (Allen, "Divine Instruction: *Of Education* and the Pedagogy of Raphael, Michael, and the Father" [*Milton Quarterly* 26 (1992), 113–21], 114); Raphael has too little control and Michael is too severe, but, Allen says, only "the Father is able to attain the desired educational end while delighting his pupil" (117).

23. Hartman observes that even in their basic function, gathering food, Adam and Eve are anxious, since they have so little to do in relation to the work of the rest of the landscape; "their noble ease is perplexed by the energy of the sun and the radiance of the stars" (Hartman, 129).

24. Empson is certain the pun exists: "The airs attune the leaves because the air itself is as enlivening as an air" (Empson, *Some Versions of Pastoral* [London: Penguin, 1995], 129).

25. Christopher Kendrick thinks of this passage the other way around: "The birds' 'choir' is made to seem born from the earth, like the smell of field and grove, while the earth itself is humanized by the metaphor of breathing" (Kendrick, *Milton: A Study in Ideology and Form* [London: Methuen, 1986], 191). His cooperative image probably works just as well as mine, although I would point out that the subject of "Breathing" is "airs" (not air): the pun suggests an even more remarkable metaphor than the one Kendrick thinks is there; not only are the birds personified, but their song is personified separately. "Vernal airs" seems to have entered the language in the gaseous meaning; the *OED* cites it in Pope.

NOTES TO CHAPTER THREE

1. Don Wolfe, ed., *The Works of John Milton* (New York: Columbia UP, 1931), vol. 2 part 2.
2. In some versions Adam does seem to participate in nature's reaction; Hughes quotes Gower: "absent Adam shook" (395n). That Milton does not have Adam participate might indicate that his version is personification (a tropic realization of the implications of the Fall) rather than anthropomorphism (the landscape actually responding as a person would). Of course, the theory of description on which I am relying here would imply that the trope can still condition the reality. In addition, Adam's not hearing might also be a reminder that the urgency of Eden is not only an issue for Adam's and Eve's work and thought but also for the narrator's attempt to reconcile worldly descriptiveness with the divine ethics of his narration. Adam's response would more clearly place the description in time; as it stands, the only time is narrative time: since nothing comes of the response directly, there is no story time.
3. "The relationship between description and time," Beaujour says, "may be trickier" than one might think ("Some Paradoxes of Description" [*Yale French Studies* 61 (1981), 27–59], 42). "Description tends to produce stable, frozen, crystalline structures, in short, *utopias*, but it can also generate transformation" (42–43). Ultimately, a large collection of this and similar paradoxes lead Beaujour to conclude that "description bears only an oblique and tangential relationship to real things, bodies and spaces" (58–59). I would accept that oblique relationship in *Paradise Lost*, except that Adam and Eve seem to articulate ideas about what they see that are based on the descriptions, not on the reality. Thus I will conclude, eventually, that what is most disruptive about the oblique relationship between description and reality is that description turns out to determine reality.
4. Genette, *Narrative Discourse: An Essay in Method*, trans. Jane E. Lewin (Ithaca: Cornell UP, 1980), 94–95.
5. *Discourse*, 105–06.
6. Riffaterre, "Descriptive Imagery" (*Yale French Studies*, No. 61, Towards a Theory of Description [1981], 107–125), 107.
7. "Hypogram and Inscription" (from the posthumous collection *The Resistance to Theory* [Minneapolis: U Minnesota P, 1986], 27–53), 43.
8. From Riffaterre's *La Production du texte*, 1979, quoted in "Hypogram and Inscription," 46.
9. "Hypogram and Inscription," 48.
10. *Allegories of Reading* (New Haven: Yale UP, 1979), 131.
11. *The Architext: An Introduction*, trans. Jane E. Lewin (Berkeley: U California P, 1992), 29.
12. For Christopher Kendrick, the shift to tragedy indicates a new interest in drama, an interest that "overdetermines the generic production of the paradise

books . . ." Thus the shift allows Kendrick's theory of the monism of creation to reveal itself in Adam and Eve themselves: "We can speak, indeed, of the psychology of creation partly because of paradise's dramatic overdetermination" (*Milton: A Study in Ideology and Form* [London: Methuen, 1986], 206). I disagree; Adam and Eve themselves believe that conversational rhetoric is opposed to the fundamental nature of creation, and there is some reason to think that they are correct, since Eden's urgency interferes with the narration of the drama itself. The effect of Milton's shift in genre is to accentuate the discrepancy between the narrative truth of the poem and its theological message. Thus the dramatic nature of Book 9 in fact makes it impossible to "speak . . . of the psychology of creation"; the only psychology of creation available is one determined by the conflict between the generic nature of the narrative and the ethical nature of the subject.

13. Describing Eden for the first time, Milton says: "next to Life / Our Death the Tree of Knowledge grew fast by" (4.220–21).

14. Revard argues that the references to classical epic constitute an invitation to consider the Fall "in terms of a failed heroic martyrdom" ("The Heroic Context of Book IX of *Paradise Lost*" [*Journal of English and Germanic Philology* 87 (1988), 329–341], 330). Ultimately, of course, the Son of God takes over that role. I believe she is reading ahead of the text somewhat; Milton claims that his subject is more heroic not because of the Christian status of its participants but because of the greater and more powerful anger of God. In other words, Milton identifies the principle subject of epic as the struggle created by the discrepancy between anger and powerlessness, and what gives his Christian epic superiority is the greater moral weight of the distance that anger creates between Man and God. But the subject is distance, not someone's ability to overcome distance.

John Steadman associates Milton's claim of superiority in part with Adam as well, arguing that "Adam represents human nature in its original perfection and therefore surpasses the heroes of Homer and Virgil, who, despite their prowess, belong to a fallen and unregenerate humanity" (*The Wall of Paradise: Essays on Milton's Poetics* [Baton Rouge: Louisiana State UP, 1985], 52). However, Milton's emphasis here is on the greater implications for Adam of his failure, so his initial perfection seems at best only to set off those implications.

15. They do not persuade each other, at any rate, though they may persuade themselves; Catherine Gimelli Martin argues that the separation scene "deludes each partner into believing in his or her own actually unbalanced self-vindication" (*The Ruins of Allegory: Paradise Lost and the Metamorphosis of Epic Convention* [Durham: Duke UP, 1998], 278). For Martin the argument produces the same effects in readers, and thus she implies that we cannot recognize the self-delusion. That strikes me as unlikely.

16. See Stanley Fish for a brief history of that critical error; Fish opposes the moralization of this scene on the grounds of its dramatic construction,

which renders the scene not an allegory but a process (*How Milton Works*, 531–32). It is a process moving not irrevocably toward the Fall, but, Fish claims, toward Adam's and Eve's self-definition in relation to the garden: "the topic is the cultivation of the garden, and the action is the cultivation of themselves by way of their discussion of cultivating the garden" (535). Fish summarizes that this is "a reading of the episode in which it signifies its own causal irrelevance" (551); on the scene's causal irrelevance he and I are in agreement. But Fish's argument is chiefly devoted to a discussion of what is right and wrong about Eve's and Adam's respective understandings of human labor in the garden; I believe that Fish errs in assuming that the function of the garden in the separation scene or elsewhere in Book 9 is merely or even principally the site of human labor. Fish's argument depends on his declaration that Eve's anxiety about the lushness of Eden is based on a misunderstanding of "the demands of her situation even as she thinks about ways to satisfy them"; Fish accuses her of thinking of the work as something "finishable" (537). But Eve is not only anxious about the task; she is also anxious about the lushness of Eden itself, and anxious that conversation with Adam does not fit into the environment as given them. That anxiety is upheld by the other characters as well as by the narration; Eden is too much governed by the extremes of its own creation to function merely as an extension of the task of mankind, and to read Eden as human homework (to read it as anything other than a distinct and poetically whole environment) is to miss the central point of the conversation, which is that the debate is a disagreement about the nature of Eden. To Eve, the pace of Edenic growth is faster than human labor; to Adam it is not. This disagreement necessarily asks the reader to consider the nature of Eden itself.

17. Joan Bennett argues that "the matter most fundamentally at stake is the meaning of human liberty" ("'Go': Milton's Antinomianism and the Separation Scene in *Paradise Lost,* Book 9" [*PMLA* 98 (1983): 388–404], 388), and that Adam errs in misrepresenting freedom. I agree that liberty is an issue, but I think that, like everything else Adam and Eve discuss, that issue is overwhelmed by the overdetermining force of the garden's urgency.
18. Diane McColley holds that the separation scene shows "Eve and Adam in just the informed and active liberty, responsibility, truth-seeking, magnanimity, and love that form the gist of any paradise" (*Milton's Eve* [Urbana: U. Illinois P., 1983], 145). Her desire to read cruelty and willfulness out of the scene forces her to stretch, I think, but I find it interesting that, like me, McColley believes that Adam and Eve are responding appropriately to their situation. Naturally the reading of that situation could not be more different.
19. Deborah Interdonato argues that Eve is interested in her own good but not Adam's here, that she is "trying overhard to prove herself as more than a decorative (and consequently inferior) partner" ("'Render Me More Equal': Gender Inequality and the Fall in *Paradise Lost,* 9" [*Milton Quarterly* 29

(1995), 95–105], 97). Interdonato defends Eve while assuming that Adam is basically right. My understanding of the nature of Eden, on the other hand, suggests that Eve is much closer to being right than Adam is, and thus my argument does not need an inferiority complex on Eve's part in order to defend her arguments.

20. It is worth questioning here whether Adam has any evidence for this kind of conversation. Mary Jo Kietzman comes closer to my reading than most when she argues that "In prelapsarian experience, Adam and Eve do not converse: they are unable to explore, understand, or share their subjective experiences" ("The Fall into Conversation with Eve: Discursive Difference in *Paradise Lost*" [*Criticism* 39 (1997): 55–88], 76). However, for Kietzman it is their prelapsarian condition that alone prevents them from having conversation, a reading that has no possible end except the fortunate Fall.

21. Defending Eve's arguments in this moment, John Reichert argues that Eve "would be indicting God's providence only if she agreed to the hypothetical description of their condition. But she does not. She is attributing the description to Adam, summarizing her sense (whether accurate or not) of *his* presentation of their condition" ("'Against His Better Knowledge': A Case for Adam" [*ELH* 48 no. 1 (1981), 83–109], 91). I agree with Reichert that this unhappy Eden is strictly hypothetical, but she is not quite attributing it to Adam. On the contrary, she is aware that Adam is not as willing as she is to read Eden as a discrete entity with particular attributes. She is accusing Adam (rightly, I believe) of failing to define Eden at all.

22. Hamlet's famous use of the same verb is a similar sleight-of-hand. He tells a suicidal Horatio, "Absent thee from felicity awhile" (*The Norton Shakespeare*, ed. Stephen Greenblatt [New York: Norton, 1997], 5.2.289); the verb suggests that death is a state toward which Horatio is being pulled and an act of will is required to keep him away from it. It collapses "felicity"—an understanding of death one associates with Hamlet and not with Horatio—and the act of suicide into a decision that no longer makes sense to Horatio (and indeed does not fit with a reader's understanding of Horatio's personality). The difference, of course, is that Hamlet's trick successfully influences Horatio's actions, whereas Adam's is a skillful piece of rhetoric without any clear agenda or effect.

23. The importance of the fact of Satan's speech apart from what he says is explored at length by John Leonard, who concludes that "the serpent's single most persuasive argument is his ability to speak" (*Naming in Paradise: Milton and the Language of Adam and Eve* [Oxford: Clarendon, 1990], 199).

24. *Imperfect Sense*, 283–345.

25. Kerrigan's emphasis. *The Sacred Complex: On the Psychogenesis of Paradise Lost* (Cambridge: Harvard UP, 1983), 157.

26. Kerrigan, 154.

27. Hughes, 259n.

NOTES TO CHAPTER FOUR

1. The trope, of course, serves multiple functions in *Paradise Lost*, to the extent that Marshall Grossman identifies synecdoche (though not about environment) as central to the entire rhetorical structure of the epic; as opposed to metaphor, he says, synecdoche asserts "identity within a larger structure" rather than mere "comparability" (*"Authors to Themselves": Milton and the Revelation of History* [Cambridge: Cambridge UP, 1987], 187), and *Paradise Lost* tends to move toward synecdoche as it progresses. In Book 10, regardless of the success of Adam's desire for synecdochic connection, the larger structure makes itself relevant; Adam finds himself inextricably bound to Eden. In a more general sense, Grossman's argument that trope can have a structuring function in the poem is an exciting one, since it enables the reader to make sense of the extent to which structure seems to overwhelm doctrinal and moral questions.
2. Many critics, such as Regina Schwarz, John Leonard (*Naming in Paradise: Milton and the Language of Adam and Eve* [Oxford: Clarendon, 1990]), and Dennis Danielson, virtually ignore Adam's despair in Book 10, even though it would seem relevant to their respective arguments about the nature of the Fall. Discussing the relationship between sex and death, Clay Daniel says that "Adam first sees his lapse's impact on sex in *Paradise Lost* 11 and 12" (Daniel, *Death in Milton's Poetry* [Lewisburg: Bucknell UP, 1994], 44), a statement I find perplexing. One must conclude that these critics disregard the soliloquy because they consider it to be an anomaly, not an organic part of Adam's postlapsarian thought; they implicitly agree with Georgia Christopher that the soliloquy is "a blasphemous apostrophe to creation" (Christopher, "The Verbal Gate to Paradise: Adam's 'Literary Experience' in Book X of *Paradise Lost*" [*PMLA* 90 (1975): 69–77], 74). To do so, however, is to ignore the passage's inner conflicts, which mark its inability to be interpretively fixed within the blasphemy of despair.
3. Reichert, 97–98.
4. Mustazza, *Such Prompt Eloquence: Language as Agency and Character in Milton's Epics* (Lewisburg: Bucknell UP, 1988), 102.
5. Fish, *Surprised by Sin*, 284.
6. See Kester Svendsen's "Adam's Soliloquy in Book X of *Paradise Lost*" (*College English* 10 [1949], 366–370) for an argument in favor of the continuity of the persona Adam expresses in his despair and that found by Michael in the final two books.
7. Rajan, 62.
8. *YCP* II:512–513.
9. For de Man, a symbol is synecdochic because "the material perception and the symbolical imagination are continuous, as the part is continuous with the whole" ("The Rhetoric of Temporality" [*Blindness and Insight: Essays*

in the *Rhetoric of Contemporary Criticism* (Minneapolis: U. Minnesota P., 1983), 187–228], 191). This continuity of perception and thought, I will argue below, is one of Adam's chief tools in his soliloquy both for creating logical entanglements and for getting out of them.
10. As Naomi Schor points out in a study of the theory of detail, "the stake of synecdoche . . . is always a question of insuring the delicate balance between the autonomy of the part and the unity of the whole" (*Reading Detail: Aesthetics and the Feminine* [New York: Methuen, 1987], 29). I would add (this will become clearer in the last section of this chapter) that synecdoche's interest in the unity of the whole can itself be a problem, making the whole assemblage that much more precarious.
11. Fish, *Surprised by Sin*, 284.
12. John Tanner associates the relationship between sin and weather with the Kierkegaardian concept of "objective anxiety": the "outward opposition of the elements mirrors new oppositions with the self" (Tanner, 97). Tanner emphasizes Adam's observation of a changed nature: "The Fall's effect upon nature is to render the objective world more polar than before" (90). Though Tanner is right that the effect of the changes to the natural world are polarizing, they also reinforce Adam's centrality (or at least, Adam can interpret them that way).
13. Culler, *The Pursuit of Signs: Semiotics, Literature, Deconstruction* (Ithaca: Cornell UP, 1981), 135.
14. The humility here should not be taken to mean that Adam is changing his mind about his earlier ideas of the desperation of his state, as Mustazza claims: "As grace works to liberate his mind and heart Adam begins to see that the real blame lies with him" (Mustazza, 103). On the contrary, Adam is more interested at this moment in the process of his own logic than he is in the question of blame, which he is about to take up again more humbly than earlier but with no more success.
15. Perhaps Adam's tentative and contradictory images of death are as close as he can get to a sense of mortality. For a discussion of the appropriateness of metaphor (as opposed to description) for Milton's conception of death, see William Engel's chapter "Imagining the Shadow of Death" (Engel, *Mapping Mortality: The Persistence of Memory and Melancholy in Early Modern England* [Amherst: U Massachusetts P, 1995], 67–94).
16. Rogers, *The Matter of Revolution: Science, Poetry and Politics in the Age of Milton* (Ithaca: Cornell UP, 1996), 157.
17. Rogers, 160.
18. Rogers, 160–61.
19. See Kevis Goodman's "'Wasted Labor'? Milton's Eve, the Poet's Work, and the Challenge of Sympathy" (*ELH* 64 [1997], 415–446) for a convincing account of the presence of the *Georgics*' sense of an unrelenting nature and of "doubtful hope" (Goodman, 420) in *Paradise Lost* 10.

20. *Daybreak,* trans. R. J. Hollingdale (Cambridge: Cambridge UP, 1982), Part II no. 117.
21. Nietzsche, *The Gay Science,* trans. Josefine Nauckhoff (Cambridge: Cambridge UP, 2001), Book 5, no. 374.
22. Or, perhaps, as Orphic song, as Heather James argues, finding the passage an expression of Adam's burgeoning misogyny (James, "Milton's Eve, the Romance Genre, and Ovid" [*Comparative Literature* 45 (1993), 121–145], 140–141). A reference to Orpheus, of course, would suggest a georgic rather than bucolic provenance, but as I argued in chapter 1 the two are compatible. In any case, the reference to the first *Eclogue* seems clear enough to make James's possibility at best an understated, trans-generic amendment of the quest for a more productive labor to the pastoral contentment Adam describes.
23. Adam's continued interest in environment here prevents a simplistic reading of the significance of his reconciliation with Eve. For Cheryl Fresch, Eve's supplication "helps Adam to recognize and then to formulate his own sinfulness in relation to hers" (Fresch, "Human and Divine Reconciliation in Paradise Lost, X-XI: The Strategy of Milton's Structure" [in Shaw, William P., ed., *Praise Disjoined: Changing Patterns of Salvation in 17th Century English Literature* (New York: Peter Lang, 1991), 259–72], 267). Fresch misunderstands the change that has occured; Adam has gone from thinking about environment as a shield for the consequences of his sin to speculating about his life in the environment of the future. Though Adam's conception of his sin has certainly changed, the direction of his rhetoric at the end of Book 10 is away from a formulation of sin and toward a more complete and more stable formulation of environment.
24. John Knott, for example, quotes from this passage as part of his insistence that Eden "cannot absorb the presence of death" (*Milton's Pastoral Vision: An Approach to Paradise Lost* [Chicago: U Chicago P, 1971], 59); Knott equates Adam's observation of the destructive winds with Michael's prediction of the final implosion of Eden, but he ignores the fact that Adam here is essentially praising what he sees.
25. John Shawcross would find "shallowness" overly kind; in opposition to a critical tradition that sees the chorus as speaking for Milton, Shawcross notes their "changeability, ignorance, self-serving, and male-orientation . . ." (*The Uncertain World of Samson Agonistes* [Cambridge: Brewer, 2001], 36). Like the passages of despair in *Paradise Lost* 10, the discussion of death in *Samson* receives radically opposed readings; the ultimate moral of these debates is surely that the pious voice in Milton's poetry, if ever present, is always hard to locate.
26. "Resisting the Chorus," John Huntley argues, "causes Samson to confront reality within himself . . . first with passive despair . . . and finally with deliberate action" (Huntley, "A Revaluation of the Chorus' Role in Milton's 'Samson Agonistes.'"[*Modern Philology* 64 (1966): 132-145], 137). Though

the Chorus should probably not be given credit for Samson's decision, there is no doubt that at his most decisive Samson ignores them.
27. In fact, as Dennis Kezar argues in a discussion of the theatricality of Samson's death, Samson's decision is clearly marked as existing outside of (and not as a response to) the debate with the Chorus that precedes it (Kezar, *Guilty Creatures: Renaissance Poetry and the Ethics of Authorship* [Oxford: Oxford UP, 2001], 149).
28. Shawcross, *Paradise Regain'd: Worthy t'have not Remain'd so Long Unsung* (Pittsburgh: Duquesne UP, 1988), 5.
29. That praise is mostly old, however; Arnold Stein participates (Stein, "The Kingdoms of the World: *Paradise Regained*" [*ELH* 23 (1956): 112–126], 117–18), quoting Cleanth Brooks in sympathy. But Barbara Lewalski is not taken in even temporarily: the passage, she says, "whatever the psychological state which prompts it, functions as a devious invitation to Christ to corrupt his kingly office" (Lewalski, *Milton's Brief Epic: The Genre, Meaning, and Art of Paradise Regained* [Providence: Brown UP, 1966], 264). I suspect she gives Satan too much credit; that is, aside from its rhetorical interest, I do not think the passage has much function, since Satan has already lost at this point in the poem, and practically admits as much here. On the contrary, it is because Satan is no longer convincing in the latter parts of *Paradise Regained* that his figuration becomes so important—the poem turns gradually from a debate into a dialectic of images of reality, in which Jesus and Satan trade metaphors without much agenda.
30. Anthony Low notes the "georgic tone and provenance" of this simile, and its anti-epic character: "Most epic similes magnify; it progressively diminishes," reducing Satan to a "nuisance" (Low, 346). Nuisances are organic in georgic; the flies are no less a part of the landscape than the bees.
31. As Christopher Grose says, "Almost from the moment of publication, it was commonplace for readers to patronize or even ignore the Satan of Milton's brief epic, primarily because he did not quite measure up to his splendidly eloquent predecessor" (*Milton and the Sense of Tradition* [New Haven: Yale UP, 1988], 104).

NOTES TO THE CONCLUSION

1. "The Return to Philology" (*The Resistance to Theory* [Minneapolis: U Minnesota P, 1986], 21–26), 24.
2. "Return to Philology," 24.

Bibliography

TEXTS

Andrew Marvell:

Donno, Elizabeth Story, ed., *The Complete Poems of Andrew Marvell* (New York: Penguin, 1995).
Margoliouth, H. M., ed., *The Poems and Letters of Andrew Marvell,* 2 vols. (Oxford: Clarendon, 1952).

John Milton:

Hughes, Merritt Y., ed, *Complete Poems and Major Prose of John Milton* (New York: Macmillan, 1957).
Patterson, Frank Allen, ed., *The Works of John Milton* (New York: Columbia UP, 1931–1938).
Wolfe, Don M., ed., *Complete Prose Works* (New Haven: Yale UP, 1953–1980).

Edmund Spenser:

Bayley, P. C. ed., *The Faerie Queene,* Books 1 and 2 (Oxford: Oxford UP, 1965).
Hamilton, A.C., ed., *The Faerie Queene* (New York: Longman, 2001).
Oram, William A., ed., *The Yale Edition of the Shorter Poems of Edmund Spenser* (New Haven: Yale UP, 1989).

Vergil:

Coleman, Robert, ed., *Eclogues* (Cambridge: Cambridge UP, 1977).
Grandsen, K. W., *Aeneid* Book VIII (Cambridge: Cambridge UP, 1976).
Mynors, R. A. B., *Opera* (Oxford: Oxford UP, 1969).
Thomas, Richard F., ed., *Georgics* (Cambridge: Cambridge UP, 1988).

CRITICISM

Alpers, Paul, *What is Pastoral?* (Chicago: U Chicago P, 1996).
Bennett, Joan S, "'Go': Milton's Antinomianism and the Separation Scene in *Paradise Lost*, Book 9" (*PMLA* 98 [1983]: 388–404).
Berger, Harry, *Second World and Green World: Studies in Renaissance Fiction-Making* (Berkeley: U California P, 1988).
Casey, Edward S, *The Fate of Place: A Philosophical History* (Berkeley: California, 1997).
Culler, Jonathan, *The Pursuit of Signs: Semiotics, Literature, Deconstruction* (Ithaca: Cornell UP, 1981).
Danielson, Dennis Richard, *Milton's Good God: A Study in Literary Theodicy* (Cambridge: Cambridge UP, 1982).
de Man, Paul, *Allegories of Reading* (New Haven: Yale UP, 1979).
de Man, Paul, *Blindness and Insight: Essays in the Rhetoric of Contemporary Criticism* (Minneapolis: U Minnesota P, 1983).
de Man, Paul, *The Resistance to Theory* (Minneapolis: U Minnesota P, 1986).
Empson, William, *Milton's God* (1961; Revised Edition, London: Chatto and Windus, 1965).
Empson, William, *Some Versions of Pastoral* (1935; London: Penguin, 1995).
Empson, William, *Using Biography* (Cambridge: Harvard UP, 1984).
Ferry, Anne, *Milton's Epic Voice* (1963; Second Edition, Chicago: University of Chicago Press, 1983).
Fish, Stanley, *How Milton Works* (Cambridge: Belknap P of Harvard UP, 2001).
Fish, Stanley, *Surprised By Sin* (1967; Second Edition, Cambridge: Harvard UP, 1997).
Flesch, William, *Generosity and the Limits of Authority: Shakespeare, Herbert, Milton* (Ithaca: Cornell UP, 1992).
Flesch, Willliam, "The Majesty of Darkness" (Bloom, Harold, ed., *John Milton: Modern Critical Views* [New York: Chelsea House, 1986], 293–312).
Forsyth, Neil, *The Satanic Epic* (Princeton: Princeton UP, 2003).
Genette, Gérard, *The Architext: An Introduction*, trans. Jane E. Lewin (Berkeley: U California P, 1992).
Genette, Gérard, *Narrative Discourse: An Essay in Method*, trans. Jane E Lewin (Ithaca: Cornell UP, 1980).
Genette, Gérard, *Palimpsests: Literature in the Second Degree*, trans. Channa Newman and Claude Doubinsky (Lincoln: U Nebraska P, 1997).
Grossman, Marshall, *"Authors to Themselves": Milton and the Revelation of History* (Cambridge: Cambridge UP, 1987).
Grossman, Marshall, "The Fruits of One's Labor in Miltonic Practice and Marxian Theory" (*ELH* 59 [1992]: 77–105).
Hartman, Geoffrey H, "Adam on the Grass with Balsamum" (*Beyond Formalism: Literary Essays 1958–1970* [New Haven: Yale UP, 1970], 124–150).

Bibliography

Hollander, John, *The Figure of Echo: A Mode of Allusion in Milton and After* (Berkeley: U California P, 1981).
Kendrick, Christopher, *Milton: A Study in Ideology and Form* (London: Methuen, 1986).
Kolbrener, William, *Milton's Warring Angels: A Study of Critical Engagements* (Cambridge: Cambridge UP, 1997).
Leonard, John, *Naming in Paradise: Milton and the Language of Adam and Eve* (Oxford: Clarendon, 1990).
Lewalski, Barbara Kiefer, *The Life of John Milton*, revised edition (London: Blackwell, 2003).
Lewalski, Barbara Kiefer, *Milton's Brief Epic: The Genre, Meaning, and Art of Paradise Regained* (Providence: Brown UP, 1966).
Low, Anthony, *The Georgic Revolution* (Princeton: Princeton UP, 1985).
Rajan, Balachandra, *The Form of the Unfinished: English Poetics from Spenser to Pound* (Princeton: Princeton UP, 1985).
Rajan, Balachandra, *Paradise Lost and the Seventeenth Century Reader* (1947; Ann Arbor: U Michigan P, 1967).
Rajan, Balachandra, *Under Western Eyes: India from Milton to Macaulay* (Durham: Duke UP, 1999).
Readings, Bill, "'An Age Too Late': Milton and the Time of Literary History" (*Exemplaria* 4 [1992]: 455–468).
Ricks, Christopher, *Milton's Grand Style* (Oxford: Clarendon, 1963).
Schwartz, Regina, *Remembering and Repeating: On Milton's Theology and Poetics* (Chicago: U Chicago P, 1993).
Silver, Victoria, *Imperfect Sense: The Predicament of Milton's Irony* (Princeton: Princeton UP, 2001).
Silver, Victoria, "The Obscure Script of Regicide: Ambivalence and Little Girls in Marvell's Pastorals" (*ELH* 68 [2001], 29–55).

Index

A
Achinstein, Sharon 8
Adam
    fall 84, 105–107
    imagination 54–57, 67–79, 123, 136, 155
    knowledge 58, 60, 71–72, 78, 124, 171 n. 12
    rhetoric 94–101
    compared to Samson 7, 148, 150
    compared to Satan 7, 118, 125, 138, 143
    soliloquy of despair 115, 117–119, 123–144
    uncertainty 6, 51, 66, 68–71, 79, 155
Adorno, Theodor 172 n. 14
Allen, Michael 173 n. 22
Alpers, Paul 23, 164 n. 9, 168 n. 33
angels 1–3, 53, 54, 59
    songs of 53, 59–66, 79, 120, 121, 156
apostrophe 65, 131–133
anthropomorphism 29, 48–50, 74, 78

B
Barrell, John 163 n. 2
Bate, Jonathan 160 n. 6
Bate, Walter Jackson 156
Beaujour, Michel 85
Bennett, Joan 176 n. 17
Berger, Harry 43, 44
Bible 106
    Genesis 111
    John 111, 113, 121
birdsong (*see also* nightingale) 46, 77, 109
Blake, William 6

Burt, Stephen 161 n. 22

C
Casey, Edward S. 5
Chaos 7, 104, 112, 170 n. 8, 171 n. 12
Chaudhuri, Sukanta 164 n. 10
cicadas 167 n. 28
Coleman, Robert 167 n. 29

D
Danielson, Dennis 58, 171 n. 10, 178 n. 2
Dante Alighieri 157
de Man, Paul 87–89, 92, 117, 124, 156, 178 n. 9
description, theory of 55, 85–88
Donne, John 14

E
echo 27–28, 32–33, 50, 115, 143, 163 n. 7, 166 n. 22
eclogue (*see also* pastoral and Vergil, *Eclogues*) 31
ecocriticism 160 n. 5
Eden
    as state of bliss 98, 128–129
    description of 1–4, 76–78, 81–82, 89, 94–96, 104, 107, 115
Empson, William 6, 9–10, 44, 45, 55, 56, 155, 161 n. 15, 173 n. 24
environment (*see* place)
epic (genre) 3, 21, 47, 48–49, 86, 90, 92, 93, 101, 114, 155, 157, 168 n. 37, 175 n. 14, 181 n. 30

Eve
  creation of 75–76
  debate with serpent 101–104
  description of Eden 81–82, 94–98
  fall 83, 105–106
Ferry, David 166 n. 24
figuration 1–4, 7, 13, 14, 17, 27, 36, 39, 48, 57, 91, 93, 117, 119, 123, 124, 127, 147, 148, 150, 152–153
Fish, Stanley 9, 12–13, 17, 53, 55, 56, 68, 118, 126, 137, 138, 161 n. 20, 162 n. 26, 169 n. 1, 169 n. 3, 170 n. 7, 173 n. 19, 175–176 n. 16
Fitter, Chris 23

F

Flesch, William 173 n. 20, 173 n. 21
Fresch, Cheryl 180 n. 23

G

Gay, David 161 n. 20
Genette, Gérard 21, 85–88, 90
genre 10, 21–31, 45, 47, 62, 90, 92–94, 106, 157, 164 n. 9, 164 n. 11, 168 n. 37
georgic (*see also* Vergil, *Georgics*) 3, 17, 26, 28–32, 35, 47, 48, 114, 139, 152, 154, 168 n. 37, 180 n. 22
God 6, 13–14, 16, 56, 57, 59–62, 64–65, 77–78, 79, 103–104, 118, 119–122, 124, 126, 150–152, 156
  Adam's account of 54, 67–71, 130–136, 144
  anger of 91–94
  debate with Adam 72–76, 99
  as light 107–113
  punishment of Adam and Eve 82–84
Goodman, Kevis 165 n. 18
Grose, Christopher 181 n. 31
Grossman, Marshall 168 n. 37, 169 n. 2, 178 n. 1
Guss, Donald 16

H

Haber, Judith 167 n. 30
Hammond, Paul 167–168 n. 31

Hartman, Geoffrey 68
Heaven 65–66, 72, 76, 89–93, 104, 108, 114, 119, 154, 173 n. 19
  difficulty of human understanding 54–55, 57–59, 63, 169 n. 2
  as place 4, 7, 13, 14
  and delay 82, 84–85, 87–88, 106, 107
Hell 7, 13, 104, 114, 143, 154
Herman, Peter C. 160 n. 15
Hiltner, Ken 6, 160 n. 5
Hollander, John 166 n. 22
Homer 4, 170 n. 14
Hughes, Merritt Y. 113, 174 n. 2

I

India 121–122
Interdonato, Deborah 176–177 n. 19

J

James, Heather 180 n. 22
Jesus 150–154
Johnson, Samuel 6

K

Kegl, Rosemary 163 n. 5
Kendrick, Christopher 6, 173 n. 25, 174–175 n. 12
Kerrigan, William 108
Kietzman, Mary Jo 177 n. 20
Knott, John 180 n. 24
Kolbrener, William 10, 157, 161–162 n. 22

L

landscape
  description of 18, 27–32, 45–49, 86–87
  personified 31–32, 36–40, 45, 49–50, 72
Leach, Eleanor Winsor 166 n. 20
Lewalski, Barbara 157, 181 n. 29
Lewis, C. S. 6
liberalism 135, 157
Loewenstein, David 161 n. 21
Loewenstein, Joseph 163 n. 7
Low, Anthony 26, 159 n. 2, 164 n. 9, 181 n. 30
Martin, Catherine Gimelli 175 n. 15
Marvell, Andrew 18, 22, 24–25, 35–45, 48, 50

Index

"Damon the Mower" 22, 36–39
"The Garden" 43–44
"The Mower to the Glowworms" 28, 39–45, 51
materialism 6
McColley, Diane 176 n. 18
metonymy 42, 71, 111, 141, 148–149
Michael (Archangel) 1, 135, 145, 146, 170 n. 4, 173 n. 22, 178 n. 6, 180 n. 24
Milton, John
  "L'Allegro" 45, 47, 162 n. 2
  Areopagitica 9, 11–17, 104, 122, 157
  "Lycidas" 48–50, 63–64
  A Masque Presented at Ludlow Castle (*Comus*) 163 n. 7
  Paradise Lost
    Book 1 5, 51, 93
    Book 3 13, 84, 87, 107–114
    Book 4 6, 76–78, 82, 138
    Book 5 58–59, 65, 172 n. 17
    Book 7 53–69
    Book 8 53, 54, 66–76, 78–79, 124, 140, 155, 169 n. 3, 170 n. 7
    Book 9 18–19, 81–107, 108, 110, 114, 116, 118–123, 124, 130
    Book 10 19, 78, 115–119, 123–147, 148
    Book 12 1–4, 154
  Paradise Regained 147, 150–154
  "Il Penseroso" 45–47
  Samson Agonistes 7, 147–150, 151, 154
  Sonnet 19 63
Morgan, Llewelyn 165 n. 16
Mustazza, Leonard 118

N

narrator (of *Paradise Lost*) 6, 51, 55, 82, 101, 107, 110–113, 116, 121, 126, 128, 142, 172 n. 17, 174 n. 2
narration
  and Adam 127
  relative to time 86–87, 174 n. 2
narrative (as distinct from figuration) 1–2, 7, 59, 92–94
nightingale (*see also* birdsong) 40–44
Nietzsche, Friedrich 5, 88, 141–142, 146

O

Orpheus 47–48, 169 n. 40, 180 n. 22
Owens, Judith 164–165 n. 12

P

pastoral 21–45, 47, 48–50, 78, 121–123, 143–144, 146
Patrides, C. A. 6
Patterson, Annabel 23–24, 26, 166 n. 23
Paul (Apostle) 15, 161 n. 22
perception 57, 123, 126–127, 138, 139–143, 146, 148
personification 72, 77, 83, 95, 145, 174 n. 2
  of environment 22–23, 29–32, 34–40, 45–50, 68, 72, 78
place (*see also* Eden, Heaven, landscape)
  as space 5, 7
  as surroundings 7, 22–24, 33, 36, 44, 51, 106, 116–117, 129, 132–135, 141–146, 147, 150
  within figuration 2, 7, 37, 123, 124, 127, 147–153
Plato 14–15, 157
prosopopeia 87
Proust, Marcel 85–86
Putnam, Michael 166 n. 19

R

Rajan, Balachandra 10–11, 122–123, 160 n. 15
Raphael (Archangel) 6, 18, 53–79, 81, 84, 89–92, 94, 106, 111–112, 119, 140,
Readings, Bill 55, 170 n. 4
Reichert, John 118, 177 n. 21
Reeves, Charles Eric 171 n. 11
republicanism 157
Revard, Stella 93, 168 n. 39, 175 n. 14
Riffaterre, Michael 87–88
Rogers, John 10, 135
rhetoric 7, 16, 18, 19, 32, 56, 81–117, 132, 136, 141, 146–48, 153, 156
Rumrich, John 162 n. 26

S

Satan (*see also* serpent) 6, 7, 13, 54, 55, 82, 114, 138, 143, 147, 155, 162 n. 26

compared to Adam 116, 118, 125
temptation of Eve 85, 94, 104
in *Paradise Regained* 150–154
Schor, Naomi 179 n. 10
Schwartz, Regina 53, 59, 171 n. 12,
Segal, Charles 47
serpent 28, 81, 82, 94, 101–105
Shakespeare, William 140, 177 n. 22
Shawcross, John 150–151, 180 n. 25
Shoaf, R. A. 55
Silver, Victoria 5, 10, 36–37, 107, 172 n. 13
song (*see* angels, songs of; birdsong)
song form 62
Son of God 13, 59, 60–61, 93, 175 n. 14
Snyder, Susan 168 n. 32
Spenser, Edmund 18, 24, 25–30, 35, 40, 45, 46, 51
   The Shepheardes Calender 26, 27
   The Faerie Queene 25
   Amoretti and Epithalamion 24, 27–32, 36, 39, 46, 51
Steadman, John 175 n. 14
Swaim, Kathleen M. 8–9
synecdoche 117–133, 139, 141, 144, 146, 147–148
Tanner, John 66, 179 n. 12
Teskey, Gordon 10
theodicy 5–6, 55, 58, 93, 124
time
   in heaven 59–61

relative to narration 86–87, 174 n. 2
tragedy 90, 93
tree
   beech 32–33, 38
   fig 121–123, 130, 144
   of knowledge of good and evil 18, 77–78, 82–84, 101–105
   of life 77–78
   oak (of Cynthia) 46
   struck by lightning 144–145
trope 7, 16, 31, 50, 84–85, 88–89, 92, 94, 117, 124, 131–132, 135, 142, 146, 147

U

uncertainty 3–6, 9–11, 25, 27, 51, 68–71, 111, 147

V

Vergil 4, 17–19, 21–51, 136, 143, 155, 157, 159 n. 3
   Eclogues 21–27, 30, 32–35, 38, 45, 48, 50
   Georgics 21, 24, 26–32, 35, 39, 47–48, 50, 136
   Aeneid 21, 48–50

W

Waldock, A. J. A. 170 n. 7
Wallace, Andrew 165 n. 16

For Product Safety Concerns and Information please contact our EU
representative GPSR@taylorandfrancis.com
Taylor & Francis Verlag GmbH, Kaufingerstraße 24, 80331 München, Germany

www.ingramcontent.com/pod-product-compliance
Lightning Source LLC
Chambersburg PA
CBHW021849300426
44115CB00005B/85